Financial Success for the
Rest of Us

The symbol depicted on the front cover is a Maori "Hei-Matau" (fish hook). The Maori people of New Zealand believe the Hei-Matau represents prosperity and abundance. They also believe the Hei-Matau is a good luck charm and a symbol of power.

Financial Success for the Rest of Us

❖

Reality Based Financial Planning for Mainstream America

Daniel J. Dorval, CFP

iUniverse, Inc.
New York Lincoln Shanghai

Financial Success for the Rest of Us
Reality Based Financial Planning for Mainstream America

iUniverse, Inc.

For information address:
iUniverse, Inc.
2021 Pine Lake Road, Suite 100
Lincoln, NE 68512
www.iuniverse.com

ISBN: 0-595-31307-8

Printed in the United States of America

Contents

v

Introduction

I wrote this book to counter much of the main stream gobbledygook that passes for financial information in today's society. The Internet, TV, radio, and print media now provide a limitless stream of "advice" and financial resources for the masses, but much of this information is skewed towards the wealthy or very high income people (but still sold to mainstream America). Most of the time this information from "financial experts" is totally generic and has no practical use for the rest of us. The media relies on getting us hooked so we keep coming back for more, because if they offered long term solutions, we would not need to watch, read, or listen on a daily basis.

Historically people sought out financial advisors to provide financial information and advice. Now you can access all the information your heart desires almost as easily as your financial advisor. This has changed the role of an advisor from a *source* of information to a *filter* of information. It is my job to pick out the bits and pieces of useful information relevant to each unique client situation and to help each client implement a reality based financial plan to give him the greatest probability of reaching his most important financial objectives.

I believe financial planning is the key concept in achieving financial success. For most of us, financial success does not mean getting rich quick or achieving vast amounts of wealth. Financial success for my family and most of my clients is simply completing the steps necessary for meeting your most important financial priorities, like financing your children's education, accumulating an emergency reserve of money, buying a home, creating a plan for retirement, and protecting your family with different types of insurance. This sounds easy in theory, but in reality, it is quite difficult.

This book is about planning. The concepts described are based on the reality of my clients and the personal planning of my family. I am a Certified Financial Planner™ professional affiliated with an independent broker/dealer and a variety of different insurance companies. I have chosen to work with primarily middle income people like nurses and engineers. Most of my clients are between 25 and 55 years of age, are married, and have children. This book is geared towards the majority of our population that fits in this category. The concepts discussed will help you get off on the right foot with your finances or will help you "fix" mistakes you might have made in the past. This book addresses the steps necessary to create a financial plan and, more importantly, to implement a plan. Most of the examples involve my own family and what we have done with our own finances. These examples are not meant to be boastful or to tell you how smart we are with money, but these examples do provide a way for you to get a glimpse into the mind of a financial planner and how a planner looks at financial problems and solutions.

Since much of this book deals with my family, I need to introduce you to my wife Tracy and our daughter Isabella. At the time of this writing, Tracy is 31 years old and Isabella is two. I am 33 years old. We live in Otsego, Minnesota (a suburb of Minneapolis). My wife and I met at college and have been married for seven years. Our daughter is the light of our lives and we focus much of our attention on her.

As you already know, I work as a Certified Financial Planner™ professional. My wife is a stay-at-home mom. She chose to leave a career as a structural engineer to focus on raising Isabella. Unlike the authors of most financial books, our family is a true middle income family. We have never had a year with more than $100,000 of adjusted gross income even when Tracy and I were both working. It drives me nuts to read financial books, and I have read many of them, where the author's only real qualification is the attainment of wealth or some form of celebrity status. These people live in another world where simple financial problems like making a house payment are not reality. I enjoy when a financial advisor touts the sense of clipping coupons or foregoing the morning latte in order to save a few bucks when that advisor will not work with a client having less than $1,000,000 of investable assets, a common minimum for many "elite" advisors.

You will find me to be extremely cynical about the financial services industry. It takes almost no formal education to become a financial planner and most firms do little to educate their people other than teach them how to sell. You may notice I will ramble at times about the "scumbags" of my business. Please bear with me as I vent, and you have my apologies. I do not mean to offend, but if you have ever had the experience of dealing with a "scumbag," you understand where I am coming from, and probably could add a few choice words of your own! At times I will probably get overly critical of the financial services industry, but my experiences have shaped these opinions over many years.

Since my family does not have unlimited money, we deal with the same issues you are dealing with in regard to financial priorities like raising a family, and living a fulfilling life. My clients are also people in the same boat as you. Most of my clients are struggling with money and need a way to get ahead in life.

I help my clients create a plan that starts with defining what is important to them. This is much easier said than done because most people have no real idea what their most important priorities really are. I know. I know. You want to retire someday, and you would like to be rich, and you would like your kids to go to college. All of these things are essentially meaningless in reality. For instance, what is "rich" to you? I can guarantee rich to you is not rich to someone else (like your planner). What will it actually cost to pay for college? When is "someday" for retirement? The point is defining what you truly want out of life is the first step, the most important step, and the most difficult step in achieving financial success. Most people make their financial decisions at random and some of those people achieve success and some do not (basically at random). The ones who make it are termed "lucky," and the ones who do not make it are "unfortunate." I strongly disagree. I think all of you could achieve your most important financial objectives if you only knew how. That is why I wrote this book. I was not commissioned to write this book, and I certainly never expect Oprah to have me on her show! I will not obtain vast wealth from this book. So why am I taking the time to commit these thoughts to paper? This is my way of trying to help regular people get through their financial struggles in life with a little less stress and a little more success. If I can help one family improve their situation in life, then this book was worth the time.

It is one thing to motivate you to spend the time to create a financial plan for your family. It is a whole different story to give you the tools to implement your plan. This is another problem I have with the typical financial planning or get rich quick book. Most books are wonderful at motivation (I particularly commend Suze Orman for this skill), but are truly lacking at giving people the tools to implement their financial plan. There is actually little substance to most financial books and few examples of how to implement a smart strategy with your finances. I know. I know. You simply buy some no-load mutual funds, some term life insurance, and some foreclosed real estate and you are good to go. How tough can it really be? Unfortunately, most people would have no idea why they have the no-load mutual funds (or how to set up an account), how much term insurance they might need (and where to buy it), and I personally would have no clue how to value foreclosed rental properties (nor am I excited about plunging someone else's toilet in order to get a rent check).

I think you will be amazed at how simple this book is and you might question why the information is valuable. If you finish the book and wonder at its simplicity, it is likely you will never implement a financial plan in your life. My hope is you will read this book and think, "I can do that! How tough can it be?" If this happens you will likely not only create a financial strategy for your life, but will likely succeed in reaching your most important financial priorities.

Simplicity is the problem for most people. Most people believe financial success is having nice things or having the appearance of wealth. If most people had the opportunity to look closer at the financial situation of the "apparently wealthy," they would realize most of those people are not actually wealthy and are truly hurting in regard to reaching their financial objectives. However, they certainly do have nice things! This is why my practice tends to focus on women over men. This was not a conscious decision, but rather a decision that was made for me by my clients. Women tend to focus much more on planning and view money simply as a means of financial security. Men tend to be driven by short term gains and view money as a means of obtaining toys. I would bet the farm that the saying "He who dies with the most toys, wins!" was first coined by a man. This means women tend to be much better with money over a lifetime (even though they have the stereotype of being spenders). Of course this is over-simplified, but I see it in my business over and over again. Men find my solutions too simple and would much rather bet their futures on stock trading (remember day trading?), options, or real estate speculation. Women typically want a plan in place and they want to know how to follow a systematic approach to achieve what they want out of life. This difference between men and women causes a lot of friction in our society which is why money is one of the primary causes of divorce. I will address this problem at length throughout this book and will give some pointers for reducing the financial friction between men and women.

If you are wondering who this book was written to help, I can give you some specific guidelines. This is not a generic, one-size-fits-all book. My target audience is any single person with an adjusted gross income less than $95,000/year and married couples with a combined family adjusted gross income less than $150,000 (these limits are as of 2003 and will change over time). How did I come up with these numbers? Simple, these are the income limits as of 2003 for making full contributions to a Roth IRA. This is also the general upper limits of income for the vast majority of my clients and it is also what I consider to be the limits on income between people who have hordes of advisors chasing after them and the rest of us, who have a tough time obtaining competent help from financial advisors. You will see the Roth IRA mentioned throughout this book as a tremendous financial tool for the rest of us, so my focus is on people able to fully utilize this wonderful tool.

Are there any minimum income limits or asset limits for reading this book? Absolutely not. In fact, the lower your income, the more this book will likely help you and the less likely you are able to get competent financial help in our society. I do not impose any asset based limits on my clients. I will do my best to help anyone who is actively seeking help in creating a financial plan they can use to guide their future decisions about money. That means there are times when I do not get paid for my services, or get paid very little. This is part of the reason for writing this book. It is not economically feasible for me to provide advice solely to very low income or low asset clients (exactly the people who most need my help). My hope is this book will help serve as a proxy for my services so all people who are looking for help can get off on the right track and make smart financial decisions.

Smart financial decisions are so much more important for those of us with limited financial resources. Think about it; if a millionaire makes a wise investment decision and makes an extra million, do you think it impacts his quality of life? Not really. It usually gets spent on a bigger house, fancier car, or some other insignificant toy. However, if a single mom with a low income can figure out a way to put away a few bucks a month for her daughter's college education and still plan for her own retirement, does this impact their life? Absolutely. If you have not already noticed in your own life, financial decisions are hard to make when you don't have any money!

We will be covering real world solutions to real world financial problems. This book is not about simply defining financial terms and, in fact, we will not even be discussing many of the financial terms thrown around by advisors and financial media like alpha, beta, Sharpe ratio, PE ratio, etc. There are literally hundreds of financial books designed to teach you about financial products and theory from basic concepts to abstract concepts. You will find the most use from this book if you also do some additional reading to learn as much as you can about all aspects of finance. However, if you only have the inclination to read one financial book, this one will give you the real world information necessary to develop and implement your own unique financial strategy.

The information I will give you is absolutely worthless unless you do something with it. Implementation of a plan is much more important than the actual process of creating a plan, although one cannot be done without the other. I want you to treat this book like a set of "how to" instructions. At some point in your life you probably had to read through a set of instructions for putting something together like a crib, or setting up a computer. If you sit down and read through the entire guide, it is probably total gibberish, but if you take it one step at a time and install each piece as you go, it all comes together in the end. What made no sense at the beginning actually became very simple by breaking it down into a series of achievable tasks.

I believe most people learn best by doing rather than reading. There is an old Chinese proverb I find particularly relevant to personal finances:

> What I hear, I forget.
> What I see, I remember.
> What I do, I understand.

Take the information I give you, apply it in your life, learn as you go, and you will have tremendous success.

Daniel J. Dorval, CFP

As for financial "experts" who know it all:

There's a story about Socrates who had been proclaimed the wisest man in Athens by the Oracle of Delphi. Not believing what the Oracle said, Socrates sought out the wisest people in Athens and asked them one simple, yet profound question, "What is truly worthwhile in life?" If somebody could answer that question, they would certainly be wiser than him. Everyone gave Socrates a different answer, but none of the answers were satisfactory to Socrates. Socrates thought they were pretending to know something they really didn't know. After interviewing all of the wisest people he knew, Socrates came to the conclusion he truly was the wisest man in Athens because he knew he didn't know it all and because of that, he would always be searching for knowledge.

This is an important lesson for the rest of us, not only with our finances, but in general throughout all aspects of our lives. Knowledge is a powerful weapon in fighting day-to-day battles. There are a lot of people who will act like they know it all (or at least know more than you), but in many cases, there is no right answer. This book is designed to give you the confidence to make wise financial decisions, not right or wrong, but wise. My hope is the knowledge you get from me will help you combat some of the drivel that passes for financial advice in today's society.

Author's Note

My original intent in writing this book was to make specific mention of financial products such as mutual funds and insurance that my clients and I utilize to implement our personal financial plans. I thought the mention of specific companies would be particularly helpful in guiding your continued research into implementing your own financial plan. I was told during the compliance review process to remove any specific names of investment companies used throughout this book because the mere mention of a specific name would constitute a potential recommendation that would require substantial disclosures. I felt these disclosures and legal disclaimers did not add to the substance of the financial planning process. Instead I have done my best to clearly describe the *types* of mutual funds and insurance I commonly use both in my family's financial plan and with my clients. I sincerely apologize for the inconvenience to my readers.

You may be wondering why other media outlets (newspapers, magazines, and other financial books) can mention specific names of investment companies and actually make specific recommendations to their audience. I was wondering the same thing! The reason, as it was explained to me, is many of those authors are not active registered financial representatives and are not under the same restrictions as me. Basically, the way the financial services industry is regulated, anyone who is not considered a financial services representative can write or say almost anything they want about investment recommendations, but an actual financial services professional cannot. Go figure.

Also, since the completion of this text, there have been substantial scandals reported in the mutual fund industry. Several major mutual fund companies have been accused of unethical, and sometimes allegedly illegal, behavior in violation of their fiduciary responsibilities. I am a strong proponent of mutual funds as excellent investment options for the rest of us and I continue to have this belief. I believe these scandals are actually good for the industry and will likely result in improvements that will benefit the rest of us. In my opinion, the media has overblown some of these issues resulting in consumers making spur of the moment decisions that may or may not have been in their best interest. I personally own shares in some mutual funds involved in these scandals. I made the decision not to sell these funds because I felt the company involved made changes to address the problem created by a small percentage of their fund managers or executives. As an involved investor, I will continue to monitor the various mutual fund companies I use for my family and for my clients, but I will not abandon the entire mutual fund industry for the failings of companies involved in these scandals.

My original intent was to include a chapter dealing exclusively with costs incurred during the financial planning process. I again found out discussing actual fees and expenses associated with financial products and services is frowned upon in a compliance review. The chapter was removed, but I will summarize eleven pages of material in one statement: Take pains to understand all costs incurred when using a financial advisor or when selecting financial products to implement your plan. You are always entitled to know these costs and you will want to be proactive in making sure all expenses have been fully disclosed to you *before* committing your time or money.

1

The Importance of Planning

"Human beings, who are almost unique in having the ability to learn from the experience of others, are also remarkable for their apparent disinclination to do so."

Douglas Adams Quote

You can learn from my experience and the experience of my clients, but it will take effort on your part (the effort part loses most people at this point!). This is the most important chapter. If you do not get the importance of creating a plan, all of the other information is merely more clutter of information to sift through. If you know what you want from life, you can get it! However, the obvious most important step is figuring out what you really want from life.

Have you ever dreamt of winning the lottery? Have you ever watched a VH1 Behind the Music episode and wished you could be the rags to riches story they document? Have you ever seen a news story about some rich athlete or musician that ended up declaring bankruptcy and is on a "where are they now" show? Do you wonder how those people could have so much money, *unbelievable amounts of money*, and now they are dirt poor? There have been numerous reports most big lottery winners end up blowing their winnings and often end up worse off than before they won. How can that be? Once you are rich, I thought all of these people could hire the best accountants, the best attorneys and the best stock brokers to make sure they would always be rich? Don't the rich just keep getting richer? I always thought it took money to make money.

I would suggest most of those people never sat down to figure out what they wanted from life so their financial decisions were made at random. I have asked my wife on several occasions what she would do with a big lottery win like $10,000,000 or more (purely a theoretical question since neither one of us buys lottery tickets). Her answer is always the same:

Buy a nice home (nothing more than $1,000,000) with cash
Put away enough money to pay for our children's education
Make sure our retirement was funded
Spend the rest!

Now $10,000,000 is a lot of money and most people think they would be super rich if they won a prize of that size. Let's take a closer look at what really happens. We start by taking about half in taxes so you are down to $5,000,000. We buy a $1,000,000 home with cash. We set aside $300,000 for the children's education (assume two kids at a private school). Another $1,000,000 gets set aside for retirement and is allowed to grow only for that purpose. There is $2,700,000 left over to spend without impacting any of our major financial priorities. At a modest 5% interest rate, we could comfortably draw $135,000/year of income, have no mortgage payment, and never spend our principal, so it would also be available for retirement or to leave as inheritance to the kids. This sounds great to us and seems more than reasonable. The lottery win would literally provide for all of our lifetime financial needs.

However, there is a problem with this approach. We actually accounted for taxes! Most people win a lottery (or get a bonus) and they think of the full amount as their money. In our example with a $10,000,000 lottery win, they believe the $10,000,000 is theirs to spend which means they can buy a much, much better home, and more extravagant cars. Say you buy a $3,000,000 home with cash and $250,000 worth of vehicles. You do some extravagant traveling, shopping, and gift some money to your relatives and friends because you feel guilty about your good fortune (let's say $1,000,000 for example since you have a huge fortune). Now the tax bill comes and about half of your fortune goes to the government. You pay the taxes, if you even have enough to do that, and you are broke, but you do have some nice things! Now a $3,000,000 house doesn't come without strings attached. There is upkeep, property taxes, and insurance. You stay at your old job that pays so poorly you cannot afford the upkeep on your beautiful home and decide to sell in order to stay afloat. Of course you are desperate which is very bad when selling high end property and you only get $2,000,000 for your house after real estate fees and other expenses. It's not so bad, you still have some nice cars and $2,000,000 in your pocket, but now you are used to living the good life so you buy a $1,000,000 house figuring you are still in good shape. Meanwhile you are still blowing through cash like you are rich and the story goes on and on until the person is broke, still working the job they have always hated, and don't have anything put away for the future. Now they are on TV complaining about money as the root of all evil and how they wish they had never won the lottery!

Money was not the problem. There was more than enough money to meet every objective they could have ever imagined. The problem was how they handled the money. Money is not evil. It is simply a tool for obtaining goods and services from society. However, what many people do with money could certainly be considered evil. The lottery example is a bit extreme because most of us will never win a big prize in our lifetime, but I think you get the idea. A more realistic example is a bonus. Many of you receive some form of quarterly or annual bonus at work. The money is "extra" money and you may often have good intentions to use that money wisely, but it has been my experience most people use their bonus simply to buy more things and many people buy those things before they ever actually get the bonus (aren't credit cards great!). All of a sudden the company decides it has been a tough year and the boss won't be able to get a new Mercedes without cutting bonuses. Sound familiar?

Financial decisions, like what to do with a bonus or a raise, become much easier when you have defined what is truly important to you. Suze Orman has written several popular financial books and has become a financial celebrity. One of her most profound messages that I strongly agree with is her consistent advice to have the following priorities:

People
Money
Things

There are a lot of things Suze Orman says that I would not agree with, but her priorities are simple and to the point. People generally get into financial trouble when they lose sight of what is truly important in their lives. Money is certainly important because it is the means to buy the things you need or want in life starting with the true necessities of shelter, food, clothing, etc. However, money should not be more important than your family or friends and, if it is more important, you will likely be unhappy in your life.

A financial plan is important for two major reasons. Planning allows you to define your most important financial priorities. By periodically reviewing your plan, you have a means to measure progress towards those priorities. These are critical concepts very few people follow in their lives.

Keep in mind the following key principles of financial planning whenever you read or discuss planning concepts:

1. Everyone's situation is at least a little bit different. We are all unique individuals or families.

2. Because everyone has a unique situation, there is no "right" way to create a financial plan.

3. Implementation of a plan is more important than the plan itself. In general, doing something is better than doing nothing. A poor plan in action can be changed, but a good plan with no action is worthless.

4. Review and revise your financial plan as circumstances change. Remember little steps. Financial plans more often require a little routine maintenance than a complete overhaul.

2

Defining Your Most Important Financial Priorities

"To begin is the most important part of any quest, and by far the most courageous."
Plato

Creating a financial plan starts with defining what is important to you (emphasis on you). In fact, creating a financial plan without knowing what is important to you is impossible. Sure I could tell you some good investments to purchase and maybe you could accumulate a nice net worth, but it doesn't mean anything until it is put in the context of what is important to you.

The first step is to set aside a couple hours with your spouse (if you are single this step is pretty simple). No distractions. Send the kids somewhere else; turn off the TV, and sit down with pen and paper. Write down what you think is most important in your life.

A typical list might be:	or maybe:
Family	Money
Faith	House
Friends	Car
Career	Boat
House	Family

Compare your lists (if you are single this is a pretty simple step). If one of you has the first list and the other person has the second list, Houston, we have a problem! If you both have the second list, Houston, we have a big problem! Notice how the first list takes little money to be happy. The second list is almost entirely based on money. I am not a psychologist, but having an honest discussion about the differences in your lists would probably be beneficial to your relationship on a number of levels.

After discussing your list, make another list together until you have some level of agreement on the different values most important to each of you. Now focus on those values that deal with money. Family (raising a family costs money), house, faith may cost money if you are charitably inclined, and vehicles (most people would consider some form of vehicle as a modern necessity in life).

What is important about family from a financial sense? Food is a good idea. Clothing would be nice. Maybe education is very important to you. Your home is likely a big financial item and vehicles certainly cost money. This process is used to figure out your basic cash flow requirements. For most of you these requirements are already set, unless you are newly married or just graduating from college. You know your rent or house payment; you have set expenses for utilities, a car payment and insurance, and your lifestyle dictates your cost for food, clothing, etc.

You will find nearly all of these things are relative. Housing costs can be very low, (I never paid more than $150/month for an apartment during the college poverty years!) or very high. Transportation costs can vary greatly (new Mercedes vs. a used Hyundai). Food could easily cost over $1,000/month if you eat out a lot or it could cost very little if you tend to cook most meals. The nurses I work with tend to spend very little on clothes (they get their work uniform from the hospital), but an attorney may have an extremely expensive wardrobe. The point is you are consciously or subconsciously making choices about money every day of your life and without setting some form of priorities, those choices can either help or possibly hurt your financial health.

I will cover cash flow in much more detail in Chapter 4, but at this point, you should be able to put some type of monetary number on what you need to provide the necessities for you and your family on a monthly basis. I am not big on budgeting and I have never used Quicken or Money to run our family finances. My system is much simpler. Our basic budget looks like this:

House	$2,400
Vehicles	$ 600
Spending Money	$1,000
Food	$ 300
Miscellaneous	$ 300
	$4,600

I will outline where these numbers come from in Chapter 4, but you get the idea. Your number may be much greater or maybe lower than our numbers. It is irrelevant what the numbers are at this point. Someone living in Manhattan might have dramatically higher numbers and someone in North Dakota, where I grew up, might have dramatically lower numbers. Notice the simplicity of breaking your life down into only a handful of categories. I once had a client who had 250 separate spending categories budgeted on a Quicken spreadsheet (right down to beef jerky as a separate category!). I thought he was extremely well organized, but I also thought he was crazy for spending that kind of time on something that silly.

You now have your cash flow priority number. It may or may not be realistic. This is priority number one. Now we can define our other major financial priorities. Most people will consider planning important for one or more of the following categories:

Emergency Reserve—how much to have in savings to cover emergencies
Education—private school or college expenses
Risk Management—insurance such as life, health, disability, and long term care
Retirement—when and how much will you need
Estate Planning—wills, trusts, and power of attorney

We have to figure out what you want from each of these categories in your life. If you don't have kids and don't expect to need any additional education for yourself, obviously you might care less about the education category.

EMERGENCY RESERVE

Nothing feels better financially than having some form of emergency reserve to fall back on when times get tough, and times always get tough at some point in life. You may lose a job. The transmission might go out on your car. Your furnace or air conditioner might break down on the coldest/hottest day of the year. All of these things can be unexpected and likely create tremendous stress in your life. The last thing you want to do in this situation is add financial stress on top of the pile.

Most people use their credit cards or a bank line of credit for emergency reserves. Not necessarily a bad approach. Let me ask you a rhetorical question: do you think banks and credit card companies make money? Of course they do and they tend to make a lot of money. Where does the money come from? Interest, fees, and late charges, all add up to big bucks for these financial institutions. If the banks and credit card companies make money, wouldn't it make sense to be your own bank? Let me use an example.

Let us assume you just lost your job. You are hurt and upset because you were with the company for ten years and they laid you off out of the blue. Bills keep coming and there is no income to offset those bills so you start to borrow money as you search for a new job. The economy is tough in your area so finding new work isn't easy. It takes you four months to find a new job with similar pay. During that time you borrowed $10,000 on your credit cards at a relatively low 9.9% interest.

Things improve, money starts flowing in and you begin paying off the debt at $200/month. At this rate, you would have the loan paid off in 65 months or about 5 ½ years. Each month the bill comes in and it reminds you of being laid off from your last job. Those hurt emotions are still there and they boil up each time that credit card payment is sent off for 5 ½ years. Also, to add fuel to the fire, you paid the credit card company about $13,000 or $3,000 more than you owed. I don't know about you, but there must be a better way.

If there had been an emergency reserve of cash set aside for just such a rainy day, the bills would have been paid during the lay off. Also, some interest would be earned while the money sat in reserve. The interest is not the important part of an emergency reserve; the important part is peace of mind. Once a new job is found, you begin paying yourself back until the emergency reserve is built back up. There are two huge advantages to this approach. The first and biggest advantage is being able to let go of the past. The layoff was a tough time in life. Having to rehash that event each month is definitely unpleasant, so why do it? Let go; move on, and leave the stress of a bad situation behind.

The second big advantage is the financial advantage. You not only earn interest on the money you have in reserve, but you also save the interest you don't have to pay to the bank or credit card company. Over a lifetime this savings can be huge and is another way to reduce financial stress in your life. Why pay $3,000 to a credit card company so a VP at the bank can spend *your* money on *his* family? Be your own bank and spend that money on your own family.

I know what you are thinking right now. "Yeah right. It's easy for you to talk about having an emergency reserve. I've got bills to pay! Things are tight and any money in savings seems to be gone by the end of the month." This is typical of most people and is why planning is so essential. If you want things to change, you have to do something different. Accumulating an emergency reserve is hard and it takes time which means it must be a priority in your life or it will simply never happen. If this is the case, you will just have to stay the bank's sugar daddy, or sugar momma.

How much is enough? This is a tougher question and if you asked ten different financial advisors how much you should have in reserve, you would likely get at least five different answers. This means there is no right answer to this question. It really depends on your circumstances: How secure is your job? Do you get paid a consistent salary or does it fluctuate with overtime, bonuses, or commissions? What are your monthly expenses? Are there two incomes in your household? These are all important considerations so the appropriate amount of emergency reserve is the amount that makes *you* comfortable. How's that for an answer!

Let me give you an example:

My wife and I operate on a single income that fluctuates greatly from month to month. We are also very conservative and feel very secure with a solid emergency reserve. We set the following goal when we got married:

Keep a minimum of one month of expenses in checking (no interest on the account)

Keep a minimum of two months expenses in savings (minimal interest)

Keep a minimum of nine months expenses in a joint mutual fund account

For us this means about $4,600 in checking, $9,200 in savings, and about $41,400 in our joint mutual fund account. Now you are truly skeptical! Many of you might be saying "If my math is right, you have about $55,200 of available money socked away; I can't possibly save that kind of money. I've got bills; things are tight, and there is never any thing left in savings at the end of the month!" We have bills too and we accumulated this money while paying off student loans, while buying a home, and without ever earning more than $80,000 of combined family income. We did inherit $10,000 early in our marriage, but I lost that money in what I like to call a "day trading accident." More on that later, but we were responsible for saving into our emergency accounts. I am not saying it is going to be easy for you and it doesn't happen overnight. It took us five years to reach this goal, but do you think it was worth it? You bet. We had to make some very conscious decisions not to spend our money on toys and other things we deemed luxuries. Here is the beauty of making this a priority:

Once you have the money saved, you don't need to save anymore. The money you were working so hard to save is now working for you. The money you were saving is now available to spend on your family (more cash

flow) and the money your emergency reserve earns is also available to spend on your family. You have become your own bank!

There are only two simple requirements for accumulating an emergency reserve. Start saving money now, no matter how small an amount, and do not spend the money you save unless it is an emergency. You will need to define an emergency, but it is not a vacation; it is not a new boat, and it isn't a new big screen TV. I don't care if it takes you ten years or more to reach your goal, whatever your goal may be. At least you are making an effort and that effort will pay off over the long term.

Now you need to discuss your goal for an emergency reserve. Here are some suggested guidelines to help you. If you have two relatively secure incomes, I would recommend the following:

Keep a minimum of one month of expenses in checking
Keep a minimum of five months expenses in a joint mutual fund account

This is obviously much easier to achieve than our goal, but you simply do not need as much set aside for a rainy day if the chances of a rainy day are slim. It is very unlikely two people would get laid off from relatively secure jobs at the same time and you would still have a sizable nest egg to get you through without needing to borrow money. You also have the ability to invest your emergency reserve more aggressively because it is more likely to be long term money (we will address investment recommendations for this type of account in a later chapter).

Start by accumulating the checking account and then begin building the joint mutual fund account. The checking account will likely earn little to no interest and you will be tempted to take more risk and try to get greater returns. Emergency money is just that, emergency money. The point is not to get great returns, but to make sure the money is there when you need it.

I would consider our family's example as the worst case example, or most conservative guideline, and the two stable income family scenario as the best case example, or the most aggressive guideline. Your goal will likely fall somewhere in between the two extremes.

Once you have agreed on an emergency reserve goal, write it down and move to the next step. It is very likely a man will want less emergency reserve and a woman will want more emergency reserve. Remember, men tend to be bigger risk takers and women see money as security. Compromise, compromise, compromise. There is no right answer to this question so respect each other's opinion and come to an agreement that suits both of you.

EDUCATION

Funding your children's education (whether private school when they are young or college costs) is certainly a noble desire, but this objective can be quite controversial. I often have spouses disagree over this priority. Some people believe very strongly that providing education is one of the best things they can ever do for a child and consider it a huge responsibility. Other people believe the child will never appreciate his education unless he pays for it (of course I mean college; it's not easy for a third grader to earn the money to attend private elementary school). I don't care which school of thought you follow, but I do care about agreement on what you plan to do in the future. A frank discussion now will potentially save huge arguments and hurt feelings down the road.

I also believe there are a lot of misconceptions about the right types of investments and investment vehicles for funding education costs. I will address these issues in a later chapter, but right now I want you to figure out your basic goals for education.

For example, my wife and I went to the same public university for Civil Engineering. I was responsible for providing my entire education through work, loans, and I was fortunate to get some sizable scholarships. My parents did not have money put away to help with my education, but they did send food and other helpful supplies along the way. My wife was mostly responsible for her education, but her parents did help pay for her tuition. We, as parents, both want the ability to help Isabella and any future kids with college costs, but we are torn over whether to have our kids go to public or private school in elementary and high school.

Here is what we agreed on for an education financial priority. We figure the most expensive scenario from a financial perspective is sending our kids to private school and then a public university. If the kids want to go to a private college, we would help, but would likely not be able to pay their full cost. We also want them to be active participants in funding their education so we expect them to work and save money for at least part of the cost.

We are saving primarily for the college costs and expect to pay for any private elementary or high school years out of cash flow (meaning my earnings had better rise or they will be in a public school). Some of our savings will be invested in such a way to allow for use prior to college to help with private high school (you will see specifics on how we save in future chapters). We base our college cost estimates on in-state costs for the University of Minnesota. The cost estimate to provide tuition, fees, books, and room and board at the University of Minnesota is about $11,000/year (based on 2003 numbers). We assume a 6% inflation rate for college costs (about the long term norm) so Isabella's four years of college would cost about:

Year 1 = $29,620
Year 2 = $31,400
Year 3 = $33,280
Year 4 = $35,300
Year 5 and beyond = Her problem!

The grand total in future dollars is about $129,600. Get the smelling salts; I think I lost a few of you on that number. Yes, a simple four year *public* education starting 17 years from now will cost about $129,600! Keep in mind; this is for just one child. How many kids do you have? If you plan on private school, double the number and you should be in the ballpark. Realistic to provide education? Maybe not, but this is our objective and we are sticking to it. Doable? Absolutely (I will show you how in a later section on investments). Easy? Absolutely not.

There are a lot of websites dedicated to estimating college education expenses. Nearly any major financial website should have a college cost calculator for most major colleges across the country. I recommend checking several different sites and do your homework before finalizing your objective.

The majority of my clients want to plan on providing some portion such as 1/2 or 1/3 of their children's education. They will plan on supplementing loans and their children's earnings. Many of these people plan on providing some form of matching funds so they can instill responsibility and help their kids appreciate their education to a greater degree. I cannot confirm or deny the validity of this belief, but I simply want my clients to agree on their goal no matter how big or how small.

At this point, you should have some basic written objective for your education priorities and we can move on to the next step.

RISK MANAGEMENT

Risk management involves the use of insurance to share life's major risks with a group of other people to make catastrophic events affordable for the whole group. Insurance is probably one of the most difficult areas to address in a plan because there are so many emotions and variables involved. If you tend to be confused about insurance, don't feel bad. The insurance industry makes policies difficult to understand and nearly impossible to compare on an apples to apples basis. The more confused you are, the more likely an agent can sell you more than what you really need.

I will preface this discussion by saying I am much more of an investment planner than an insurance planner. However, this is an area relevant to virtually all of my clients so I have been forced to become knowledgeable about the various types of life, health, disability, and long term care insurance. I am not an expert on property and casualty insurance (car, home, boat, umbrella policies, etc.) so I will not address these areas. Please find a competent, trusted agent to help you with your property and casualty insurance (preferably a referred agent) and compare at least a couple different agents.

Insurance is not fun to talk about, but it is extremely important in a properly constructed financial plan. I always tell clients to plan for the worst and expect the best out of life. Insurance is the part of your plan where we plan for the worst case scenarios like a premature death, a life altering disability, or a serious health condition.

As with property and casualty insurance, I will not cover health insurance in much detail. Nearly all of my clients have some form of comprehensive health insurance through work. If you are like me and have to purchase health insurance on your own, talk to a specialist and do not, I repeat, do not go without coverage. A major medical policy with a high deductible will at least insure you can financially handle a major health care issue without declaring bankruptcy.

Many people have the misconception that group health insurance is dramatically less expensive than personal coverage. This is true if you have health problems and cannot obtain reasonably priced coverage on your own. However, if you are healthy, personal coverage is not outrageous and can often be cheaper than group insurance. Our family coverage costs us $305/month to cover the three of us. We have a $1,000 deductible per person to a family maximum of $2,000. We pay the deductible out of pocket until medical expenses exceed the deductible. At that point, we have to pay 20% of additional health care costs up to a family maximum of $5,000 out of pocket. Our worst case scenario on an annual basis is $305/month in premiums and $5,000/year in total out of pocket expenses (which would rarely occur). Regular physicals for my wife and me and regular well checks for Isabella are entirely covered by the insurance company. As a business owner I am able to write off the cost of health insurance as a business expense, so the premiums are even less on an after tax basis.

Health insurance options vary greatly from state to state so you will need to do your homework if you do not have coverage through work. Also, health insurance is continually changing so it is difficult to stay on top of new advancements. If your employer provides group coverage, but you are on the hook for paying premiums, make sure the group rates are competitive with what you could obtain by shopping for a personal policy. Again, the group rates will be very good if you have a major health problem, but the personal policy may be less expensive if you are healthy.

Life and disability insurance definitely need to be addressed in any comprehensive financial plan. The way to approach insurance is to have a frank discussion about what would realistically happen if you were to get seriously disabled or die prematurely. If you are single, disability is much worse than dying. Dead people don't have bills, but disabled people often have higher bills. In a married couple, disability insurance is still important, but at least there is the possibility of two income earners to help spread the risk. Life insurance becomes very important to a married couple, especially if children are involved.

For now we are simply trying to come up with the proper amount of insurance and not the proper type which will be discussed in a later chapter. Determining the right amount of insurance is relatively easy for a single person. Most single people tell me they do not want to be a burden to someone else, but unless they have kids, they are also not responsible for anyone else. This means you should have enough life insurance to cover any current debts and any final expenses. Add up all of your outstanding debts; throw in a number for final expenses (usually around $10,000); add any amount you would like to leave someone else, and you have your insurance objective.

Disability insurance is more complicated, but I normally recommend single people have at least a long term disability policy that covers 65% of their current income. Short term disability insurance is great if your company provides coverage, but if you don't have it provided through work, do not buy your own short term disability policy (use your emergency reserves for short term emergencies and save the premiums). Long term disability coverage is very important to help protect your ability to earn money. This is an area where group insurance tends to be much less expensive than personal coverage, but there are many group policies that really stink. Again, this is an area where you will want to discuss your options with a disability insurance specialist (even if you have coverage through work) and do not skimp on coverage.

For married people, life and disability coverage become much more complicated. The emotions involved in talking about a premature death or serious disability are extreme and can cause irrational decisions. Insurance salespeople are often taught to prey on these emotions and I have seen many inappropriate policies sold to people based on their fears rather than their personal situation. I recommend spouses seriously sit down and discuss what would happen if either of them would die or become disabled and discuss what the other spouse would want or need in that scenario. Do this before talking to an insurance agent. Develop your objective and then figure out how to address the objective.

For example, we have a fairly unique situation. I personally do not carry long term disability coverage (I probably just lost credibility with any financial planners reading this book). How can a financial planner with a family be so irresponsible to not carry a long term disability policy? My wife and I discussed this issue at length and came up with a couple conclusions (not necessarily right or wrong, but this is how we discussed the issue). My wife is a structural engineer so she has the ability to earn a good income if I became disabled. Her income would mostly replace the money I currently earn. This helps hedge our risk, but still is not enough. My profession is not a physical profession meaning it would take a very serious disability for me not to perform my job (basically a disability that kept me from doing *any* type of job). If that happened, social security would likely qualify me for disability benefits, but it is extremely difficult to get approved for social security disability benefits. Most people are denied at least once. This would lead most people to believe I should purchase a long term disability policy, but there is another less obvious issue to think about. I personally believe most disability insurance companies are, how should I say it, less than ethical in dealing with their policy holders (I am trying to be nice). Personal disability insurance is expensive to buy and I am not entirely convinced the coverage would pay off unless I suffered a truly debilitating disability. I am not saying this is the right way to feel about disability insurance, but it is the way we feel about disability coverage.

That being said, I am currently investigating group long term disability coverage through my broker/dealer. This is a new option that recently became available to us. If the prices are reasonable, I will likely purchase some type of policy to supplement my wife's earning ability. I am thinking $2,000/month of benefits would pay for help with our daughter (since my wife would be working and I may be too disabled to watch Isabella) and would cover some supervision for me. Health insurance should cover my increased medical expenses if any. I have run through this scenario with disability insurance agents and they gasp in horror at my ignorance. They immediately bring up the worst case scenario and claim I am being absolutely irresponsible for not better protecting my family. This may also happen to you, but you need to remember how these people get paid. They can only get paid if you buy a policy meaning they have no vested interest in your financial security; they have no interest in learning your unique situation, and they only get paid if they can convince you there is a need. They also make more if they convince you of a greater need meaning more insurance and higher premiums.

Hopefully you have a decent long term disability policy through work so you don't have to deal with talking to an agent. If you do not have coverage through work, talk to at least two disability insurance experts before making a decision. I also recommend thoroughly investigating the company they recommend to see if there is a history of complaints against the company for not paying justified claims. You might consider calling your state insurance commissioner or commerce department. They should be able to give you an idea if a large number of complaints have been received for the company you are investigating. They won't make specific recommendations to you, but they have good insurance information for consumers.

Life insurance for married couples is also an emotionally charged issue. This is another area where men and women think very differently. Remember, men tend to be risk takers and women generally want security. When you buy insurance, you are transferring risk from yourself to the insurance company in exchange for premiums. This means men tend to minimize life insurance and women tend to maximize life insurance (certainly not always the case, but this has been true in my experience). I have had many men with inadequate life insurance tell me their wife would simply need to remarry if they died. Really! Usually the wife gives the death stare and the husband starts to rethink his comment. What is the dating scene like for a 35 year old woman with three kids? Maybe life insurance is a better solution in this scenario because getting married might be a hit or miss proposition.

So how do you come up with an answer for the "how much" question. There is no right answer and there is no scientific method for determining your need. Your need is dependent on your unique circumstances and your individual comfort level in taking risk. My wife and I have the following objectives which helped us figure out our needs:

If I die first:

Tracy would like to be able to stay home with our kids until at least school age, but we want enough insurance to give her the option to not work full time until the kids go to college. This is an expensive objective because we not only have to pay off debts and future education costs using insurance, but we have to replace enough of my income for the family to get by with a decent lifestyle. We also have to make sure Tracy will have enough for retirement since she may not be working much during her primary earning years.

Note: Future marriage for Tracy did not enter into our assumptions!

Our total current debt and final expenses would result in about $150,000 being spent right off the top. Another $50,000 would be set aside for future education costs. With all debts paid off, we figured she would need about $32,000/year in today's dollars to live a similar lifestyle to our current lifestyle. This number includes $500/month in spending money and includes 25% assumptions for federal and state taxes (no social security tax if she is not working). If we assume Tracy draws 5% income from the investments, she would need about $640,000 to provide income without eating into principal and hopefully the investments do better than 5% to account for future inflation. The kids would also receive social security payments until they are eighteen, but I didn't include those numbers in our assumptions. This adds a conservative safety factor to our calculations and accounts for increased future debt if we buy a bigger house or take on auto loans.

We decided $800,000 (rounded down from $840,000) of life insurance would be adequate for Tracy to do what she wants.

If Tracy dies first:

I want to continue my profession which means I would definitely need help with the kids and help keeping up the house until the kids are old enough to help out with chores. My income should be adequate to do these things, but I own my business so I suffer when times are tough. We figured paying off all debts would be nice and providing some money for future education would take that burden off my shoulders. As mentioned previously, our estimate for total debt and final expenses is $150,000. We assumed another $50,000 for future education costs and we threw in another $50,000 as an emergency reserve for help around the house the first couple years. We decided $250,000 of life insurance would be adequate for me to do what I want.

Note: Future marriage for me did not enter into our assumptions!

At this point we are simply determining an appropriate amount of insurance to give some peace of mind for both of us. I will address types of life insurance in later chapters and tell you how our life insurance is structured to meet our objectives.

There are also a million variables involved with our assumptions and many life insurance agents would consider our family under insured. It is not your agent's place to decide what is over or under insured, but rather your comfort level in the total amount and type of insurance. The agent is only there to help guide you through the decision process and to help get you the best insurance to fit your ultimate objectives. Remember, most insurance decisions are based on fear and guilt feelings and agents are taught to play on these emotions. If you feel pressured by an agent to do something that makes you uncomfortable, I strongly urge you to meet with another agent. I also recommend meeting with independent agents that do not have a conflict of interest to only recommend one company's products. This may help you save money and give a greater level of comfort in working with the agent.

RETIREMENT

Retirement is a lot more fun to talk about than insurance. Now instead of planning on dying early, you actually get to live and ultimately enjoy the fruits of your labor. Clients are always much more excited to talk about retirement than life insurance (I start to get worried when a client is excited about the life insurance discussion!).

How do you define a retirement objective? This is tough because retirement, or financial independence, is a very abstract thing in the minds of most people. It is a utopian ideal, far, far in the future. I often hear things like, I want to retire early; I want to be comfortable; I want to travel, or I want to cut back at work.

These all sound like retirement objectives, but they really are not objectives and they certainly are not attainable in their current form. How early? How comfortable? Where do you want to travel? How much do you want to cut back? When and how will it affect your income? These questions are much better at defining what you will need to meet your individual retirement objective.

My wife and I are in a unique position in regard to retirement. Remember, I own my business so I do not hate my employer! I also love what I do for a living so retirement is not a "sanity" issue for me. I will likely never truly retire. I may cut back and we may travel more, but I will likely continue to earn some form of income for the rest of my life, or until I become senile and my clients fire me. For this reason we end up in a fundamental debate whether to save in retirement accounts or say the heck with it and use our money for more immediate needs. Because our situation is different from the typical reader, I will use my typical client as an example for creating a coherent retirement strategy.

The first question is when you want to retire. Of course none of these priorities are set in stone and you certainly can modify things in the future (and probably will), but we must have a starting point and a finishing point to chart a course. My most common answer to this question is tomorrow (and the age of the client doesn't seem to matter). I often wonder why the most common answer is not today, but I have been told it is because today is over, or close to over, so it can be tolerated while tomorrow is still waiting and is dreaded. The most common realistic answer falls between ages 60 and 65.

The second important retirement issue is how much you will reasonably need in today's dollars to live the way you want to live. You are the only one who can answer this question and I notice many people have no idea how to answer this one. I usually suggest starting where you are today, meaning if you retired today, would you be comfortable with your current lifestyle. Most people answer "yes" and very few people have the financial determination to retire with a greater lifestyle than they currently have. Most people in our society are forced to retire with less than their working lifestyle, but they normally don't have a choice in the matter.

Before you come up with a monthly income number, which is what we are trying to obtain, I want you to consider a couple of things. Most media gurus and financial advisors say you will only need 60–80% of your pre-retirement income during retirement. There are a number of reasons why, but reduced taxes, no kids at home, no need to save for retirement, and maybe your home is paid off are the most cited reasons for reduced expenses. All of these issues may or may not be relevant to you, but what most people forget is retirement means you do not have to work anymore, *so you have seven days per week to spend money*. Most people do not spend a lot of money when they are working and for most, working takes up a significant amount of their week. I like to say "retirement means you have seven days per week to spend money rather than two days per week." Unless you plan to sit on your butt for most of retirement, you will likely spend more "spending" money on activities than you spent before retirement. My experience is most active retirees spend between 80–100% of their pre-retirement income even if the kids have moved out and their house is paid off.

The point is if you let other people define your objectives for you, the chances for future disappointment have been greatly increased. How does anyone know your circumstances better than you?

Our retirement objective (although I may never formally retire) would be $4,600/month of expenses or about $6,150/month of gross income ($73,800/year) in today's dollars. Why do I keep saying "today's dollars?" Rarely, if ever, does someone properly account for inflation when they talk about future financial objectives. Historically (since 1926), inflation has averaged about 3 1/2%. As of this writing, inflation is very low compared to historical standards, but inflation was very high during the late 70's and early 80's. We have no way to estimate future inflation because it certainly is not dependent on historical records. All we can do is assume a number and hope our assumption is close. If inflation turns out to be lower than your assumptions, you will have more than you thought and you will be pleasantly surprised at your good fortune. If inflation turns out higher than expected, hopefully you periodically review your plan and make modifications as needed, or you will be unpleasantly surprised. Either way, we have to start somewhere and I usually use 4% inflation until retirement and 3% after retirement. Retirement expenses tend to be high early in retirement, but they tend to level off a bit as people age and they become less active.

Have you come up with a monthly income number in today's dollars? If you haven't and don't know where to start, I recommend using 100% of your current gross income as a starting point. This may be an unrealistically high number, but it is always better to shoot high and miss than to shoot low and probably still miss, but miss lower. In our assumption of $73,800/year and assuming my age 62 (I am now 33), we would need about $240,000/year in 2033 to live the same lifestyle we currently live just based on 4% inflation. $240,000! This is a bit hard to comprehend because wouldn't you be rich making $240,000/year? This is why I want you to use today's dollars for all of your discussions. It is too hard for us to comprehend future dollars after accounting for inflation. We still account for inflation, but we would have no idea how to make decisions based on the seemingly huge numbers needed in the future. The overall size of the requirement also creates a sense of being overwhelmed and when most people are overwhelmed, they ask, "What's the use?" and never get started on the path.

I want you to always use today's dollars as you work through your financial plan and then account for inflation only after your objectives have been defined. If you have no idea how to account for inflation, please contact a financial advisor and figure out what inflation will do to your finances. The problem is many financial advisors are only taught how to sell "stuff" so they might not know any more about inflation than you do. Do everything you can to make sure the person giving you advice is competent and able to spend enough time with you to thoroughly address important concepts like inflation.

At this point you should have a specific retirement objective written on your sheet of financial priorities. The objective should give an age and an amount for you to retire and live the lifestyle you wish to live. Remember, this is only a starting point to give you a target to shoot for as you experience life's adventures. It is very likely your objective will change as circumstances change and it will be extremely important to periodically review and modify your objective as priorities evolve.

ESTATE PLANNING

This topic is a lot more difficult to discuss from the perspective of defining your priorities. Estate planning is a legal topic and, as most of you know, legal discussions are full of fancy words no one understands and it takes fifteen pages of text to accomplish a seemingly simple objective (and it still is likely a gray area). Most people, including me, do not fully understand all of the ramifications involved in creating a proper estate plan. Having a will is nice, but it really doesn't do the important things needed in the case of a premature death. There are several other issues more important for the typical family.

This is an area where an estate attorney's help is invaluable. The problem is I have seen many responsible people go to an attorney knowing they need to do something about their estate. Some of those people walk out with a ream of documents laying out an extremely complex plan that cost a fortune and probably won't work effectively anyway because no one can understand what it says. You need to find a competent, reasonably priced attorney to help your family. I will discuss competency and a reasonable price in a minute.

My goal in this book is not to give you a legal course on estate planning. There are many terms used that you may not understand or know exactly what I am talking about. That's fine. If I tried to explain all of the terms and tools used in the estate planning profession, we would be looking at many hundreds of pages and you would still be confused anyway (the legal profession is just plain confusing). My goal is for this book to be a practical guide to your finances. In order for anything to be practical, it cannot get bogged down in the minutiae of legal detail and definitions. I simply want to get you thinking about estate planning and let you know when it might be appropriate in your life to contact an attorney and what documents you might consider creating for your own peace of mind. As previously mentioned, you will need to supplement this book with other sources of information. There is no "holy grail" of financial planning books although many authors have the arrogance to claim their book is "the only financial book you will ever need!" Arm yourself with information from your own life experience and research, and find advisors you trust so you can obtain the information you need to make wise financial decisions.

You may also be asking, "I thought this book was for the rest of us and not the wealthy? Isn't estate planning only needed if you are rich?" In my opinion, the general media, attorneys, and advisors do a horrible job of educating the general population about the importance of creating a proper estate plan. An estate plan is appropriate for anyone who expects to die someday! If you fit in this category, you just might need to do an estate plan.

You are right though about the rich doing estate plans. The complexity of an estate plan is somewhat based on the wealth of the person needing the plan. For instance, an unmarried recent college graduate with no net worth certainly doesn't need a will, but she should still know who her beneficiaries are on her retirement accounts (if any) and she may want to consider a health care directive or possibly a power of attorney in case something happens to her.

Before we had Isabella, my wife and I had each other as beneficiaries on our various retirement accounts and life insurance policies, and we owned everything else jointly (house, savings, checking, investments, etc.). If one of us had died prematurely, the surviving spouse would have been able to access all aspects of the estate in a relatively simple manner. Probate, the legal process for distributing an estate, would have been minimal and there was really no reason for a will. A will does not avoid probate, but helps guide the court through the probate process. We did not have any formal estate plan, but we were comfortable with our situation.

When we had Isabella, we knew enough to figure our circumstances had changed dramatically from an estate planning perspective. Our level of financial responsibility had changed and we felt the need to do something to make sure Isabella would be fine if something happened to both of us. Remember, financial planning is about anticipating and preparing for the worst case scenario, but hoping for the best case scenario. We sat down with an attorney client of mine that we trusted and she led us through a discussion of what we wanted to happen if the worst case scenario occurred. My wife and I agreed on the following objectives for our circumstances:

- If one of us died, the surviving spouse gets the money and would take care of Isabella (nothing magical about this one).

- If both of us died:

  1. We wanted my wife's sister and her husband to be the legal guardian for Isabella and any future children.

  2. We wanted my wife's dad to handle the money for our kids until they were old enough to take care of themselves (my father-in-law is also a financial advisor which is a bonus).

  3. We wanted to make sure the kids had enough money to provide for their health, welfare, and education until they were old enough to make and live with their own decisions.

- If one of us was incapacitated, but still alive, we wanted to have our health care wishes on record and we wanted the other spouse to have the power to make decisions in his or her best interest.

I have found many of my clients have these same objectives (or similar), but most of my clients have never created a formal estate plan. They usually tell me they thought estate planning was only for the rich. The other reason for not doing an estate plan is the morbidity of the whole process. No one likes to have a lengthy discussion about being dead.

That being said, if you have a family and you care what happens if you, your spouse, or both of you prematurely die or get seriously disabled, I strongly urge you to see an attorney and create a formal estate plan. We ended up with the following documents to help meet our primary objectives:

1. Last will and testament for each of us leaving all assets to the surviving spouse.

2. The will named legal guardians and successor guardians for Isabella and any future children.

3. We created health care directives, health care power of attorney, and durable power of attorney.

4. The wills outlined contingent trusts in case both of us die prematurely to detail how our estate can be used for the children. The contingent trusts name trustees and successor trustees who have the responsibility for making financial decisions in the best interest of Isabella and our future children. The trust assets will be distributed to the kids 1/3 at their age 21, 1/2 at age 25, and the remainder at age 30.

Of course our legal documents come in a huge binder and there are numerous other legal notes and details, but the previous list describes the basic documents in our plan. We keep our legal documents with our other financial documents so they will be easily found in case something happens to one or both of us. Our attorney also has a copy of all documents.

Again, you might think estate planning isn't for you because you don't have any money. When my wife and I had Isabella, our investable net worth (retirement accounts and other investment assets) was about $50,000. Our other major asset was our house with equity of about $50,000. Do those assets make us rich? Certainly not, and I am guessing you may have more. What you may forget about is life insurance, whether group insurance through work or your own personal policies. Remember, if both of you die, the kids get all of your life insurance lump sum in cash. In our case, life insurance on both our lives is $1,050,000.

Let's say we have two children and my wife and I die in a car accident. We have no estate plan and the kids are five and two years old. What happens? First off, the courts decide a whole lot of things because we did not have the foresight to make those decisions for our family. The process is different in each state, but the court decides who will be legal and financial guardians for the children. Sometimes this process becomes a court battle if two or more relatives want custody. Also, the kids get their portion of the money on their eighteenth birthday. The age of majority differs from state to state, but it is usually 18 or 21 years old. Now I don't know about you, but an 18 or 21 year old with over a half million dollars sounds like a time bomb waiting to go off. We hope to do a great job raising our children (but we are dead in this assumption so we don't have much say in the matter) and we hope they become responsible adults, but at eighteen years old, I would question nearly anyone's ability to handle a significant lump sum of cash. We wanted to be responsible and make those important decisions for ourselves to insure the health and best welfare of our children if something happens to us.

Our estate planning documents cost us $1,000. Some attorneys will certainly be less expensive and some attorneys will be more expensive. This is not an area to skimp on. I see ads in the paper for all estate documents at $250 with a coupon. A coupon? You must be kidding! This is an extremely complex area of law and the attorney takes a coupon? There are also a large number of do-it-yourself software programs available for estate planning. I have been asked if these programs are an appropriate way to do estate planning. Maybe. I don't really know. We spent the money and the time to do it right. If you feel comfortable trusting your children's future to a software program, go for it. The whole idea made me a bit queasy and I like to think I know more about estate planning than the average person. I wanted to make sure my wife and I had a good relationship with a competent attorney so I have the peace of mind that if I die, my family will have a knowledgeable, honest person to act on their behalf. I didn't see that benefit from software.

You will also need to periodically review your estate plan as things change in your life. Divorce is a big deal when talking about legal documents. One of the first people you should see if you get divorced is your estate attorney. Everything typically changes and becomes dramatically more complicated. Also, if you get remarried, see your attorney and make the appropriate changes to your plan.

The point here is to take responsibility for your own actions, no matter how unpleasant they may be. If you are married and have children, take the time, spend the money, and get your estate plan in order.

◆　　　◆　　　◆

A sample list of objectives (these happen to be ours):

1. Review our cash flow and net worth

   Accumulate and maintain a minimum of one month of expenses in checking
   Accumulate and maintain a minimum of two months expenses in savings
   Accumulate a minimum of nine months expenses in a joint mutual fund account

2. Have the ability to fund 100% of the cost for four years of college at the University of Minnesota ($11,000/year in today's dollars). We assume a 6% inflation rate and two kids.

3. Review our risk management plan

   A. Maintain health insurance coverage for our family

   B. Consider purchasing a disability insurance policy on me. We determined $2,000 of coverage with benefits payable until age 65 would be adequate.

   C. Determine the appropriate amount of life insurance

      If I die first:

Tracy would like to be able to stay home with our kids until at least school age, but we want enough insurance to give her the option to not work full time until the kids go to college. We also have to make sure Tracy will have enough for retirement since she may not be working much during her primary earning years.

If Tracy dies first:

I want to continue my profession, but I want all debts paid off and money set aside for the children's education.

4. Our retirement objective, although I may never formally retire, would be $4,600/month of expenses or about $6,150/month of gross income ($73,800/year) in today's dollars. We assume a retirement age of 62 for me and sixty for Tracy. We also assume a 4% inflation rate up to retirement and 3% inflation after retirement.

5. Estate Planning—our objective is to create wills, health care directives, health care power of attorney and durable power of attorney for both of us. We want to make sure these documents address our desire to take care of our children in case something happens to Tracy and me.

This is the most important chapter in this book because there is no way to meet your objectives if you don't know what they are. Once your primary financial priorities are on paper, you can start to do something tangible to meet those objectives and can begin to measure progress. The remainder of this book will describe practical, real world solutions to help you achieve your unique priorities. Keep your list of priorities handy as you continue reading. This will help you stay focused on the book recommendations that are specifically helpful for you.

3

Elements of a Comprehensive Financial Plan

As you can tell by now, a comprehensive financial plan is much more than picking some mutual funds, contributing to your 401k at work, and picking up some life insurance here and there. Creating a plan gives you a map showing where you are and where you would like to be. Having a map doesn't get you to your destination, but it sure helps determine the best way to reach your destination. The process of implementing your unique plan is much more important than the financial products you use during implementation. The process is what allows you to measure progress and make modifications as your priorities and assumptions change.

When you travel to another city, you have to determine the best way to get there. You might consider several modes of travel like driving, taking a bus or train, or flying depending on several factors like how far you need to travel, how much it will cost, and how long it will take. You would probably take some time to figure out the cheapest, shortest, and quickest route to take. If you decided to fly, you might use the Internet to get the "best" price and would snap up a bargain ticket if you found a good deal. The whole travel planning process might take hours depending on the type and length of trip.

Most people spend more time planning their vacation than planning their financial life. Why? There are probably a number of reasons, but if I had to guess, I would say planning a vacation is fun for most people and planning your finances is not fun. We like to do fun things and tend to procrastinate or avoid doing things that are not enjoyable. I (along with a small minority of my clients) like to deal with finances. I get a sense of comfort knowing we are making progress towards our goals. Most of my clients do not like to plan their finances which is why I have a job doing what I do. The process is not easy and can definitely get confusing, but I believe people would be so much better off if they took the time to plan.

Hopefully you now have some idea of your most important financial priorities. If you skipped the first chapter, it probably doesn't make sense to go any further. Sure you might get some interesting tidbits of information and may even find something useful, but if you don't know where you are going, it probably wouldn't matter. This is why I am so critical of most "get rich quick" books that have no basis in planning.

The financial services industry spends billions of dollars each year to determine the best way to sell you "stuff." Financial media bombards readers and viewers with the opinions of financial "gurus" who all seem to differ in their opinions, but who are all right (of course). How the heck do you keep track of it all and what does it mean for you and your family? I would contend most of what you read, see, or hear about financial services or financial planning is just sales advertisements in the disguise of advice. As with all advertisements, they are mostly sales gimmicks and certainly do not indicate the quality or benefit of what is being sold.

The classic example in my mind is the huge debate over "load" or "no-load" mutual funds. I read the Minneapolis Star Tribune business section each Sunday; I get the Wall Street Journal each weekday, and I do tremendous amounts of Internet research every day, trying to stay on top of the ever-changing financial services industry. I also watch CNBC and listen to their financial experts discuss various financial topics. During my research I will generally run across at least one, and sometimes several, articles per week debating whether a person should invest in load or no-load funds. In my opinion, the debate is totally irrelevant to most investors, but it certainly is an excellent way to confuse people.

I will cover mutual funds in a later chapter about investing, but for now, a load mutual fund is simply a mutual fund that charges some form of commission to compensate a financial planner, broker, or agent. The load can come in many forms and is often hidden, meaning you would not see the charge on your statements. A no-load fund is a mutual fund with no commission charges generally sold directly through the mutual fund company. The media contends most people are better off with no-load mutual funds because they can often be less expensive since there is no commission. The financial services industry contends load funds are better because you get the help of an advisor in one relatively inexpensive package (the commission is usually built right into the fund so it is a convenient way to pay an advisor). I have oversimplified the argument, but it really just comes down to a debate over expenses. I believe neither one is better than the other and no one can predict your future returns from two comparable mutual funds whether they are load or no-load. If you want your advisor's help, it would be nice if he could be compensated and stay in business long enough to help you over the years. Your advisor may get his compensation from the commissions on mutual funds in which case, load funds would be used. If you are a do-it-yourself investor who doesn't need the help of an advisor, it would be silly to pay a commission to someone else, so you would probably be better off in a no-load fund. Neither investor is smarter or better than the other and only time would tell who ended up doing better.

The point is both sides are missing the real reason for buying a mutual fund in the first place. A mutual fund is simply an investment tool used to help you meet a future financial priority. I say "simply," but mutual funds are actually very complicated partly because there are so many of them. This means the priority itself is much more important than the mutual fund or funds you select to help meet the future priority. How do you know which fund is right if you don't know what you are investing for?

The financial services industry would say I am validating their argument for the use of load funds to compensate a broker or other type of financial advisor. This is absolutely not true! I believe most brokers and so called financial advisors are glorified salespeople. Their job is to sell stuff and make money for themselves and their firm. Financial planning is at most a secondary issue with most advisors. In my opinion, the financial services industry does not make enough money from financial planning to justify wasting time doing proper planning for clients. They make a lot more money when they sell you something. If you are paying an advisor, make sure he is doing something worth his compensation, whatever form of compensation your advisor chooses to utilize.

On the other hand, no-load funds have to sell their product too and their big pitch is being cheap (or I guess they would rather say "inexpensive"). Most no-load fund companies believe financial planning is a simple concept and everyone knows exactly how to save for their future priorities without any help other than a 1-800 number and a website with some generic investment information. For this reason, why would you ever pay for the help of an advisor? You are just wasting money! Buy a no-load fund and you will be better off in the long run. Keep in mind they are not selling a service; they are selling a product. The product is only a tool so they are missing the big picture of financial planning.

Don't get me wrong, the expenses you pay for investments or insurance are certainly important, but they aren't the most important thing. The process of planning and defining what is truly important to you is the most important thing. No one knows which tools you should use to help achieve your priorities without first knowing your priorities.

Here is an excellent example. *How much do you need to retire?* I hear this question a lot and have heard many financial experts debate this issue. It seems to me the prevailing wisdom claims you need $1,000,000 to retire "comfortably" today. This type of garbage makes me downright angry because it screws up people's lives. Who are these "gurus" to think they know what *you* think is comfortable and what *you* want during retirement?

I had a person call me this past fall to help her with planning for retirement. She was 62 at the time and was concerned about the decline in her investments the past couple years and wanted to know if she would ever be able to retire. I met with her and we started a financial planning process together. I discovered she had done an excellent job of controlling her debt. Her house was paid off and she had only a small loan on her relatively new car. She had also done a good job of saving for retirement. Her investments totaled about $250,000. She had heard on a local financial radio show that she would need at least $1,000,000 in investments to retire and was very concerned because she was already 62 and didn't want to work forever.

In our discussion, I asked her to talk about all the things she would like to do if she could retire today. We spent an hour talking about grandchildren and gardening, but she really didn't have any extravagant wishes for retirement. We developed a rough conservative estimate of the income she would need during retirement and it was about $3,300/month, keeping in mind she was going to pay off the car and would have no debt for several years until she needed another car. I assumed 3% inflation throughout retirement and we assumed a mortality age of ninety. Her estimated social security benefit at age 63 was $1,040 and she had a pension through her union with a benefit of $1,385/month.

The pension and social security payment add up to $2,425/month so she would only need to get about $875/month from her investments or about $10,500/year. This means she would need to draw about 4.2% from her retirement investments to get the income she desires without tapping into her principal. As of this writing (2003), interest rates are very low and the stock market has been in a three year bear market, but we should still be able to find investments that could realistically give her a 4.2% return and still provide some additional growth to account for future inflation. Some people might debate this conclusion with me, but I think most rational people would agree she certainly does not need $1,000,000 to support her current "comfortable" lifestyle.

I told her I thought she could retire whenever she would like or she could cut back at work whenever she would like. She set a retirement date of her next birthday and immediately cut back on her hours at work. She was very happy and a few months later told me she enjoyed her work more because she knew she could retire when she wanted, meaning she wasn't tied to her job and wasn't locked into her decisions by money.

In this particular case, the gurus were wrong and they were causing this poor woman to worry unnecessarily about the "grim" prospects of her future. I have also had other cases where $1,000,000 would not have been nearly enough to provide the desired lifestyle of my client. Planning is a unique process for everyone which is why mass marketed financial advice is not appropriate for most people.

I think you are getting the idea. You are the most important person in determining your own financial future, but it takes some time and effort on your part.

Back to the elements of financial planning. You can see from the priorities you wrote down after Chapter 1 that your priorities dictate the primary elements of a comprehensive financial plan. Most people's primary objectives revolve around debt reduction, retirement, life insurance, education, buying a new home, etc. Some of these objectives are more important to you than your neighbor, but most people have to deal with these financial issues at some point in their lifetime. Wealthy people have a whole slew of other financial issues to worry about such as business succession planning, tax shelter planning, and trying to preserve their estate for themselves and future generations. They usually are not worried about making a tuition payment for the kids or if they will be able to retire someday. They are more likely to worry about not having a fifth stall on their garage for another Mercedes.

Most of my clients deal with the same issues you are concerned about in your life. The primary financial issues fall into three categories: Cash Management, Insurance, and Investments. This is a bit oversimplified because there are a number of issues that fall under these broad categories, but we have to start somewhere.

Cash management includes your basic day-to-day cash flow. What you do with your money on a day-to-day basis is probably the most important aspect of your financial life. There are literally hundreds of money decisions made every week. These decisions are sometimes very minor and sometimes quite important. Some decisions are made consciously and others are made without even noticing. Net worth would also fall under cash management, but net worth is really a measure of how well you control your cash flow. You could be the world's greatest investor, but if you live paycheck to paycheck and never put any money away, it wouldn't matter. This is what makes cash flow the most critical aspect of any successful financial plan.

Insurance is the risk management aspect of your financial plan. All of us have some form of insurance, whether it is car insurance, home insurance, health insurance or pet medical insurance. If you don't have any type of insurance at all, I would be surprised. Risk management is certainly an important aspect of any successful financial plan, but a person could go broke buying insurance. Risk management is about sharing risk with a group of people rather than transferring all risk out of your life. Transferring all risk would be prohibitively expensive so we must find a balance. Since there is no right or wrong balance, insurance is mostly a philosophical debate and depends largely on your own risk tolerance.

Investments cover a broad range of issues. It takes investments to provide the money necessary to meet future financial objectives like paying for education, retiring, or buying a home. The term investment is generic and can often be confusing. How you invest can vary dramatically with the type of objective you want to achieve and there are thousands of different investments available. Some are good, but many are bad. Some of the best appearing investments may actually be shams. Enron was one of the most widely promoted stock investments the year prior to going bankrupt, taking the life savings of many shareholders down with it.

The following chapters will deal with each element of your financial plan in greater detail along with specific recommendations to help you achieve success. Many of the reasons behind these recommendations are philosophical so keep an open mind and remember, there is no right way to do a financial plan or everyone would do it!

4

Cash Management

If you master cash flow, all of your other financial decisions will become amazingly easy. If you cannot master cash flow, all of your financial decisions will become amazingly difficult. Simple as that.

I have done comprehensive financial plans for hundreds of people (none of them would be considered "wealthy") and it always strikes me how easy it is to plan for people who live within their means and how difficult my job becomes when people live beyond their means. The concept is simple enough—don't spend more than you make and you will be better off financially. If it is that simple, why isn't everyone doing it?

There is more than enough blame to go around. The media and our advertising culture certainly should get some credit. They have turned shopping into a hobby rather than a chore. But in the end, you are responsible for your own financial decisions so the ultimate blame lies with each of us. You have the power to control your own financial destiny, but it won't be easy because you will be in the minority and it is always so much easier to be in the majority than trying to be different.

I am sure you have heard it all before. You may have even tried to set up a budget. There is probably a Quicken or Microsoft Money program on your computer that you used for a month or two, but never got in the habit. For most people cash management is a lot like their eating habits. Nearly all of us have tried some form of diet in our lives, but most diets fail and we revert back to our old eating habits. Budgeting and diets are both tough to implement because they are nearly always restrictive in nature. It is a scarcity mentality rather than an abundance mentality which means you don't have control anymore. As human beings, we want what we can't have and budgets make us want to spend more just like diets make us want to eat more.

I don't believe in formal budgets. Not because they wouldn't work for my family, but because I am too lazy to spend hours each month analyzing and processing every aspect of our day-to-day spending. I would rather spend time with Isabella than input how much we spent on chewing gum this month. I will discuss our family "budget" in more detail in a few moments, but right now it's time for some clichés (a few clichés and everyone will feel just a bit better!):

Any interest you pay is money you can't spend on yourself.
Clearing up debt is short term pain for long term gain.
Make compound interest work for you, not against you.
Pay yourself first.
A penny saved is a penny earned.
Borrow only for things that appreciate in value.

Well there you go. We don't need to go any further. Just follow these simple pieces of advice and watch the money roll in.

Clichés are nice and they certainly make sense, but they are better for a thirty second media sound byte than they are in reality. It is one thing to say something that sounds great, but how do you implement that concept in a practical manner? There are thousands of books on dieting and financial planning, but most people keep getting fatter and poorer. I am not sure exactly why this is, but I am guessing it has something to do with beer, doughnuts, lattes, pizza, and cheeseburgers.

Are you ready for some statistics? Things are going to get a bit preachy so bear with me. The following information comes from the American Bankers Association, myvesta.org, the Consumers Bankers Association and cardweb.com and was compiled in July-August of 2002. They found the average household now owes 104% of their after tax income. The national savings rate fell from 8.7% in 1992 to 1% in 2000. The following are average debts as of 2002:

Household credit card debt	$ 8,367
Auto loan size	$ 20,650
Mortgage loan size	$184,000
Refinanced mortgage loan size	$208,000

At least we have nice cars, nice furniture, and a nice place to live! What else do you need in life? I don't care who you are; there has been some point in your life when you wanted to buy something you didn't actually need because it was nicer than what you have and you saw someone else who has it. This isn't wrong; it's human nature. Being financially responsible doesn't mean you have to skimp on everything or feel guilty whenever you spend money.

One of the major issues with spending comes down to plastic becoming the chosen source of currency. Remember when purchases were made with cash? If you are like my wife, you may never have actual cash on hand. Why would you even need it? There is a credit card, debit card, and checks as a last resort. When was the last time you actually saw your paycheck? You probably have direct deposit so you don't even get to enjoy depositing your check at the end of the pay period. Plastic money is a bit like casino money. It's not actual money, but a bit more like monopoly money.

How many of you have your Internet, cable, and cell phone services automatically billed on your credit card? Nothing wrong with a little interest charged for the sake of convenience. Must be a good trade off and just think of the 37 cents you save for each stamp you didn't have to send! We stop for a few groceries and end up with an $87 bill because we loaded up on frozen convenience foods, gourmet coffee (how could you possibly drink anything else), and pop (or soda in some parts of the country and just plain "Coke" in some places). No worries, put it on the credit card. It's nothing frivolous because we definitely need to eat and you can't skimp on food.

I believe people would be much better off financially if we went back to the old days of paper money being the primary currency. It's pretty easy to know when the money is gone when you deal with paper! It's hard to know when the money is gone on a credit card and of course your credit limit is more than you have in checking and savings. It is also tough to control spending if you use your ATM card as a check card.

I will stop with the ranting. I think you get the point. So what do we do? There are a number of books dedicated to teaching ways to save more money so I won't get into a whole dissertation on how to budget or how much you should budget. I am all about being practical which means anything we talk about with cash management must be systematic or it probably won't work in real life.

I am going to use our family as a real life example. Again, I am not trying to say what we do is right or wrong, but I think it will help most of you get a feel for a different way of managing your month to month cash flow situation. This discussion will be primarily geared towards married couples rather than singles. There are a couple reasons for this: first off, my wife and I are a couple so it works best to give the example as a couple and second, it is much easier for singles to adapt these concepts to their way of life because there is only one opinion to consider.

I am always interested to see how people manage their money. Now when I say manage money, I am talking about their checkbook, spending, and their savings (not investments or any other aspect of their lives). I can learn a lot about a couple just by discussing their cash management system. Let me explain what I normally find.

The most common system I find is some form of joint checking and joint savings. All of the money goes into the joint checking and all of the spending comes out of the joint checking. Pretty simple and straightforward. There is nothing inherently wrong with this system which is why most people do things this way. In reality, one common problem typically comes to light with this form of money management. Most couples that utilize this system tend to compete over spending money. People tend to have at least a subtle competitive nature to them and this tendency really comes out when dealing with money. What do I mean?

This may or may not relate directly to you as a couple, but most of my clients admit this occurs to some extent in their lives. Let's say you like to do some form of crafting as your hobby and your spouse likes to fish as a hobby. You go out and spend $100 for crafting material that your spouse finds, how do I say it, kind of stupid. So if you can spend $100 on your hobby, your spouse can spend $100 on a new fishing rod that you find—kind of stupid. And the race is on. Now you feel justified in spending more money on something else because your spouse spent money and probably criticized your initial spending in the process. The spouse comes back with another purchase to offset your purchase and usually the amounts get bigger and bigger. In many cases the competition is who can spend the money the fastest until the bank account is drained. This also happened in the old days, but when the cash was gone, you each had to wait until the next payday to get more cash. Not so in today's society because when the cash is gone, there is always the credit card. Now the competition can go beyond what you have and can cause a lot more problems than your typical money argument over dinner. This type of spending pattern can cause real financial problems that can create enormous financial stress unless dealt with early in the process. Also note the beauty of this system: It doesn't matter how much you make because we can always spend more.

I hope you can relate to my example on some level and if you are like most of my clients, you have never truly thought about it in this kind of detail, but it happens. The next question is how you change the system so this doesn't happen. That is not an easy question which is why there are so many budgeting "gurus" who try to develop the next best way to manage money. Tracy and I have found a way that works for us, and you will need to find a way that works for you. If that means you use some things we use and develop your own way for other things, great. That means you have taken the time to think about cash management and have come up with something that works for you.

Let me set the scene. When Tracy and I first got married, we were each employed with good jobs (we were both engineers each making in the mid $30,000 range). I was 26 and she was 24 so we were a few years out of college, but we both were still in the college mentality meaning we didn't spend a lot of money. Most college kids are broke and we were no different. When most people graduate from college and get their first real paying job, they go on a spending spree. A new car is a necessity and a move from the dumpy college apartment to a new place is also a necessity. The wardrobe also has to change and shopping has now become fun because there is money to spend on new things you could never afford before. Fortunately for Tracy and me, we agreed this wasn't what we wanted to do. Before we got married, both of us made a serious effort to pay off our student loans, meaning we drove crappy used cars and lived in questionable apartments to save enough money to pay off our loans. Neither one of us had any debt when we got married.

We bought our current house and a brand new car when we got married which caused us to have substantial debt. It was the first time in our independent lives (meaning away from our families) that we had some nice things. This was an important time because having nice things makes you want to have more nice things. We sat down and had a frank discussion about how we wanted to handle money as a married couple because we both knew the problems that stem from a bad money system in a marriage (the most cited reason for divorce).

The first thing we did was tally up our fixed expenses. This is the easy part. Fixed expenses include mortgage or rent, utilities, car payments, insurance, gas, food, etc. These are the basic month to month expenses you should be able to closely track. When we first got married, our fixed expenses totaled $2,450/month.

House	$1,250/mo. (includes mortgage, taxes, utilities, repairs and insurance)
Vehicles	$ 800/mo. (includes payments, insurance, gas, and repairs)
Food	$ 200/mo. (only groceries, not eating out, which is spending money)
Miscellaneous	$ 200/mo. (extra fluff to cover unanticipated expenses)

The last part of a budget is the generic category of "spending" money. This is where most problems occur because spending money is not easily quantifiable for most people. Most people deem spending money to be the amount left over after all other bills have been paid. This means no matter how much money you make, it will all get spent. We knew both of us were early in our careers and we anticipated pay increases in the future, but we didn't want future pay increases or bonuses to translate directly into more spending. Our big conclusion was spending money had to become a "fixed" expense. We also concluded we both wanted to have some control over our own money so neither of us would feel guilty about spending "our" money on something just for one person. Tracy was particularly concerned about wanting to buy me a present from "her" money rather than taking the money from a joint account. In her opinion, if the money came from the joint account, it was like me buying a present for myself.

Based on our mutual objectives about spending money, we devised a system for fixing our spending expenses. First off, I asked her what she thought an appropriate monthly amount of spending money would be for her to do the things she would want to do. Keep in mind this was only a short time after college so we were still in the college poverty frame of mind. Tracy said $300/month would be more than enough for her. I agreed, but thought we should build in some fluff for expenditures we did not anticipate because of our poverty mentality and our mutual objective of wanting to do some traveling together. We finally agreed $500/month for each of us would definitely be more than enough to cover all of our individual spending.

With $1,000/month of spending money ($500/month each), our total budget included five line items totaling $3,450/month. Our base combined take home pay after maxing out my retirement plan at work (Tracy did not yet qualify for her plan at work) was $3,600 so we had room to spare with an extra $150/month available for savings.

STRUCTURING BANK ACCOUNTS

Now we had to design our bank accounts to fit our budget. Keep in mind most people have a joint account for everything. We set up a joint account and put all paychecks into that account and also paid all joint expenses with that account. We also set up an individual checking account for each of us to use for month to month spending money. Our accounts looked like this:

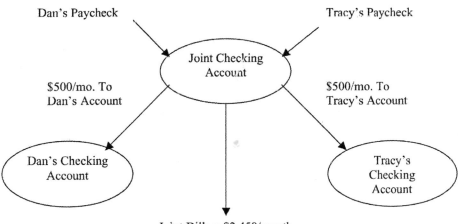

Note the subtle advantages of this system and how it met our objectives.

1. Our individual spending money is our own and we cannot criticize how the other person spends money. There is no incentive to compete.

2. We set a control on how much each person can spend and the amount was agreed upon by both of us. If the individual account runs dry, that person cannot spend anymore until the next month's transfer.

3. The income part of the equation is somewhat irrelevant as long as it is enough to cover all fixed expenses including spending money.

4. We are able to retain our unique spending values while still working together jointly for the common financial good of our marriage.

There was another subtle advantage of this system that works well for us from a planning perspective. One of our primary marital goals was to start a family at some point and to plan for Tracy to stay home with the kids for at least one year and hopefully longer. This scenario presents a challenge for most two earner families because it throws off the financial balance of the couple. If one income is lost, most families struggle with how to account for joint and individual expenses. Let me illustrate with an example.

My mom and dad struggled with money most of their lives while trying to raise a family. There were three kids and mom stayed at home for many years while dad was the sole bread winner. There wasn't much money to go around, but they made things work. Since mom did not work for an income, it was commonly accepted that she basically had no right to spend any money on herself. She had to ask for money from dad. As dad made more money and their finances improved, dad spent more money, but mom still had to ask permission to spend. Dad blew a lot of money at the bar and had no problem spending money on other individual hobbies like hunting and fishing. My mom was incredibly frugal and almost never spent any money on herself. In today's society this type of relationship would probably not work, but it was common back then. It is still that way today. Dad continues to spend tons of money while mom spends little on herself. It continually amazes me that dad doesn't see anything wrong with this system. It apparently makes sense to him.

It may have made sense to dad, but it didn't make sense to me. I wanted to make sure these spending injustices didn't happen in our marriage. This is why we created a system that didn't depend on who made the money or how much money we made as a couple. I didn't want either of us to think of "our" money as "his" or "her" money no matter where the money came from in the first place.

This past Sunday I read an article from Wall Street Journal about family finances and how to account for "found" money like bonuses, inheritances, or big winnings. The article focused on the debate about who gets to spend the money. Should it be the person who made the money or both of you? I actually got angry as I read the article because most of the people responding to the question said it is the money of the person who received it and they should have sole discretion over how it gets spent. Are you kidding me! If you run money this way you are just asking for trouble. There will be fights; there will be distrust, and there will be a sense of paranoia proliferated in your marriage.

No matter where the money comes from, it should be considered family money and get put into the joint account. If I want to spend money on myself, I do it from my own individual account. Same goes for Tracy. The joint account is used for joint purchases meaning both spouses have a say in how it gets spent or how it gets saved. Obviously there are times when compromise is an absolute necessity, but having a system in place takes care of a lot of the little problems in managing money.

I absolutely do not understand the concept of somehow splitting bills between spouses. You know what I mean, "You pay the phone bill and I'll pay the cable bill" type of thing. The spouse who makes more pays more of the bills so it is all "fair." The spouse who makes more also gets to spend more on themselves because it is "fair." If this system works well for you, I would not only be shocked, but I have to tip my hat to you for making a crummy system work. The sharing bills system seems anti-marriage to me. Why aren't the bills joint bills? Why not just live together and run totally separate financial lives? Why get married? I really don't understand and I think the sharing system is a money crisis waiting to happen. What if the bill you pay steadily rises while the other person's bill stays flat (mortgage payments tend to be flat while other bills rise)? How do you account for the difference over time? The feedback I get from clients is it most often gets resolved with a fight. Why do this to yourselves?

Why am I taking the time to discuss something as mundane as your checking account and paying bills? I believe it is an incredibly important aspect of your life that helps build a foundation for all of your other financial planning activities. As I have previously said, I do a great deal of financial research and I run across a lot of articles about cash management in some form or another. Most of the articles talk about ways to save money or ways to be frugal, but I never run across articles that tell you how to actually set up a system. It is probably a taboo subject because most writers don't want to be perceived as telling you how to manage your own money. They are fine with making some suggestions or giving some advice, but you need to decide what works best for you. As you can probably tell, I am not like most writers. It is incredibly difficult to learn anything about money as a young person (particularly for young married couples trying to get off on the right foot financially) because no one wants to talk about money. Most people probably have a decent idea about the sex lives of their best friends, but I find most people would not have a clue as to the financial health of their best friends. I have been at parties where the topic of money comes up, I mean personal topics of money, and the room usually clears in a hurry. Everyone seems to think other people have more or are smarter with their money and they don't want to be embarrassed talking about their debt or why they had a fight about spending. Men in particular often like to talk about investing, but they would never tell you about their credit card debt or how big their mortgage is.

I believe money should be discussed openly with the people closest to you. You talk about recipes, maintaining your car, how to build a deck, and what to feed your baby, all in an effort to learn, but most people won't talk about money in order to learn what to do. This is why I am using our own family examples throughout this book. It is likely our family is different from yours, and you probably have your own unique challenges, but getting the opportunity to see into our finances may help you get a better idea for how to deal with your own finances. I don't know about you, but I learn best by example.

So back to our story. We have three separate checking accounts at our bank. None of the accounts earn interest because we hate having to maintain minimum balances or limit transactions in order to earn $1.38/month before taxes. One penalty from the bank can practically wipe out a year's worth of interest. Don't worry about interest on these types of accounts because they are meant for practicality and convenience rather than money making. All of our accounts are linked and we do online banking (one of the best things I have ever done) so transfers usually take a couple minutes each month on the computer. I usually do the transfers when I am using our online bill pay so it really doesn't take any extra time.

Tracy and I are each responsible for balancing our own individual check books and I tend to take care of the joint account and all joint bill paying. I think most families will designate one person to keep track of the joint account because it is easier, but I like the idea you are both still responsible for your own account. This keeps both spouses involved with money on a month to month basis.

Both of us have cash cards for our individual account, but there is no cash card for the joint account. Tracy and I operate very differently with our individual accounts. She likes to use her debit card and to write checks while I operate almost exclusively on cash. The cash machine was truly a great invention in my opinion. I balance my checkbook about every 4–6 months and it usually takes about 5–10 minutes because I just add up all of my cash receipts and all of the transfers to my account. All of the transfers are $500 each and nearly all of my cash withdrawals are for $100 each. There is rarely a problem with an addition error or an error in entering an amount in my checkbook so it usually balances on the first try. Neither of us is right or wrong in how we do things. What I do works for me and what Tracy does works for her. That's all that matters.

The joint account has a check book, but most transactions occur online with our bill pay system at our bank. We are not charged a monthly fee for bill pay because we usually maintain more than $5,000 in all of our combined bank accounts. Otherwise, the charge would be $5.95/month. I absolutely despise fees like this and you need to keep a close watch on this nickel and dime crap. A lot of $5.95 charges add up to big money over time. If our balance does drop below $5,000, our bank is usually right there with a charge, but it rarely happens, so I call them and they are usually pretty good about taking back the charge. Don't be afraid to ask for money back from vendors, especially banks and credit card companies, because there are a lot of them to pick from. Late charges and other penalties can often add up to significant money so why not take the time to see if they will give you a credit for being a good customer.

I hope this all makes sense to you. I find it very difficult to translate real world applications into words. It all makes sense in my own mind, but it is truly a talent when someone can get words to paint a true picture of reality.

Finally we get to the spending money component of our expenses. This is where I get the most questions from clients. They are usually intrigued by the concept, but they get caught up in the minutiae of details like: Is gas a joint or individual expense? How do you cover joint entertainment expenses like eating out or going to a movie together? How does it work when you travel? Who pays the baby sitter?

These are all valid questions Tracy and I also had to address, but the answers will likely be different for everyone. We originally planned on gas being an individual purchase since we both had about the same amount of driving. This didn't work well because I paid with cash and Tracy tended to use her credit card. I told her to pay with cash, but she liked the convenience of paying at the pump, and I couldn't argue the point. I basically let it go. I also tended to pay for eating out and movies because Tracy almost never has cash on hand and it just seems right for the man to pay (don't ask me why in today's society of sexual equality). We do tend to pay for big traveling expenses out of the joint account because we always seem to travel together. Because of these little things, I tend to spend more money on a monthly basis than Tracy so my account depletes faster than her account. Not to worry because I came up with a better way to balance the little things over time.

Once or twice per year, I rebalance our accounts back to an equal amount. Neither one of us tends to spend our $500/month so both accounts build up over time. This is a natural result of us setting a number higher than we really expected to spend. Since we are not in a spending competition, there is no reason for either of us to spend down our accounts just to get "ahead" of the other person. It is almost the opposite where each of us likes to see our accounts bigger than the other account. It is almost a competition to see who can spend the *least* money. The money has already been set aside for spending so when the accounts get big (nice technical term), I periodically balance them.

As an example, let's say Tracy's account is $1,500 and my account is $1,100 (pretty common numbers for us). I will ask Tracy if she plans on buying anything relatively major for herself like clothes or other things that result in sizable one time charges. If she doesn't have anything planned, I will transfer $100 from my account to the joint account and $500 from Tracy's account to the joint account and we are both at a $1,000 balance. Now you might say, "A ha! You are cheating and getting to spend more money than Tracy." Not so my friend! Before ever making any transfers, we discuss what to do with the $600 that was transferred to the joint account and decide together how to spend the money on *us*. Remember, this money was specifically set aside to be spent so we spend it! The only time we don't actually spend the money is for an investment like our Roth IRAs or Isabella's Education IRA, but that is a topic for a later chapter. The $600 might get spent on furnishings for the house, or landscaping, or a smaller trip (Duluth for the weekend or maybe Las Vegas for a few days—of course I mean before Isabella came along because we haven't traveled much since we had her). The point is we both decide how to spend the money. We do this together. Dr. Phil would probably have good things to say about us making these types of decisions together rather than individuals with different values making random decisions on his or her own.

This system has worked extremely well for us during the six years of our marriage. We never fight about money. More importantly, as our incomes increased, our spending did not increase. We had more resources available to invest and there were no arguments about spending versus investing the extra money because we already had set amounts put aside for spending. This allowed us to invest large sums of money in anticipation of starting a family and still allowed us to travel and have a good time without feeling guilty about spending.

If this system works so well, why don't more people do it? I am not exactly sure, but I would say they are commonly doing what their parents did. Since no one really talks about money, people tend to do what they saw in the past or what they have always done. They don't know another way so they stick with what works, or more likely what doesn't work.

Out of the hundreds of people I have helped, I have only run across one couple that works their cash management similar to us. I say similar because they have some differences, which is natural, but the concept is the same. They have been married for 36 years and claimed there has never been a serious fight over money. I wasn't surprised by their results. It doesn't mean you will never fight about other things, but taking one extra point of contention (and usually money is a big point of contention) off the table will likely help your relationship.

For single people reading this book, you might be feeling left out right about now. The same system will also work for you, but on a much simpler basis. There is no joint account to set up. You really don't even need two accounts, but if you have trouble controlling discretionary spending, I would recommend setting up two checking accounts. The first account pays all of the bills and the second account is for discretionary spending. Everything else works the same as for a couple. Setting up a separate discretionary account will help you control how much you spend and also gives you a built in means for tracking your overall spending without a formal budget. If the account is down from the previous month, you spent more than you normally allow and you know exactly how much more you spent. If the account goes up from the previous month, you spent less than you allow (pat yourself on the back) and you know exactly how much less you spent.

I honestly believe this topic should be taught in the senior year of high school. Cash management is important to absolutely everyone. I also believe engaged couples should take a cash management course before getting married so there is an opportunity for their spending issues to get resolved before walking down the aisle. The problem is no one has come up with a decent course and there probably isn't any money in teaching the course (which is probably why no one has done it). Why would any self respecting, high producing financial advisor actually take the time to help young couples? Everyone in the business knows young couples don't have any money! For many financial advisors, it is not about helping people who need help, it is about helping people who are *profitable*.

◆   ◆   ◆

Have our expenses changed over the years? Absolutely. We are currently in the process of purchasing a lot where we will build our new house. The new house will have higher mortgage payments, higher taxes, and higher insurance. We also have one child which costs some money, but I don't understand why people say babies are expensive. The diapers, food, clothes, and toys are relatively small items and are easily covered in our budget by our discretionary spending allowance. I think most parents would agree they do less overall spending on entertainment when they have children and we are no exception. Our idea of a big night is ordering a pizza and getting a couple movies, not exactly high expense entertainment. We do have the advantage of Tracy being home, and me working out of the home, so we do not have daycare expenses, which can be huge. Children get more expensive as they get older, but they aren't very expensive as babies.

All things considered, our original budget included five items amounting to $3,450/year and our anticipated budget including the extra expense from the new house will be about $4,600/month (net of all taxes). We still have only five spending categories, but the spending in each category has changed over the years and will continue to change in the future just like your spending will change through life's journey.

	New Budget	Old Budget
House	$2,400	$1,250
Vehicles	$ 600	$ 800
Spending Money	$1,000	$1,000
Food	$ 300	$ 200
Miscellaneous	$ 300	$ 200
	$4,600	$3,450

Note how some of our most important spending items have increased as our income has increased, but discretionary spending remains the same and will continue to do so for the foreseeable future.

Will we actually spend $4,600/month? No. There will likely never be a month where we spend exactly $4,600 and most months we will spend considerably less than $4,600. This means there will be some excess (gravy) along the way. I am a huge believer in budgeting for worst case scenarios. It is rare the worst case scenario will actually occur, but if it does, you planned for it. If the worst case does not occur, you will always have some extra money left over. This is a good thing, but it is not easy to do and it will likely take your family quite a while to change your own spending habits to fit within this system. For newlyweds who have not created their own spending habits, this system should be fairly easy to implement.

As life throws you some curves, you will need to make slight modifications to the numbers in your budget, but the system remains the same. The system is what works, not the numbers in the system. There are a lot of people who think I will tell them how to spend their money as a part of their financial plan. It's their money; why would I care how they spend it? What I do care about is whether they have a realistic plan in place to reach their main priorities. In many cases their current cash flow picture is not aligned with what they tell me their main priorities are, so I need to bring them back to reality. If this happens, I make some suggestions for changing their system, but they are ultimately responsible for making their own money decisions. Some people listen to me; others don't. Some people will read this book and make beneficial changes to their finances; others won't. We cannot change human nature.

Notice I have not even talked about any investments yet. Everyone thinks investments are the most important part of a plan, but this is not the case. Getting a handle on your cash management is so much more important than making investments. In fact, good cash management makes picking investments much easier because you have more to work with and don't need to make investment decisions in panic mode. Some of you may have done this over the past three year bear market.

NET WORTH

The next aspect of cash management is net worth. Net worth measures how much money would be left if everything you owned was liquidated and all debts were paid off with the proceeds. I calculate net worth in all of my client's plans, but only as a means to help measure future progress in our relationship. Net worth is essentially a worthless number at any given time unless you are talking to a banker and trying to obtain some type of loan.

How can net worth be meaningless if it is a measure of your true wealth? I believe it is meaningless because money alone does not allow you to necessarily reach your financial objectives and often the people you think are the richest are not truly rich. Let me give you an example:

Couple number one lives in a $1,000,000 house, drives a new Mercedes, sends their children to private school, and they both dress very nice. Their total assets are $1,500,000.

Rich, right? In our society this couple would certainly be perceived as being rich, but we didn't get a chance to see their liabilities. Net worth is assets minus liabilities and their liabilities are $1,200,000. They are also cash flow negative which means their net worth may be declining. Basically they cannot afford private school, but they have to keep up their wealthy façade.

Couple number two lives in a $200,000 house, drives a three year old Buick, sends their kids to public school, and they both dress nice, but not designer nice. Their total assets are $400,000.

Not rich, right? Yeah, you are probably right. This couple does not meet society's definition of wealthy because they do not have all the trappings of wealth. However, liabilities are $100,000 so their total net worth is $300,000. This happens to be the same net worth as couple one, but couple one is rich and couple two is not rich. How can that be? Couple two also has positive monthly cash flow so their net worth should be increasing. In my opinion, couple two is in a much better position to meet their financial priorities than couple one, yet couple one is considered rich. This societal paradox causes a lot of problems for many people because they strive for the wrong thing—a perception of wealth rather than true wealth. The situation is similar to young women starving themselves to look like super models because society, or at least the fashion industry, defines beauty as how thin and tall you are.

Your financial priorities are your own and don't let anyone take that away from you. Money means different things to all of us. Couple one is not wrong for doing what they are doing and couple two is not right. The point is society judges couple one as being somehow "better" than couple two.

I have an excellent example of this comparison fresh in my mind because it just happened a couple days ago. I was outside working in the yard when a solicitor came up to our house to ask me some questions about possible hail damage on our house. He worked for a siding company and he wanted to inspect our house for hail damage. Nice guy. We walked around the house for awhile and got to talking in the driveway when we were done. I found out he was 33 years old, married, and had no children yet. He found out I was a financial advisor. He asked what I was recommending to clients for investments. This is a typical guy question considering a lot of men think financial planning is all about getting the best return, not about putting a system in place to reach objectives. I said it depended on the client and he asked if I was recommending real estate. I said "no" because real estate was very expensive and most of my clients, myself included, do not know enough about real estate to justify the risk of such a large investment.

He began to brag about the rental properties he owned and how much money he not only made at real estate, but also how well he was paid to sell siding. I guessed he was probably doing very well, but had a chip on his shoulder about being perceived as unsuccessful because he was doing door-to-door sales for a siding company. He told me about the $1.2 million dollar house they were building in one of the prestigious local developments on a lake and how the people in my neighborhood were "schmucks" for living in our "crappy" homes. We certainly do not live in a "wealthy" neighborhood, but it is a nice suburban location with hard working, middle class residents. Of course, he didn't even realize he was insulting me since I lived there. I changed the subject and asked him what he would do if the siding market changed and things got tough for awhile. He said that could never happen and was hoping to buy more real estate, but did not have any available money since he was building a new home. We talked for a few more minutes and he left on pleasant terms. I noticed he drove away in a brand new 4x4 truck with all the trimmings.

This is typical guy talk I experience all the time (no offense to other guys). This person had a high paying job; he had made some excellent decisions in purchasing real estate, and was basically living the American dream. He had a beautiful home; his wife also had a high paying job, and he judged our neighborhood as "schmucks" because he appeared wealthier than the rest of us. I hate to judge because it puts me at the same level as him, but if I ever sat down with this couple I would expect a couple things to come out in our conversation. The first thing I would expect is extremely high debt levels. You can always afford payments when you have a good income so why would you ever pay something off when you can use the money to buy real estate and help increase your net worth? I would expect there is little to no contingency plan in place for a major life altering event such as a job layoff, disability, or premature death. Finally I would expect no real financial strategy between the two of them. Times are good; money is plentiful, and everything is going great. Why would you need to plan when everything is rosy? I have seen and heard it all before. I hope things work out well for this couple, but more often than not, they will eventually go through tough times together and, if it happens, their financial stress will go through the roof. High debt levels can wreak havoc on a marriage and having the appearance of wealth doesn't pay the bills.

Most people plan for the best and never prepare for the worst. It is always sad when the worst case happens. Unfortunately, I fear this particular couple has not prepared for the worst case scenario so I sincerely hope they never have to experience a major financial crisis.

The basic point of this chapter is to focus on creating a cash management system that works for you. The ultimate goal of a successful cash management system is to create ongoing positive cash flow and to reduce stress created by unbalanced spending. Focus on cash flow much more than your net worth. Cash flow is the tool to reach your most important priorities while net worth is simply a measure of your overall wealth.

By now you should have a realistic estimate of your expenses and you should also know your typical take home pay. Comparing the two numbers gives you an indication of your cash flow. If your cash flow is consistently negative, you have a problem and unfortunately I cannot tell you how to fix the problem (your spending decisions are yours, not mine), but something must be done or your financial health will slowly (or quickly) deteriorate. If cash flow is positive or neutral, you are in a position to start focusing on efficiently using the excess money to help reach your financial objectives.

I want to focus on those of you with negative cash flow or high debt load. There are many times when people come to me for planning services and want to know how they should be investing. In the fact finder meeting, I discover they have high consumer debt. Consumer debt is discretionary debt rather than mort-gage debt. I may also find their cash flow is negative. This is a double whammy that absolutely must be fixed before we worry about investing. Realistically, spending habits must be changed or the problem will only continue to get worse as time goes by. Also, any extra cash flow should be utilized to pay off the credit card debt in order to create a future positive cash flow to help them reach their other priorities.

These are two separate issues: Paying down debt and reducing spending. I will give you some advice for doing both, but the advice is worthless unless you decide to make the changes necessary to improve your situation.

PAYING DOWN DEBT

When I talk about debt as discretionary or consumer debt, I am usually talking about high interest credit card debt, but it could also include high interest second mortgages, boat or motorcycle loans, and higher interest car debt. It usually does not include mortgage debt or student loan debt which I usually consider useful debt since the mortgage gives you a home and the student loans hopefully improved your earning capabilities. Also, mortgage and student loan debt tends to be at lower overall interest rates than consumer debt. Don't get me wrong, your mortgage and student loans are still very important to pay down, but you usually benefit far more from paying off consumer debt first.

The first step in paying down debt is to do an inventory of all you owe. Com-pile a list of every creditor you have including your mortgage and student loans. Make a list showing what the loan is, how much you still owe, the interest rate, the minimum monthly payment, and how long you have left to pay. Now you get an idea where you stand. If you have debt problems, this may be a painful step, but it is critically important to understand the depth of your debt issues.

If there is not enough cash flow to cover all minimum payments, you need to take more desperate measures. If your debts cannot be paid and you don't expect your income to increase soon, your situation will only get worse unless something is done to change the situation. I don't have many clients in this situation so I am no expert on alternative means for reducing debt, but I am talking about debt consolidation services or even bankruptcy. If you are in this critical situation, you need to talk with an expert in the area of debt reduction to discuss your options and how they impact your future financial decisions. Obviously, bankruptcy or even debt consolidation programs should be the last resort, but these programs exist to help people who got in over their heads financially and, if you fall into that group, these programs may help you long term.

I will assume most of my readers have the ability to at least pay minimum payments on their debt and hopefully more than the minimums. If this is the case, I normally recommend the following steps:

1. Reduce spending as much as reasonably possible until your debt position has improved and limit adding more debt to credit cards or other consumer loans. The next section covers some common ways to help reduce spending.

2. If you can, consolidate higher interest cards or loans onto your lower rate cards. Call the credit card companies you use (and maybe some new ones) and discuss your situation and ask what they can do for you in regard to lower interest rates or even an interest free introduction period. Every dollar you save in interest helps reduce debt quicker.

3. List the debts in order from highest interest rates to lowest interest rates. If two cards or loans have the same rate, order them from smallest balance to largest balance.

4. Pay any extra cash you can on the highest interest, smallest balance credit card or loan until the loan is completely paid off.

5. Take the money you were paying on the first loan and immediately apply that amount to the next loan on your list (in addition to the minimum payment you were already paying). Pay this loan off as quickly as possible.

6. Continue with this process until all of your consumer debt is gone.

It is like a row of dominos, just keep knocking them down as you go and know that it may take time, but when you are done, think of how great you will feel. I have several clients who are on schedule to pay off their debt over three to five years. It is sometimes difficult to stay focused on your goal for five years or more, but there are huge benefits to living in a fiscally responsible manner. Once the debt is gone, think of all the positive cash flow you will have available to spend and also to invest for your future.

If you are married, please work through this process together. I cannot stress this enough. Even if one of you is much more responsible for the debt than the other, you both need to take responsibility and work hard to get back on track together. It is never easy to spend several years paying for past expenditures, but it must be done to improve the financial health of your marriage. Improving the financial health of your marriage will likely improve the overall health of your relationship which is important to both of you.

REDUCING SPENDING

There are many books on how to budget and how to save money on day-to-day spending. Many of these books provide guidelines on how much to spend on common items like your house, vehicles, food, etc. I am not a big believer in these guidelines because everyone is different and everyone has unique values about spending. How would anyone go about creating spending guidelines? They sure didn't talk to me! I don't care how my clients spend their money and I would never try to push my values on them because it wouldn't work and would probably annoy them. My job is to explain how their current spending decisions might impact their overall finances so they can make their own spending priorities.

If you want a $500,000 house and you can make the payment, but it means you will both drive used cars, that is a values based decision for you to make. Maybe you are good at repairing vehicles and know you can maintain a used car (definitely not me). Another person might want to live in a less expensive home, but if they travel a lot, they might want a brand new luxury car. There is no right or wrong, but there are different spending values.

I believe the first step in reducing discretionary spending is to "fix" your spending account using the previously mentioned techniques. However, it is often difficult for people to fix a spending category where they have no idea what they are spending. If this is you, it may take a couple months tracking expenditures to get an idea of your comfort zone in regard to discretionary spending. This process is rather unpleasant and would be comparable to counting calories. Did you know a tablespoon of butter has 100 calories? The non-dairy additive I put in my coffee each morning has sixty calories! In many cases it's not what you eat that makes you fat, it's what you put on what you eat that gets you. It is the same concept with spending. We tend to categorize large spending items, but it is often the little nickel and dime items that really hurt our monthly budget. Putting a limit on your monthly spending will help eliminate the common financial problem of runaway spending on little things.

What if you feel the discretionary spending number you come up with is too high to sustain and still allow you to reach other financial objectives? This is the painful part because you will need to cut back. Fortunately there are a lot of relatively painless ways to save more money without significantly impacting your current lifestyle. This is because our society has created such a tremendous focus on money wasting activities. The following list of common spending mistakes is from "The Rookie's Guide to Money Management" by Carolina Edwards and Ray Martin (1997) and can be found on the AmericaSaves website (www. americasaves.org):

- Buying from a TV ad with a credit card
- Leaving appliances on when you are not at home
- Buying extended warranties on appliances
- Buying additional dealer protection packages on a car
- Leasing your phone from the phone company instead of buying a phone
- Dry cleaning clothes that could be washed at home
- Joining a book, video, or CD club
- Paying for premium grade gasoline
- Eating out more than five meals per week
- Carrying more than $100 cash in your wallet (it can burn a hole until you spend it)

Maybe you only do a couple of these things, but a few bucks here and there makes a difference in the long term. Also, if you feel your spending is out of control, I would recommend trimming the eating out suggestion down to a couple times per week. I was brought up to think eating out was a luxury to be cherished rather than a daily routine to avoid having dirty dishes. The AmericaSaves website also offers some guidelines for how much money can be saved by making a few simple changes to your daily routine:

TIP	Monthly Savings
Save $0.50/day in loose change	$15
Cut soda consumption by 1 liter/week	$ 6
Substitute a coffee for a cappuccino	$40
Bring your own lunch to work	$60
Eat out 2 fewer times per month	$30

Borrow, rather than buy, one book per month	$15
Maintain checking account minimums to avoid fees	$ 7
Bounce one less check per month	$20
Pay credit card bills on time to avoid late fees	$25
Pay off $1,000 of credit card debt to reduce interest	$15
Total Savings	**$233/month**

I would also add clipping coupons for some common grocery items you use every week and buying groceries once per week or even more frequently. My wife and I don't use a lot of coupons, but we do watch for sales and use coupons on things we commonly use like cereal, pop, meat, and frozen pizzas. We almost never pay more than $2 per box of cereal (and Tracy eats a lot of cereal); we tend to stock up on meat when it is on a big sale; frozen pizzas could literally break us except we tend to stock up when they go on sale, and I don't remember paying more than $5 for a case of pop since we have been married. Buying a separate freezer can be a great investment if you like the idea of stocking up on frozen goods when there is a great sale. We figure being smart consumers with these few grocery items saves us about 15% of our typical grocery bill without taking up a substantial amount of time messing around with coupons or shopping around for deals. If the typical family of four pays about $400/month in grocery bills, the monthly savings would be about $60/month.

We don't actually save or invest the money we save on groceries because it was already budgeted to be spent. We tend to use the savings to treat ourselves to eating out. We also use a fair number of dining deals where you can "buy one get one free" or get some other form of discount. For example, TGI Fridays sends us a $5 off coupon for lunch every couple months. I know a lot of people eat there anyway and it is the same food, so why not save the extra $5. The coupon cuts our typical lunch from $20 down to $15 and we save about $30/month on groceries so we get to eat out twice per month just on our grocery savings. Isabella is usually a very well behaved little girl in restaurants so this is one way for us to get out of the house, enjoy a nice meal, and not have dishes or the kitchen to clean up.

Another great way to save some extra money is on long distance charges. We don't use a lot of long distance, but there are still savings to be had. I absolutely despise long distance companies. They seem to be some of the shadiest characters around. We finally got so disgusted with phony claims and misrepresentations that we entirely changed how we do long distance. Our system works like this. We have AT&T for basic long distance. No discounts, no monthly fees, and no minimum usage requirements. I think we are billed something like $0.17/minute or some ridiculously high charge. The reason I don't know for sure is because we never use our regular phone long distance to make calls unless there is some type of emergency. We use our cell phone with free long distance for many of our calls, but when we don't want to use the cell phone, we use an MCI calling card we bought at Costco. The card costs a flat $0.035/minute with no taxes or other fees. We can recharge the calling card at any time for the same flat rate using our credit card and the calling card can be used both at home or when we are traveling. Since we went to this system for long distance, I would guess we save about $10/month and I have not noticed any real loss of convenience. If you are a big long distance talker, this little change could save you 40% or more on long distance charges.

Another great way to save is to avoid the trendy health club memberships. You don't know how many clients I meet with who have no available cash flow and don't know what they are going to do about their credit card debt, but they can afford $50/month on a health club membership they rarely, if ever, use. Personally, I am an extremely unmotivated exerciser. I know I should do something, but I will find nearly any excuse to avoid exercising. If I had to drive even five minutes to a local health club, there is no way I would go (at least after the first week or two when I would be gung ho about the whole idea). Tracy and I do our best to exercise for free. We go for a lot of walks with our daughter, we ride bike (sometimes); she does Tae Bo; she runs, and I do the occasional weight lifting, push ups, and we both do crunches. We splurged on a recumbent bike for winter exercising and have been extremely pleased with our purchase. It is quiet and low impact enough for me to read while I sweat up a storm. Multi-tasking at its finest. We also bought a weight bench and an Olympic set of weights for home workouts. I figure all of our exercise equipment combined cost us about $900 in six years of marriage or about $12.50/month. This is far less than the typical membership fees of $50/month or more for two people at a health club. If you decide to work out at home, please do not get sucked into buying every piece of exercise equipment touted on infomercials or you might as well just join the gym.

The other major spending trend I cannot understand is the whole gourmet coffee scene. I often wonder if anyone ever notices how much it costs to buy a Starbucks latte. I am no coffee connoisseur, but I always thought most people got on the coffee kick for the caffeine. I make my own coffee in the morning and splurge on vanilla flavored non-dairy creamer. I get my caffeine fix, decent flavor (hope I didn't lose any "coffee snobs" with that claim) and spend about $7 per month. If you spend $3.50 per day on the local coffee shop latte, you not only take in a lot of extra calories, but you spend about $98 per month more to get your chosen form of caffeine. $98 per month! If money is tight, wouldn't $98 per month help the situation substantially? If you are addicted to overpaying for coffee, maybe you could consider cutting back to splurging once or twice per week rather than every day or maybe a couple times per day. You will truly appreciate the better quality on the days you splurge and will save about $50/month on coffee. If you invested $50/month in an account that earned a constant 6% over the next twenty years, there would be about $23,100 in your account. It could cover a year or two of college for one of your children.

Maybe some readers are shocked with these suggestions and are worried about being "cheap." I would prefer the term frugal, but if I am considered cheap for spending habits that allow us to still live a comfortable lifestyle based on our values, call me cheap. We use the extra cash flow to help reach priorities we consider more important than gourmet coffee!

◆   ◆   ◆

I have devoted a lot of pages to cash management because it is so very important in all of our lives. You may have never invested a penny in your life, but every one of us has made some form of spending decision nearly every day of our lives. I am a huge believer that working together to get a better handle on cash management would actually save a lot of potentially doomed relationships and could definitely improve the overall quality of life for most people.

You have made it almost a third of the way through this book and still no investment recommendations, no get rich quick schemes, and no magical wealth building strategies. Everything so far has focused on defining the financial priorities most important to you and your family and also defining the basic financial resources available to help you reach those priorities. The remainder of the book discusses more specific recommendations to position your available resources to meet those priorities. The emphasis will continue to be practical recommendations you can easily implement to improve your current financial position, no matter how good or bad it may be.

5

Risk Management—Otherwise Known as Insurance

"If you can't sell them what they need, then sell them what they want. Just make sure you sell them something!"

Actual quote from a life insurance seminar I attended early in my career

There are a couple important concepts I want you to understand about insurance. The first important concept is—insurance is one of the most complicated things ever created by humans. The second important concept is—insurance is generally expensive.

When you combine these two concepts you end up with something few people understand that costs a lot of money. Talk about a recipe for disaster! Let me elaborate on the two important concepts of insurance.

Insurance companies create incredibly complicated policies with page after page of definitions, riders, terms, conditions, legal mumbo jumbo, and escape clauses. Few clients ever take the time to read all of this garbage. They are forced to trust the agent, but unfortunately, most agents are not able to understand all of the ramifications of a typical insurance policy (whether it be life, health, disability, or property and casualty insurance). A good insurance agent has been taught to sell and market. They know how to play on emotions, and ultimately, how to close the deal. Insurance companies often use confusion to sell, plain and simple.

Every insurance company is just a little bit different which makes comparison shopping almost impossible. Rarely is there a situation where an apples to apples comparison can be made where price ends up being the ultimate deciding factor. There is almost always some difference in two competing policies that end up creating confusion during the decision making process.

Health and disability insurance are two of the biggest offenders in the confusion area. At least with life insurance, there is an ultimate deciding factor in when the insurance company pays a claim: when the insured dies. With health and disability, the claims paying process is not so cut and dried. Let me give you a couple real life examples.

When Tracy left her job to be home with Isabella, we needed to shop for health insurance because we lost her group health insurance coverage through work. I didn't expect the process to be incredibly complicated because I am in the business and understand most of the terms and concepts. Keep in mind; I rarely deal with client's health insurance policies because nearly all of my clients get their health insurance through some type of group policy at work. For this reason, I called an acquaintance who is an expert in individual health insurance policies (health insurance is all he sells). I told him what we were looking for as coverage (high deductible, major medical type policy). He made some suggestions; we discussed some scenarios, and he ran some quotes with several different companies. I thought the decision would come down to the lowest premium for the same coverage, but the process wasn't that simple.

He faxed me a page with a matrix of different quotes based on deductibles, co-pays, max out of pocket for individuals, max out of pocket for our family, Medical Savings Accounts, Major Medical Policies, and the list goes on and on. My head started to ache as I sifted through some of the numbers. I am used to evaluating insurance quotes so things slowly started to make sense and one of the companies really stood out based on our priorities for health insurance. I just assumed all of the companies provided essentially the same health coverage and only the deductibles and premiums were different based on the company's niche market, but I was wrong. I called my agent friend and started asking questions. I told him which company I was interested in and asked him why it was so much less expensive. He said they were relatively new in Minnesota and were trying to "buy" business (that was fine with me). He also said they had some administrative issues, but nothing major that he was aware of. The company also had more restrictions on who you could use as a family physician and out of network expenses were sometimes greater than other companies. I asked him to check specifically for our doctors and they were all included in the plan so I was fine with everything he told me. I told him to send an application and we would get the process moving.

I got the application, filled everything out and was ready to send it in. Before mailing it off, I took a little time to glance through one of the literature pieces that accompanied our paperwork. There was a confusing paragraph about covering future pregnancies that concerned me so I called my agent friend to get an explanation. He wasn't sure about the provision so he called the insurance company and got back to me. It turns out we would not have been covered at all for any future pregnancy costs! The literature didn't say it quite that way and I am sure many people would have glanced over that piece of information. I nearly did. I was irritated with the agent for not telling me this rather important piece of information earlier in the process and I expressed my irritation to him. He explained there was no possible way he could keep up with all of the policy changes and provisions for the many different companies he could offer. He went on to say there were no standards between different companies and he often got misleading answers from the companies themselves when he would call to get more details on policies. I have found it common for insurance company employees to give different answers to the same question and finally admit they don't know the answer. I normally recommend using an independent insurance agent, but sometimes these agents represent so many companies, they have trouble keeping things straight. However, I still believe independence has advantages for consumers usually in regard to competitive premiums.

Fortunately we found out about the pregnancy issue before submitting the application, but if we had purchased the coverage and decided to have another baby, we would have had a nasty surprise when the bill came.

I also rarely deal with disability insurance, but I had one client who was self employed, was the sole bread winner in the family, and was making very good money in his business. He had no disability insurance coverage. We discussed disability insurance as an important part of their financial plan and they both agreed disability coverage should be a priority so I began to investigate insurance options for my client. Since I am not a disability insurance expert, I called an insurance agency that specializes in helping independent agents like me with getting the proper disability coverage and disability insurance company for my clients. I explained the circumstances of this particular case and they went to work on compiling recommendations and quotes from a number of companies.

They came back with a very reasonable quote from a respected disability insurance company. I didn't ask a lot of questions because they were the experts and I figured they had done their due diligence and research on the case. The client agreed the quotes were very reasonable and we met to complete the application process. During our implementation meeting as the client was filling out paperwork, I noticed a provision in the policy summary that disturbed me. It appeared there was a gray area on whether my client would get disability payments for a certain disability common in his business. I called the agency and we did a conference call with a representative of the disability insurance company. The client sat right there with me as the disability insurance representative explained she had no way of knowing whether my client would actually have any type of coverage unless a claim was submitted and she had all of the facts. I told her it was a hypothetical case and I wanted to know what the insurance company would do for my client if that case ever occurred. She would not say whether my client would receive disability payments even though he would definitely be disabled. The exclusion clause may or may not apply to my client.

I recommended my client not purchase the policy. Why pay premiums if you don't even know what the policy covers? As you can probably imagine, my client was not particularly impressed with my services and he ended up getting a disability policy from another agent. I have no idea if the other policy is appropriate for my client, but I wasn't about to argue with him.

This is the primary reason I don't currently have disability insurance coverage for me. As I said earlier, I am investigating a group policy, but there will likely be no way for me to know if the insurance company would truly step up if I got disabled.

These are just a couple real world examples why I am uncomfortable trusting insurance companies. Most of my clients have had a bad experience with insurance companies or an insurance agent in the past. Finding a competent agent you trust is sometimes difficult, but can be a real asset in your financial planning process.

As for insurance being expensive—I usually talk about one thing most clients can relate to when discussing the expense of insurance companies. If you live in a larger metropolitan area, have you ever noticed how many very large, beautiful buildings are owned by insurance companies? If you have, did you wonder how those companies can afford to buy those buildings and how they pay all of those employees? That's right, they pay using your premium dollars. As an agent, I also get solicited by a lot of companies talking about their superior commissions and great trips they offer for high producing agents. How does the company pay for these high commissions and fabulous trips? You are right again. They use your premiums. Insurance is expensive!

However, noting the problems of insurance still does not change the fact that most people require some form of insurance during their lifetime. Insurance is an extremely important part of everyone's financial plan so it is important to make wise insurance decisions. A big part of my job is to explain these issues to clients, help them define what their insurance priorities are, and help them select the most cost effective insurance policies to help meet their specific priorities. I know most agents would probably agree with this job description, but you need to be aware of conflicts of interest inherent in the business. I would suggest most agents have been indoctrinated to sell, sell, sell, and if the client doesn't like what you are recommending, sell them something else, whether or not it meets their needs.

I understand my views on insurance are quite cynical, but if you have ever sat down with an insurance agent and got the full sales pitch, I think you understand why I feel this way. There was an event in college that helped solidify my views at a young age.

I was nineteen years old and was struggling along trying to pay for college. My Grandpa had bought a life insurance policy for each of us kids when we were babies to help us pay for future costs of college. Back in the 60's and 70's it was common for people to purchase life insurance policies as investments. My Mom told me the policy had about $2,000 of cash value and Grandpa wanted me to use the money to help pay tuition. I called the insurance company to cash out the policy and they told me I had to meet with an agent before they would release the cash. I knew I was headed for a fun meeting.

The agent was an extremely polite, middle aged gentleman with a rather luxurious office. He was very pleasant and asked a lot of questions to help put me at ease. It was incredibly easy to talk to him and I soon began to enjoy the meeting. We discussed why I wanted the cash. I said it was to help pay for college, which was the original intent of the policy, and he understood, but said cashing out the policy would be a huge mistake. It would be a short sighted decision I would grow to regret later in life. He said life insurance was a great investment in my future and since the policy was paid up, it would provide important benefits over my lifetime.

I was a little confused at this point because it seemed to me the only real future benefit of my policy would come if I died, and it certainly wouldn't come to me! I stated this rather obvious fact and he almost became angry with my ignorance. He proceeded to show me an example where I could use the policy to purchase a larger policy and use the cash value to leverage my existing coverage. If I only paid $2,000 per year until I was 65, I could accrue a substantial retirement benefit and still have coverage the whole time.

$2,000! Who was this guy trying to kid? If I had $2,000 to spend on life insurance premiums, I wouldn't be there trying to cash out a $2,000 policy to pay for college.

He seemed to think the decision was a no-brainer. Why wouldn't I want the extra life insurance? The fact I had little to no debt and no dependents made little difference to this guy. He was after a commission and he laid a number of very good sales pitches on me in an attempt to close a totally ridiculous sale. The sad part is the sales pitch was so effective, and he beat on me so relentlessly that I started to at least consider doing what he recommended. I was nineteen years old and didn't have a clue. This guy was an established professional and maybe I was wrong.

In the end I came to my senses and told him to cash out the policy for me. A couple years later when I started to date Tracy, I had the opportunity to discuss this particular incident with my father-in-law who was a financial advisor for many years and had gone through life insurance training in the early 80's. He could almost guess exactly what the guy said to me because he had been through all of the life insurance sales training also. It was almost funny except when I sat back to consider how many people got sucked in by this guy's sales pitch. How much money ends up being wasted because a slick salesman sells something you don't need? I don't know how some of these agents sleep at night. The brain washing must completely destroy their conscience and greed takes over from there. I think you get the point. You need to be careful with insurance decisions!

Most of the time I am dealing with the *life* insurance needs of my clients. I have little background in property and casualty insurance so I won't address that aspect of insurance in detail. As you can tell from a couple of my stories, I rely on experts to help my clients with disability and health insurance. These agents deal exclusively in their own area of expertise. Plus, most of my clients are nurses and engineers so they often have decent group health and disability insurance through work.

Long term care insurance has become much more prevalent the past few years and I do have a decent background in this area, but certainly I am not an expert. Also, I anticipate most of my readers are more concerned about other financial priorities than long term care insurance at this stage of their lives.

You might be saying, "What good are you? It sounds like you don't know anything about anything!" In a way you are right. My education as a Certified Financial Planner gives me a background in a wide variety of topics, but does not make me an expert in any particular area of insurance. For this reason, I view my job as the facilitator of a comprehensive financial plan for my client, and once the priorities are defined, I rely heavily on "experts" in each area of insurance to best address those priorities. Insurance is an extremely complex area and I believe it is almost impossible to become an expert in each unique area and still have time to help my clients. For this reason I choose to rely on specialists who are supposed to know everything there is to know about their area of expertise. I think my clients are better served with this approach.

I do an objective analysis of the recommendations provided by the specialists and my client and I recommend a course of action. Remember there is no right or wrong way to select insurance so we do the best we can to address the most important concerns of the client.

DISABILITY INSURANCE

Although I am rarely involved in purchasing disability insurance policies, I want to take a couple paragraphs to discuss the importance of having some form of disability coverage in a properly constructed financial plan. The biggest mistake you can make is to have no coherent plan for a future catastrophic disability. Note I said plan, not necessarily rely on insurance.

Long term disability coverage is very important to help protect your ability to earn money. As I said in Chapter 1, disability insurance is an area where group insurance tends to be much less expensive than personal coverage, but there are many group policies that are not competitive. Again, this is an area where you will want to discuss your options with a disability insurance specialist, even if you have coverage through work, and do not skimp on coverage.

One problem with group coverage is taxation. If your employer provides you with coverage and premiums are paid with pre-tax dollars, your future benefits will be taxable as income. For example: Say you make $50,000/year and your company provides you with long term disability insurance providing 60% of your current income in benefits. Your monthly benefit would be $2,500 or $30,000 per year. You might be satisfied with this coverage, but just remember income taxes will be due on your benefits. If your spouse also makes a good salary, much of your benefit might be lost to taxation. If we assume your total state and federal income taxes are 35% and do not change after you are disabled, your take home pay under disability would be $1,625/month compared to $2,708/month before you were disabled. This is a big difference in income when you consider family expenses often rise when one of the family members suffers a debilitating disability.

On the other hand, a personal disability policy is usually paid for with after tax dollars so all future benefits are income tax free. This means a personal policy providing 60% of your current income in benefits will provide a substantially greater after tax stream of income than a taxable group policy. Make sure you are comparing apples to apples when you discuss coverage with your agent or with your company disability representative.

Remember from Chapter 1, I do not currently have long term disability insurance. My wife and I discussed this issue at length and came up with a couple conclusions (not necessarily right or wrong, but this is how we discussed the issue). My wife has the ability to earn a good income if I became disabled. Her income would mostly replace the money I currently earn. This helps hedge our risk, but still is not enough. Just since writing Chapter 1, our situation changed enough for us to revisit the discussion of disability insurance and decide I should obtain some supplemental coverage to help protect the family. We put money down on a lot and are building a new home. The new home will have a higher mortgage so our expenses are about to rise (the new house was actually included in the previously mentioned budget of $4,600/month). I recently applied for a $2,000/month long term group disability insurance policy with a 180 day wait. Benefits are payable to age 65 and there is a residual disability rider. This rider allows me to continue getting benefits once I go back to work assuming it takes me awhile to get back up to full speed. The benefits will help supplement reduced income during the time when I am not up to my pre-disability earning level. The premium is $470.25/year which I thought was reasonable. I am now waiting for the policy to be issued. The premiums are paid with after tax money so the $2,000 monthly benefit will be an after tax benefit or "take home" pay during a disability.

You might be saying, "Why the 180 day waiting period?" We have a solid emergency reserve in place which allows us to pay any expenses during the first 180 days of disability with our own savings. There are big benefits to being your own bank. The premiums go down the longer the waiting period before benefits begin. We are essentially buying coverage only for a catastrophic disability that impacts my earning ability for a long time. Any other type of short term disability will not trigger coverage, but will also not devastate our family because of our substantial emergency reserve (which is in place for just such an emergency). This is one example of how a comprehensive financial plan fits together like a puzzle with all of the various pieces needed to make the picture complete.

You should have come up with your own disability insurance priority in Chapter 1. The first thing I want you to do is get a detailed statement of benefits from your group policy or policies. Make sure you have an understanding what the policy really provides as coverage. Most people know they have some type of disability coverage at work, but hardly anyone knows what the coverage actually provides, until a disability occurs which is a bad time to find out you don't have decent coverage. I want you to know what will happen before a worst case situation occurs and I want you both to have a comfort level with your coverage now, rather than later. If the coverage is adequate to meet your priorities, we can move on to the next issue (this is the case for most of my clients and I expect for most readers). If the coverage is not adequate, you unfortunately need to investigate further options.

You will need to sit down with a competent disability insurance agent to discuss your situation. Have an idea of what you need before meeting with the agent. Know the monthly benefit amount, a comfortable waiting period, and how long you need the benefits to run. I normally recommend benefits run to age 65 instead of some fixed term like five or ten years. The benefit to age 65 costs more, but it insures you for what you are concerned about, a catastrophic disability. If you suffer a permanent disability that keeps you from having the ability to earn income, a five year benefit probably won't provide much comfort if you are thirty years old.

The agent will almost always recommend more insurance than you want. Remember how these people get paid. The agent makes more if they convince you of a greater need, meaning more insurance and higher premiums. Listen to the agent with an open mind because they may think of something you didn't consider when you established the need on your own. If not, stick to the amount of coverage that provides you with an adequate comfort level. Talk to at least two disability insurance experts before making a decision. I also recommend thoroughly investigating the companies they recommend to see if there is a history of complaints against the company for not paying justified claims. As previously mentioned, you can contact your insurance commissioner or department of commerce to get valuable consumer information about insurance in your state.

You now have covered the possibility of a serious disability. Pat yourself on the back and move on to the wonderful world of life insurance.

LIFE INSURANCE

There are lots of books covering life insurance as a single topic meaning there is way too much information for me to possibly cover in one chapter. As with most financial planning topics, there is no right or wrong way to purchase life insurance. There is no cut and dried way to calculate how much you need or what type to purchase. In fact, if you consulted several competent advisors, they would probably all vary in their recommendations and you would walk away more confused than you started.

We start by going back to Chapter 1 and revisiting the life insurance objectives you created. When dealing with a tremendously confusing topic like life insurance, it is extremely important to stay focused on what is important. This is especially important if you are talking to an agent because they will tear you apart if you come unprepared. You might walk into the office feeling good about yourself and know you aren't going to buy any insurance, and you walk out dazed with your checkbook in hand wondering why you just bought a whole life insurance policy with outrageously high premiums!

Life insurance was created to give you peace of mind and a reassurance that everything will be fine financially if you die prematurely. Make sure the priorities you created in Chapter 1 are adequate to give you peace of mind. In its most simple form, there are three important aspects to life insurance: How much? How long? What type?

How Much?

Good question. Depending on the complexity of your family situation, the estimate of how much life insurance you need could range from a couple hundred thousand to a couple million depending who you talk to. I always ask clients how they determined their current amount of coverage and almost always they say "it seemed like enough coverage." This is the response I get even if they worked with an agent. In this case the peace of mind aspect is covered knowing they have some coverage, but not by knowing whether or not the coverage is enough or the right type. Determining an appropriate amount of life insurance sounds easy, but gets quite complicated for a number of reasons.

The first difficulty is figuring out when you are going to die. I always ask clients when they are going to die and no one has given me a definite answer. If I know when you are going to die, I can come up with a solid number for how much insurance you need. Since no one will commit to a date of death, we have to make assumptions. Are the assumptions going to be right? I am not a palm reader; I have no crystal ball, and the only cards I have are not tarot cards, so I have no idea when you will die. We have to figure out the worst case date of death for our assumptions.

The second difficulty is considering life insurance in a lump sum amount rather than as an income stream. As a single person with no dependents, you can consider life insurance as a lump sum. Adding up all of your debts and estimated final expenses minus your available assets will give you a lump sum number your heirs will need to settle your estate. Pretty easy. If you are married with kids, things get more complicated because you are normally buying insurance to provide for your family long term. Your income has been lost and your family still needs to pay bills. For this reason, the life insurance must be considered as a means of supplementing income rather than as a simple lump sum amount.

The third difficulty is estimating all available future income sources if you die. Will your spouse continue to work full time, part time, or not at all? And for how long? Will your spouse stay home with kids until they start school and then go back to work? How much will the kids get from social security benefits until they are eighteen? There are many questions and variables in trying to estimate future income sources.

The fourth difficulty is estimating all future family expenses after you die. Will your spouse use the insurance to pay off the house and reduce monthly expenses? Will there be increased daycare expenses? Do you want to pay for future college expenses? What will the inflation rate be over the next thirty years? Again, there are numerous estimates and variables in trying to determine future expenses.

The inability to know these variables is what makes life insurance a philosophical issue. Some people will over-insure just to make sure everything will be fine if they die and of course they will pay higher premiums along the way. Some people will under-insure to save on premiums knowing they are never going to die anyway (typically guys feel this way). I have people tell me straight out they simply don't believe in insurance. This is always confusing for me because I don't understand what they mean. Do they not believe the insurance company will ever pay out or do they believe everything will just work itself out without insurance? I'm not sure.

I consider all insurance as a tool in completing a comprehensive financial plan. Whether or not you believe in insurance, it can serve a function in meeting some important financial priorities. My personal philosophy on insurance is to purchase the minimum amount of coverage that provides your family with a similar standard of living under worst case assumptions. The challenge is coming up with the right type of coverage and the right amount to meet these objectives and give you a decent balance between protection and premiums. This is obviously easier said than done which is why there are hordes of insurance agents running around trying to sell the stuff.

One rule of thumb I like to follow when deciding how much life insurance to buy:

Overestimate your life insurance need when using term life insurance and underestimate your need when using permanent life insurance.

This rule of thumb might be confusing so let me elaborate. First off, I will get to definitions of term and permanent life insurance soon. But for now, term life insurance can provide large amounts of coverage for low premiums so overestimating your need will probably not cost a lot more. Permanent life insurance provides long term coverage, but is very expensive compared to term. Underestimate your need when using permanent life insurance to help control costs.

How Long?

This is a much easier question to handle, but this is where a lot of people make a mistake, sometimes because of their agent and sometimes because they were not thinking about long term ramifications. This is essentially the common "Term vs. Permanent" debate, but also how long of a term policy if you go that route. I will cover the "Term vs. Permanent" debate in the next section so for now, we need to determine when life insurance coverage will no longer be needed.

The classic example of this question with most of my clients deals with their children. Most people want some type of life insurance protection while they have minor children. If one spouse dies, the other spouse might struggle trying to work, raise children, and help the kids through college. In this case, most people want to make sure the protection is there for a defined period of time. Namely, until the kids leave home. This type of insurance is usually best provided by term insurance, but the term needs to match the amount of time you need the policy.

I see a lot of people with ten year term policies purchased when their youngest child was one. What good does that do them? You will likely still need insurance when the ten year term is over and what if you aren't insurable anymore? In this case, it would have made more sense to buy twenty year term or even thirty year term and make sure you had coverage until the youngest child was independent. Why would people buy the ten year term? Because the ten year term will be less expensive than the twenty year term. Why would the agent sell you ten year term? Because the agent often will sell whatever it takes to get some type of sale regardless of your personal situation. The agent may also sell the ten year term with the intent of converting the term to permanent insurance at some point in the future. We will talk about conversion and why it is promoted in the industry later in this chapter.

Another classic example is purchasing life insurance to cover the mortgage on your home. If you have a fifteen year mortgage, you might consider fifteen year term insurance to make sure coverage is there over the whole term of your mortgage. Be careful of life insurance policies sold by your mortgage company. Most of these policies are called declining term policies meaning the amount of coverage declines over time as your mortgage balance declines. This coverage is often easy to get and seems inexpensive. However, if you are in good health, it is often substantially less expensive to purchase an individual term life insurance policy. If you are in poor health, an individual policy might be more expensive than the mortgage insurance. Keep this in mind the next time your mortgage company solicits you about mortgage insurance.

What if you want life insurance to pay eventual funeral and estate expenses or want to make sure you leave a set amount of money to one or more of your heirs? Term insurance really wouldn't make sense unless you knew exactly when you were going to die, so we would likely cover this objective with some form of permanent insurance.

For now, you need to discuss why life insurance is important to you and how long the importance will remain relevant. Then we can move on to what type of insurance you might consider to meet your objectives.

What Type?

This is not only the "Term vs. Permanent" debate, but also what type of term or permanent once you have made the first decision. We need to start with some basic definitions. Term insurance is pure life insurance protection with no associated cash value. With term you pay the insurance premiums and the insurance company promises to pay a death benefit to your beneficiary if you die while the policy is in force. There are two common types of term insurance:

1. Annual renewable term—this type of term policy is active for a certain maximum number of years as long as you continue to pay premiums each year. The premiums are not fixed and will rise as you get older.

2. Level premium term—this type of term has a fixed death benefit and a fixed premium for a set period of time (ten year level term or twenty year level term are common periods). No matter what happens to you, the coverage cannot change over the length of term. Be careful here to make sure premiums are guaranteed for the whole period of time because many policies are called level term policies, but the guarantee period might be only five years or some other period less than the policy period (for instance: twenty year term with a ten year guarantee means the policy cannot change for twenty years, but the insurance company

could raise premiums on the policy after ten years). The possible rise in premiums could make for an unpleasant surprise.

The alternative to term insurance is permanent cash value insurance. There are a wide variety of permanent life insurance policies. These policies are meant to be permanent and they are generally much more expensive than term policies. As soon as you hear they are more expensive, you should know this is the form of insurance pushed most frequently by agents. Why? Follow the money. The more premiums you pay, the more commissions go to the agent. The agent has a vested interest in getting you to pay the largest premium possible.

Permanent style cash value policies all start with the same basic concept. A piece of your premium goes to pay the cost of insurance, fees, and other expenses associated with the contract (there could be quite an extensive list of expenses depending on the policy). The remainder of your premium creates cash value in the contract. Why is there cash value in the contract? Good question. The cost of insurance rises as you get older because you are statistically getting closer to dying, but most policies are designed with level premium payments. At some point, usually many, many years into the contract, the cost of insurance becomes greater than the premium payment and the pot of cash value is used to pay the excess premium charges. Usually the policy is designed for you to stop paying premiums at some point (age 65 is common) and the goal is to have enough cash value in the contract to pay the premiums for the rest of your life. If the cash value runs out, you either have to pay more premiums or the policy "dies" meaning you no longer have coverage.

The difference in permanent policies is what happens to the cash value. The life insurance industry has evolved over time to give consumers more choices in how to invest their cash value life insurance. There are now four primary types of cash value policies. I will not bore you with a long definition for each policy, but a summary is necessary to give you a basic understanding of how each one works.

1. Whole Life Insurance (also called Traditional Life Insurance along with a variety of other creative names)—whole life is the oldest type of cash value policy. The old style whole life was used to give people "guarantees." As long as you paid an illustrated premium, the insurance company would credit your policy a certain amount of "guaranteed" cash value at relatively low, but guaranteed interest rates. Some companies also credited additional dividends if they experienced returns greater than the guaranteed return. The word guarantee is important because it means the insurance company is taking the risk of investing your money

for you. Transferring the investment risk of your money to the insurance company is comforting for some people, but it doesn't come free. The insurance company will always be compensated for taking risk (this is how they make money). What are the fees? Who knows, because most of the fees and expenses are buried inside the contract and cannot be determined. This is similar to a Certificate of Deposit at the bank. There are definitely fees, but you don't know what they are. All you typically care about is the interest rate you get. These polices were hugely popular with people who experienced the Great Depression. Many of those people did not trust banks or most other financial institutions, but life insurance companies with their guarantees were often considered trustworthy. Whole life is the type of policy my Grandpa bought each of us kids as an investment for college.

2. Universal Life Insurance—in the late 1970's the United States experienced some very difficult economic times where interest rates and inflation ran wild. People with whole life policies were getting paid very low guaranteed interest, but they could get guaranteed treasury bills from the government paying double digit interest. As you can imagine, many people took cash from their whole life policies and invested in other safe investments at much higher rates. Insurance companies certainly are not stupid so they made a fundamental change in their policies to take advantage of the economic times at hand. Universal life was created as a more flexible policy where the return on your cash value could fluctuate with interest rates. The life insurance company still takes care of the investments for you, but there are fewer guarantees (fewer guarantees means you are taking greater risk, but the expenses are generally less because of the reduced risk to the insurance company). Universal life became very popular because of much lower premiums than whole life due to the higher interest rates being credited and lower expenses charged. Many unscrupulous, or maybe just misinformed, insurance agents sold these policies with very low premiums to entice buyers with the assumption high interest rates would never decline. As interest rates declined in the 80's and 90's, many of these policies ran out of cash and people lost their coverage or had to pay additional premiums to keep their policies in place. It has been common the last few years to see large insurance companies getting sued in class action law suits because of irresponsible sales practices associated with universal life when interest rates were very high.

3. Variable Universal Life Insurance—as interest rates declined, the stock market started to do very well and people began to pull money from whole and universal life policies and put their cash in the stock market. Again, insurance companies rolled with the punches and developed the next wave of permanent insurance. The variable universal life policy took a different approach to investing cash values. Variable life had all the flexibility of universal life, but the investment decisions were left up to the policy holder (typically with little to no guaranteed minimum return). The life insurance company provided a list of investment options (essentially mutual-fund-like subaccounts) to choose from including stocks, bonds, real estate, and money markets. The policy holder has total control over the investments and therefore takes most of the investment risk in the account. The combination of flexibility with the 90's bull market made these very popular policies.

4. Equity Indexed Universal Life Insurance—a lot of people liked the concept of variable universal life while the stock market went straight up, but they didn't like the lack of guarantees when the market eventually declined. Some enterprising insurance companies created equity index universal life to address this issue. This type of policy gives you essentially two investment options: a fixed bucket (bond portfolio of the insurance company) and an equity index bucket (tied to some type of stock index like the S&P 500 Index). The policy holder is forced to put some money into the fixed bucket to cover cost of insurance and fees and to provide some minimum guaranteed return. The rest of the cash value can be invested in either the fixed bucket or the equity index bucket (your choice). You get some of the upside potential of the stock market with some of the minimum guarantees of universal life or whole life. This is a simplified description because there are some complicated components to equity index universal life, but I think you get the general idea.

These are the four basic types of permanent style life insurance, but there are thousands of variations within the basic policies.

So what do you buy? Most periodicals and media experts recommend term insurance because of the low cost and the ability to afford a greater amount of coverage. I believe most agents would recommend permanent insurance because of the greater peace of mind in knowing a death benefit will be paid someday (and the higher commissions). Who is right?

Personally, I think the debate itself is wrong. There is no right or wrong in the choice between term and permanent insurance. The different types of policies provide different financial tools to meet your objectives. If they are used properly, neither type of policy is better or worse than the other. If they are used improperly, bad things happen and unfortunately, I see life insurance used improperly all of the time. It comes down to one of two things being important to you:

If your goal is to have a guaranteed chunk of money go to your heirs when you die, then use permanent life insurance.

If your goal is to provide a death benefit safety net for your heirs over a defined period of time, then use term and try to match the term of the insurance to the term of your need.

Why is this confusing to so many people? I would say mostly because of the conflict of interest inherent in selling life insurance. Agents are after the greatest amount of premiums to increase their commissions. On the other hand, the media is unable to mass market proper life insurance recommendations because they think cheaper is always better. Agents also have a whole bag of tricks at their disposal for selling permanent style policies which also confuses the issue. One of the biggest gimmicks is the tax treatment of life insurance.

Life insurance death benefits are usually paid income tax free (if structured properly) and the cash value inside a permanent style policy grows tax deferred and can often be accessed tax free (again, if structured properly). For these tax reasons, many agents promote permanent style life insurance as an *investment* rather than *insurance*. It is often easier to sell investments than insurance so if an agent can muddy the water about what you are buying, it is often easier to make the sale.

Is life insurance a good investment? Frankly, yes! It is a great investment, but not for you! You have to be dead to collect the death benefit. Life insurance should never be about you; it should always be purchased for someone else. Why is life insurance a good investment? When all things are considered, including taxes and inflation, life insurance is probably the best long term investment you can make on behalf of someone else. Where else do you get a guaranteed return with virtually no risk and no taxes on the gains? The tax free nature of death benefits can truly provide impressive average annual returns if used properly which makes life insurance a great way to build family wealth (note I said family and not your wealth) if that is your objective. One problem is many agents think life insurance is an excellent investment for increasing your *own* wealth meaning you aren't buying it for the death benefit, but rather for the tax free nature of the investment inside the contract. Sometimes this makes sense (especially in a corporate setting), but I don't believe this approach makes sense for most family situations.

So what's the problem? If life insurance is such a great investment, wouldn't it make sense for nearly everyone? No, unless you are very wealthy. Since this book is about the rest of us who are not ultra wealthy, life insurance rarely makes sense as an investment. The ultra wealthy are often concerned about transferring wealth to future generations and preserving the family estate. The ultra wealthy are also very concerned about taxes. The rest of us usually are not concerned about transferring wealth and taxes are often a secondary concern after providing security to our families. This means term insurance generally makes more sense for the rest of us than permanent insurance because the lower premiums allow term insurance to provide a greater death benefit within confined cash flow. Term insurance usually is a more efficient use of our financial resources to meet specific objectives.

What happens when a good agent (and by good, I mean a good salesperson) sells permanent life insurance to the wrong person? Usually the policy gets cancelled or expires (runs out of cash) before the person dies. Permanent insurance provides some wonderful financial benefits, but it isn't cheap which means people eventually get tired of paying high premiums. I read one study claiming about half of all whole life policies are cancelled in the first ten years. Once a permanent policy is cancelled (usually to save money on premiums), the coverage is lost and you essentially purchased extremely expensive glorified term insurance. It would have been better to buy term insurance in the first place and use the savings from lower premiums to help meet some other financial objective.

Also beware of the agent who sells term insurance with the intent of eventually converting the policy to a permanent policy. Let me explain. Most good term life policies have a provision where the policy holder can, at his discretion, convert the policy from term to one of the life insurance company's permanent policies without proof of insurability. This provision makes a lot of sense to have available, but should rarely be used. There are two times the provision should be used and one time when it should not be used:

When to use conversion:

1. Conversion works very well if you become uninsurable while you own the term life policy and will need life insurance beyond the original term

period of your policy. My father-in-law had this happen with one of his clients. He had a young husband with ten year term insurance designed to help his spouse and kids if he died. In the eighth year of the policy this young, healthy person was diagnosed with an inoperable brain tumor. Doctors had no idea exactly how long he would live, but they estimated less than five years. The client converted his term policy to a permanent policy with no evidence of insurability to lock in his coverage. The conversion requires much greater premiums because now the policy is a permanent policy rather than a term policy about to end. The client died a few years later (after the original term would have expired) and his wife and kids received the tax free death benefit. This is a relatively rare scenario, but knowing this option is available can provide an extra sense of security in buying a life insurance policy.

2. Conversion also works well in the scenario where your objectives are best met by a permanent style policy, but for now, you cannot afford the higher premiums associated with the permanent policy. Maybe you are a young executive who expects a substantial pay increase in a few years and your goal is to provide guaranteed life insurance for future final expenses and estate costs. You might buy a term policy with substantial coverage to protect your family now and convert the policy once you get the big promotion. The term policy provides inexpensive coverage for a few years and locks in your insurability rating for the eventual conversion. This scenario is unusual for my clients because most of my clients work in regular jobs without the prospect for future huge pay increases. For the rest of us, our financial picture rarely changes in such a dramatic fashion, although an inheritance could also make this happen.

When not to use conversion:

Many agents will consider everyone to meet Scenario 2 described above. They sell whatever your cash flow can support now and if they find out your cash flow has improved in the future; they will try to convert some or all of your term policies to permanent policies. Why would they do this if the term policies were designed to meet your original objectives? Commissions, plain and simple. The conversion allows them to get paid on larger premiums. The system for agents is all about getting more premium dollars so they can earn higher commissions. If the original term policy meets your objectives and you don't fit the two scenarios described above, why would you do a conversion?

The best weapon in the life insurance agent's selling arsenal is fear. A good agent has a horrible story to tell for nearly every possible scenario. The horrible story usually relates some form of worst case scenario to really scare the crap out of you. Once the agent has your emotions boiling, it is much easier to make a sale because you aren't thinking rationally. An irrational decision could cost your family a great deal of money over the long term. Creating realistic life insurance objectives (like we did in Chapter 2) is the best defense against irrational fear. If you have a strong comfort level with your goals before meeting with an agent, you are more likely to be happy with the outcome and the agent will likely serve you much better.

As I said previously, life insurance is incredibly confusing so I could go on and on with definitions and theories about different types of coverage, but I will save you the pain. This discussion is about practical uses for life insurance, not about the in's and out's of all types of policies.

WHAT DO TRACY AND I OWN?

I think one of the best teaching methods is through example, so I would like to share what my wife and I have done with our life insurance. Not to say we are right or wrong, and your circumstances will certainly be different, but just to give you an idea of how the reasoning might work when picking life insurance policies.

We need to start with revisiting the objectives outlined in Chapter 2:

If I die first:

Tracy would like to be able to stay home with our children until at least school age, but we want enough insurance to give her the option to not work full time until the kids go to college. This is an expensive objective because we not only have to pay off debts and future education costs using insurance, but we have to replace enough of my income for the family to get by with a decent lifestyle. We also have to make sure Tracy will have enough for retirement since she may not be working much during her primary earning years.

Note: Future marriage for Tracy did not enter into our assumptions!

Our total current debt and final expenses would result in about $150,000 being used off the top. Another $50,000 would be set aside for future education costs. With all debts paid off, we figured she would need about $32,000/year in today's dollars to live a similar lifestyle to our current lifestyle. This number includes $500/month in spending money and includes a 25% assumption for federal and state taxes (no social security if she is not working). If we assume Tracy draws 5% of income from the investments, she would need about $640,000 to provide income without eating into principal and hopefully the investments do better than 5% to account for future inflation. The children would also receive social security payments until they are eighteen, but I didn't include those numbers in our assumptions. This adds a conservative safety factor to our calculations and accounts for increased future debt if we buy a bigger house or take on auto loans.

We decided $800,000 (rounded down from $840,000 mentioned above) of life insurance would be adequate for Tracy to do what she wants.

So how did we address these objectives to meet Tracy's comfort level in case I die first? When Tracy and I were first married and did not have Isabella, we each bought thirty year level term life insurance policies. These policies were designed to allow the surviving spouse to keep the house if the other died. Tracy's policy is for $100,000 and the premium is $114/year. The premium is guaranteed level for thirty years until 2029. My policy is for $150,000 and the premium is $145.50/year also guaranteed level for thirty years until 2029. There was no meaningful reason I remember for my policy being bigger since we each made about the same amount of money.

So I had $150,000 of thirty year term coverage when we had Isabella and our objective was $800,000 so we needed an additional $650,000 of coverage on me. We started by figuring out when the bulk of the need would occur. If you notice from our objective, most of the insurance is needed to protect Tracy while our children (I say children because we assumed one more future child—my mom will be so happy) are at home. Like all parents, we hope our children will eventually be independent and we assumed this would happen at age 22. If we have our second child before 2007, the thirty year term insurance we bought would help Tracy until both kids were at least 22.

Some people would argue our entire life insurance need is term insurance because after the children are independent, Tracy doesn't need life insurance. I don't necessarily disagree because if we have done our planning, our investments should be adequate to protect Tracy after the kids have left home. I don't dispute this, but I also understand if I die, it may take some time for Tracy to cope with her loss. I was not excited about her being forced to sell investments in order to pay bills and funeral expenses while she was grieving. For this reason, I thought *some* permanent life insurance made sense.

We decided to buy an additional $500,000 of twenty year level term life insurance and $150,000 of permanent life insurance. There was no scientific reasoning behind the amounts, but here was our thought process. If I die in the next twenty years, Tracy has $800,000 of coverage to meet her needs. If I die sometime between years 20 and 26, Tracy would have $300,000 of coverage to protect her (at that time, both kids would be almost done with college and our mortgage would be substantially smaller). If I die after both term policies have expired, Tracy would have $150,000 to cover final expenses and bills for quite a long time without having to sell any investments. By that time, the mortgage should be paid off and we assumed our investments would be adequate to support Tracy during retirement. The children were assumed independent by the time the two term policies expire.

The $500,000 term policy cost us $305/year and will be level until 2021 when Isabella will be nineteen years old.

So what type of permanent policy did we select? Personally I think whole life is ridiculously expensive and Tracy and I were comfortable in taking some of the risk for investing our life insurance. I believe most people should nix the whole life option (I also have never sold any whole life to any of my clients). As an advisor, I also understand the power of investing in the stock market over long periods of time so I nixed the universal life option. It came down to variable universal life and equity indexed universal life. I ran what I considered to be an apples to apples (as close as I could get) comparison between the two types of policies with several different companies and decided on the equity indexed universal life. The variable life policies have greater upside potential which means we may end up paying less premiums, but the equity indexed universal life policy had greater downside risk protection. In my mind, the upside potential of variable life was not as attractive as the guaranteed downside protection of equity indexed universal life. We weren't buying life insurance to maximize the amount of cash value (which would likely be better accomplished by variable universal life). Our investments accomplish that separate objective. We wanted this coverage to be in place permanently so we opted for some guarantees provided by the equity indexed universal life. We still had some investment exposure to the stock market, but with less risk.

There is one more difficult question to answer when considering any permanent life insurance other than whole life. How much premium to pay? Most types of universal life insurance are considered flexible premium policies which means you are not locked into paying a set amount of premium. However, if you do not pay enough premiums to keep the cash value intact, the policy will eventually die, and you will lose coverage. It is a bit of a crap shoot coming up with an appropriate amount of premium to realistically keep the policy alive for the rest of your life. First off, we don't know how long we will live, and the second thing is we have to assume a rate of return on the cash value portion of the policy. What if our assumed rate of return is greater than we actually experience? We would likely have to pay more premium in the future or the policy would probably crash and die at some point (either of these results would not make me happy). Therefore, I am a big believer in over-funding universal life policies upfront to get the most bang for your buck early in the contract. The more cash working for you in the early years of a life insurance policy usually means the quicker you can stop paying premiums in the future. Let me illustrate this concept using my equity indexed universal life policy.

The minimum premium required to guarantee my coverage for fifteen years no matter what returns we got was $595/year. This means the performance of the cash value investments is totally irrelevant for the first fifteen years as long as the minimum premium is paid each year. However, there is a relatively good chance the cash might be gone after fifteen years and my policy would lapse if I didn't pay substantially higher premiums. This would result in a very expensive fifteen year term policy, rather than the permanent coverage we wanted. As a comparison, my $500,000 term policy only costs $305/year and is guaranteed level for twenty years. You want to make sure permanent policies are permanent, or they become a huge mistake. For this reason, you will want to pay a greater premium than the minimum to increase the probability your policy will eventually pay a death benefit no matter when you die. I decided to pay $960/year in premiums which provided a substantial margin of safety for keeping the policy in force over my lifetime. The minimum guaranteed return on my particular policy is 3% annually and I cannot remember exactly, but the $960/year of premium guaranteed the policy into my age 70's assuming the absolute worst case scenario. The worst case scenario is negative returns in the stock market for the next forty years or so—if this actually happened, the United States would probably not exist in its current form.

The reason I don't remember the illustration is because life insurance illustrations are nearly worthless as a predictor of future performance. This is why you should over-fund the premium. If you get good performance in the future, you can stop paying premiums early. If you get poor performance, the over-funded premium will provide additional assurance the policy will stay in force. Since illustrations are almost worthless, it is very important with permanent insurance to periodically review how your policy is doing. By periodically, I mean at least every 3–5 years. This will allow you to know if the policy is doing so poorly that premiums should be increased in time to save the policy.

I also selected a rising death benefit for my policy to age 65 and then we assumed the death benefit would level off. This is another confusing aspect of permanent policies for many people. You basically have two options when you buy permanent life insurance. The first option is a level death benefit. This type of policy will pay a set amount of death benefit no matter how much cash is in the policy (as long as the policy is in force). If you have a $150,000 policy and the cash value is $20,000, your beneficiary would get $150,000 when you die (cash value doesn't matter). The second option is a rising death benefit option. In this option, your heir receives the cash value along with the face value of the contract. If you have the same $150,000 policy with $20,000 of cash value, your beneficiary would get $170,000 (the death benefit plus the cash value). A rising death benefit option is more expensive than a level death benefit option because the "at risk amount" covered by the insurance company never decreases.

Our assumption is to increase the death benefit to age 65 and then level it off. Why would this make sense? It is a way to control premiums. If we assumed a rising death benefit until death, the policy would be much more expensive. However, I want Tracy to get the cash we put in the contract if I die prematurely (I consider dying before age 65 as premature).

Also, based on our assumptions, the premium will end at age 65 and there should be enough cash value in the contract to pay premiums for the rest of my life. Actually, I expect we will be able to stop paying premiums before age 65, but this was my worst case assumption.

See how complicated life insurance can be and how many different things you need to consider? No wonder so many people make mistakes in this area. Here is a summary of my life insurance:

Type of Policy	Amount	Expiration Date	Annual Premium
Thirty Year Level Term	$150,000	2029	$145.50
Twenty Year Level Term	$500,000	2021	$305.00
Equity Indexed Universal	$150,000	Permanent	$960.00
	$800,000		$1,410.50

There are a couple other things to mention. Note I always say annual premium. You typically have the option to pay premiums monthly, quarterly, semiannually, or annually. Most people opt for monthly payments, but we pay annually. Most companies charge some type of fee to process payments which means the fewer payments you make each year, the lower your overall charges. Sometimes the difference is negligible, but it can sometimes be substantial. I have seen many term life illustrations where paying annually can save you 15–20% over monthly payments. If you know the premium has to be paid anyway, we figured it was better to pay a lower premium one time per year than a higher premium twelve times per year.

If an advisor is reading this book, they might note I did not make any assumptions for social security in our life insurance calculations. If I die while the kids are under age eighteen, the children, not Tracy, will receive social security benefits until they reach age eighteen. Tracy would control the money on behalf of our children. When I do life insurance calculations for my clients, I include social security benefits in the calculation. However, for our personal planning I assumed any social security benefits would be gravy. I tend to plan very conservatively for our family and since there is no way to estimate the exact life insurance need, I wanted to make conservative assumptions. I am also not a big believer in relying on a government program to take care of my family. If I die and the children get social security, great. If they don't get social security for whatever reason, I want to know they will be fine without it.

The other thing to mention is one of my personal philosophies about the term versus permanent debate. There are many people who would criticize me for buying some permanent life insurance because it is more expensive. However, term life insurance is cheap for a reason. All companies are betting you will not die during the term of your policy and life insurance companies are very good at playing these odds. In most cases people pay their term premiums and the policies die before they do. In our case, my family is guaranteed to get more out of life insurance than we ever put in. Let me say that again. My family is absolutely guaranteed to get more from the life insurance company than we will ever pay in premiums. I like that idea compared to paying substantial term premiums over much of my lifetime and probably not collecting a death benefit, in fact, hoping not to collect a death benefit. Who wants to die early so their family gets some money? This personal philosophy leads me to recommend some combination of term and permanent insurance for many of my clients.

Based on our current life insurance plan, I will have paid $44,065 in life insurance premiums by age 65. If our assumptions are correct, I will not pay any more premiums after age 65. When I die after age 65, my family will get at least $150,000 in tax free death benefits, or more than three times what we paid in premiums.

If Tracy dies first:

I want to continue my profession which means I would definitely need help with the children and help keeping up the house. We figured paying off all debts would be nice and providing some money for future education would take that burden off my shoulders. As mentioned previously, our estimate for total debt and final expenses is $150,000. We assumed another $50,000 for future education costs and we threw in another $50,000 as an emergency reserve for help around the house the first couple years. We decided $250,000 of life insurance would be adequate for me to do what I want.

Note: Future marriage for me did not enter into our assumptions!

The scenario for Tracy dying first is dramatically different than for me dying first. I would continue to work and should be able to make enough to provide for us. For this reason, Tracy's insurance is an added safety net during the time when we need financial security the most—when the kids are young and we have not had enough time to accumulate money for their education. In our opinions, this meant term insurance for Tracy.

So how did we address these objectives to meet my comfort level in case Tracy dies first? Remember when I said Tracy had a thirty year level term policy from early in our marriage. Tracy's policy is for $100,000 and the premium is $114/year. The premium is guaranteed level for thirty years until 2029. This means we needed an additional $150,000 of life insurance to meet our objective.

Since most of our life insurance need will be in the early years of raising a family, we went with a $150,000 twenty year level term policy. The premium is $126/year and will remain level until 2021.

You might be asking why Tracy doesn't need any permanent life insurance. It certainly would not hurt our financial situation to have some permanent coverage on Tracy, but we felt the extra premium dollars would be better utilized to save for future college expenses. Tracy will have at least $100,000 of coverage until she is 56 years old. We figured if Tracy dies after age 56, our obligations to our children will be over and we will easily have enough in our investments to cover funeral expenses for her. As a financial advisor, I am much more suited to handle the financial implications of Tracy's death after her age 56 and I will also still be working so there will be income to offset any short term extra expenses. For now, the combined $250,000 of term insurance is the most cost efficient means to meet our objectives. We may reconsider some amount of permanent life insurance for Tracy if our situation changes (maybe a future third child born much later than the first two kids—this event would change our future planning significantly).

Type of Policy	Amount	Expiration Date	Annual Premium
Thirty Year Level Term	$100,000	2029	$114.00
Twenty Year Level Term	$150,000	2021	$126.00
	$250,000		$240.00

It always amazes me when I run across uninsured people who have young kids. They often tell me they cannot afford life insurance, but that argument doesn't make sense when you consider how inexpensive quality term life insurance can be. Granted my wife is very healthy and qualifies for the best underwriting rates, but her total cost is $240/year for $250,000 of coverage. Twenty dollars a month to make sure our family will be fine if she dies! It is ridiculous not to have coverage. The problem often comes from a prior experience with a life insurance agent. The agent usually ends up recommending some form of permanent life insurance that costs too much for the family to afford. Instead of offering some inexpensive protection, the agent simply gives up and moves on to the next prospect while the family goes without coverage and thinks life insurance is too expensive for them.

If you add Tracy's life insurance premiums to the premiums we pay on my coverage, we will pay $50,005 over our lifetimes ($44,065 for me and $5,940 for Tracy). Our family will still be guaranteed to get tax free death benefits three times greater than our total life insurance premiums. This makes sense to us and makes a compelling argument for most families to have at least some minimal permanent life insurance protection.

◆   ◆   ◆

Congratulate yourself on making it through the most boring topic covered in this book! For most people, insurance is their least favorite aspect of a comprehensive financial plan. Insurance decisions are based on worst case scenarios filled with doom and gloom, but it is absolutely essential in providing the base of a coherent financial strategy. The remainder of this book will cover investments and their uses. Investments are usually more fun because they are geared for the best case scenarios where the future holds promise and hope for a better life.

I will close this chapter with a summary of guidelines you might consider when creating and implementing your risk management strategy along with a general description of how Tracy and I have addressed each issue.

Health Insurance

- Absolutely do not go without health insurance (you may be tempted especially if you are young and healthy)

- Health insurance is not an area to skimp on to save money on premiums

- Group insurance is much less expensive if you have a major health issue

- Personal policies can sometimes be better than group policies if your health is good

Our family coverage costs us $305/month to cover the three of us. We have a $1,000 deductible per person to a family maximum deductible of $2,000. We pay the deductible out of pocket until medical expenses exceed the deductible. At that point, we have to pay 20% of additional health care costs up to a family maximum of $5,000 out of pocket. Our worst case scenario on an annual basis is $305/month in premiums and $5,000/year in total out of pocket expenses (which would rarely occur). Regular physicals for my wife and me and regular well checks for Isabella are entirely covered by the insurance company. As a business owner I am able to write off the cost of health insurance as a business expense so the premiums are even less on an after-tax basis.

Property and Casualty Insurance

I did not get into any detail about property and casualty insurance, but I can give you a couple quick guidelines.

- Select the highest deductible you can reasonably afford in an emergency scenario (higher deductibles reduce premiums)

- Comparison shop (rates can vary widely from company to company)

- Talk to at least one independent agent before buying

- If possible, consolidate all of your property and casualty insurance with one company to get maximum premium discounts

- Review your policies every year or two and periodically get new quotes from other companies

- Consider an umbrella policy if you have substantial assets (discuss this issue with your agent to determine if it is appropriate for you)

- It is often substantially cheaper to pay premiums less frequently (we pay every six months rather than monthly and save $4.35/month on premiums)

All of our property and casualty insurance is with one company. When we first got married, this particular company was the least expensive option when comparing several different companies. We have done at least three evaluations over the past six years and our rates have remained competitive.

Our homeowner's coverage is for replacement value of our home rather than actual value (very important to confirm your policy is for replacement value). We selected a $500 deductible. There is a rider on our policy to cover Tracy's wedding ring. Be careful when purchasing riders on scheduled personal property. These little policies often are very expensive and can really add up over time. Our annual premium is $553 for homeowner's insurance.

We currently have comprehensive car insurance on both of our vehicles (I drive a five year old Chrysler Sebring and Tracy drives a three year old Oldsmobile Alero). Our coverage provides $50,000 per person up to $100,000 per accident. Many insurance agents would recommend greater coverage, but this is an area where we skimped a bit. We will likely up our limits in the future, but we are comfortable for now. We pay $812.40 every six months.

We do not currently have an umbrella policy, but we will likely consider purchasing one at our next insurance review (once we get settled in our new home). A typical umbrella policy is $1,000,000 of coverage and might cost $15–$25 per month. This is a relatively inexpensive way to help protect your family against potential lawsuits.

Disability Insurance

- Group insurance will almost always cost less than a personal policy.

- Hopefully you have disability insurance through work, but if you must purchase a personal policy, choose at least a ninety day elimination period (and preferably a 180 day elimination period), get benefits to age 65, and select some form of inflation adjustment rider.

- If you have a specialized profession, select an "own occupation" definition of disability.

- Work with an agent who specializes in disability insurance to help you get the most appropriate coverage for your circumstances.

- Investigate your disability insurance company to see if they have a good claims paying history.

We do not currently have long term disability coverage. I have submitted an application to purchase a group long term disability policy on me. The coverage will be $2,000/month (tax free benefit because we pay premiums on an after tax basis) with a 180 day elimination period, benefits payable to age 65, and for my own occupation. I did not put an inflation protection rider on the policy, but I do have the ability to purchase a larger benefit in the future if our situation changes.

Life Insurance

- Have your objectives well defined *before* meeting with an agent.

- Over-insure with term life insurance (great way to buy a lot of coverage for low premiums).

- Under-insure with permanent life insurance.

- Match the type of life insurance with your need.

- A mix of term life and permanent life insurance is often a good mix (the bulk of coverage in term with a smaller permanent policy).

- Do not procrastinate! The longer you wait, the higher your premiums and you take the risk of becoming uninsurable over time.

- Personal life insurance policies are often better long term solutions than group insurance unless you are a smoker and/or you have a major health issue.

- Single individuals often don't need life insurance (or maybe a group policy at work is enough).

• Families almost always need some type of life insurance.

Here is our life insurance portfolio as previously outlined:

My Policies	Amount	Expiration Date	Annual Premium
Thirty Year Level Term	$150,000	2029	$145.50
Twenty Year Level Term	$500,000	2021	$305.00
Equity Indexed Universal	$150,000	Permanent	$960.00
	$800,000		$1,410.50

Tracy's Policies	Amount	Expiration Date	Annual Premium
Thirty Year Level Term	$100,000	2029	$114.00
Twenty Year Level Term	$150,000	2021	$126.00
	$250,000		$240.00

Long Term Care Insurance

I did not cover any long term care insurance issues, but this is an area of increasing concern for many people. This is also insurance coverage most appropriate for the middle class. Wealthy people can often self insure for eventual long term care expenses and poor people often cannot afford decent long term care insurance premiums so they must rely on government programs (Medicaid) to help with the costs of long term care.

• I recommend dealing with this issue after the age of fifty (many agents would say you should purchase coverage as young as possible, but I believe there are generally more important financial issues at younger ages).

• Develop a written strategy for dealing with long term care expenses and include at least one of your children in the discussion.

• Long term care insurance is particularly important for women (women tend to live much longer than men and are often on their own by the time they need care).

• It is often best to partially insure for long term care. Sharing some risk with an insurance company while keeping some of the risk on your own will help keep premiums down while still providing additional peace of mind.

- If you are under age seventy, make sure there is some form of inflation protection on your policy. Over age seventy, inflation protection is nice, but does not offer as much bang for the buck and premiums are already outrageously high by seventy.

- Talk to a long term care insurance specialist to get the facts about different types of coverage. Be careful you do not end up buying too much coverage. Long term care insurance agents are very good at overestimating how much coverage is appropriate (more coverage results in higher premiums which mean more commissions).

We do not have long term care insurance and will likely not deal with the long term care issue for another twenty years or so. I have been told by several agents that Tracy and I should already have long term care insurance coverage, but I personally consider college and retirement as more important and more immediate financial objectives.

6

Investments—An Introduction

We need to revisit our primary objectives from Chapter 2 before proceeding into the wonderful world of investments. The basic five financial categories of importance for most people include:

Emergency Reserve—how much to have in savings to cover emergencies
Education—private school or college expense
Risk Management—insurance such as life, health, disability, and long term care
Retirement—when and how much will you need
Estate Planning—wills, trusts, and power of attorney

Risk management objectives are usually best met through the use of insurance and estate planning objectives are usually met through legal planning. This leaves us with establishing an emergency reserve (I include short term saving objectives like saving for a house under the emergency reserve category), planning for education expenses, and planning for retirement. These three objectives usually involve some form of investment to achieve success.

In my opinion, successful investing is all about focus. I am often asked what investments I am recommending to my clients and it is an impossible question for me to answer because I may recommend many different types of investments on a weekly basis. My attempt is to always recommend investments I feel give the greatest opportunity to meet my client's unique financial objectives. This is where focus comes in. Focusing your investment activity on meeting your own financial priorities will help you make intelligent decisions and will help you cut through all the noise that passes for "expert" advice.

Your objectives from Chapter 2 should now be well defined and for most people, there should be three areas of your finances that directly involve investing:

- Emergency Reserves (including accumulation for certain spending priorities)

- Education

- Financial Independence (otherwise known as retirement)

If you can keep your investments focused on these three areas, the decisions become much simpler. Mistakes are most commonly made when you lose focus. Let me give you an example of losing focus using one of the most commonly held investment beliefs.

YOUR HOUSE AS AN INVESTMENT

I often hear people say their house is their best investment. In fact, I am hearing this statement more frequently considering the recent bear market in stocks and the current environment of very low interest rates. If you look at your house strictly as an asset on paper and look at the long term appreciation, then I would agree that your house has likely been the single best investment you have made in your lifetime. However, if we look at the three reasons why most people invest, I think you will find your home has not been a very good investment and should not even be considered an investment.

A house is where you live. Its primary purpose is to provide shelter for your family. The decision to buy or sell a home should not be made based on the investment ramifications, but rather on the merits of providing shelter and security for your family. The investment element should be a secondary consideration or even no consideration in your house buying decisions. This is a controversial statement and there are likely many readers shaking their heads in disbelief at my obvious ignorance.

Buying a home is often a wise financial decision, but rarely does buying a home help you meet the three primary financial investment priorities of a typical family. In most cases, buying a home is actually an impediment to your investment priorities because many people buy too expensive of a home and become "house poor." Being house poor means you probably have a very nice home, but it eats up so much of your available cash flow that there are little to no financial resources left over to meet other financial priorities. This is very common in today's society of bigger always being better.

If you have owned a home during any period over the past decade, you likely experienced some excellent appreciation in your house value (depends on which part of the country you live in). At the same time, your other investments probably have not fared very well which is why your house might be considered your best single investment. But let's take a closer look at your appreciation and what that means to your family in relation to your investment priorities.

I will use our housing situation as an example because our situation is similar to many of my clients. We bought our house in the spring of 1997 for $113,000. It was an exciting time because we had just gotten married and now we had a nice new home. There was lots of space compared to all of the cramped apartments we had lived in through college. We felt our house definitely helped improve our overall quality of life and was a great purchase. It is now spring of 2003 and our house is worth about $200,000. The $87,000 gain in value amounts to a 77% return on the original value of our house. Not a bad gain in six years! We also had the added benefit of having a nice place to live over those six years compared to an apartment.

Keep in mind, we did pay about $75,000 in mortgage payments, property taxes, homeowner's insurance, and utilities over those six years, but the gain in value still outpaced what we paid to live in our home. I also forgot we spent about $13,000 on various home improvements like a deck, a fence, a new refrigerator, a new stove, paint, flower beds, and miscellaneous other little things for around the house. Anyone who has recently bought a house probably knows where the nearest Home Depot can be found.

Now our expenditures are greater than the appreciation on our house, but I didn't account for the tax deductions for mortgage interest. Ah, the great mortgage interest deduction! One of the greatest financial myths ever propagated in our society. The logic goes something like this: Buy the most expensive home you can afford and make payments for as long as possible and refinance all of your consumer debt into your mortgage because the interest paid for mortgage debt is tax deductible. Great idea, right? Not exactly, and let me explain why. Remember my dislike for banks and why I recommend you try to become your own bank? Banks make money off the interest you spend on debt. Any interest payments you make, directly reduce the amount of money available to use for other important financial priorities. True, but what about the great tax deduction.

This is difficult to explain in written form, but let me give it a shot. Growing up I went to a little tiny school in western North Dakota. There were seventeen people in my graduating class (twelve boys and five girls so competition was fierce when prom rolled around). Many of our teachers were "old school" and thought a common sense education was important in life. Our math teacher was particularly good (thanks Mr. Hushka). I remember one of his most common sense quotes was, "You give me two apples and I give you one apple, and we can trade all day!" Who eventually ends up with all of the apples?

This is how mortgage interest works. Let's say you give the bank $100 in interest. The government gives you a tax break so you might save $30 on your taxes. The bank gets $100; the government lets you keep $30, so it sounds to me like you are still out $70. Where do I sign up? The bank is happy; the government doesn't care (they will hit you somewhere else anyway), and you end up in the poor house. In a perfect world, you should have no mortgage debt at all, but obviously we don't live in a perfect world and big, fancy houses don't come cheap, so we will all continue to make mortgage payments for most of our lifetimes. The bigger the house, the more interest you will likely pay, and the quicker you become house poor.

Back to our $87,000 of appreciation on our house. We are in the process of building a new home and selling our current home. The price appreciation on the current house, minus real estate fees and moving expenses, will be applied to the new mortgage as a down payment and we will start paying mortgage payments on the new house. Did we benefit from our home appreciation? Absolutely. It allowed us to move into a larger home that will hopefully provide a better quality of life for our family. That is certainly a benefit to us. Did our fortuitous home appreciation help us meet our investment objectives? No. Any appreciation we realized was rolled into the new house and the only way to tap into that equity is through some form of loan (bigger first mortgage, second mortgage, home equity line of credit, etc.). All of these loans require interest payments which gets us right back to the "trading three apples (interest to the bank) to get back one apple (tax deduction from the government)" theory. In fact, the new home will actually result in a larger monthly expense for us which hurts our ability to meet our other important financial priorities. In our case, the new house fit into our financial plan and we will still have enough cash flow available to meet our other objectives, but without a financial plan, we may have paid for too much house and would have hurt our overall financial position over the long term.

The point is your home is where you live and is truly an important part of your life, but it is not an investment.

Why do people lose focus when they invest? It is very easy to lose investment focus and I believe most people have no real connection between their investments and their objectives (no matter how rich they might be). The main reason people lose focus is because they never create a financial plan in the first place. Fortunately, you are reading this book and are creating your own financial plan so you won't fall into the first trap. But even for you, it will be very easy to lose focus for two primary reasons: the media and your own emotions.

THE MEDIA

Not only are there hundreds of financial books that describe various forms of investments, but there are also hundreds of financial articles written each day in the noble pursuit of trying to better inform investors. Unfortunately this mass of information often makes the attainment of knowledge harder because there are such varied "expert" opinions on how people should be investing. Some gurus adamantly recommend real estate; others strongly believe in the stock market as the only way to go, and there are even a handful of people saying most of your money should be in gold. It is nice all of these people have taken such an interest in your financial well being, but how could they possibly know what makes sense for your situation if they don't even know who you are.

One of the primary reasons I wrote this book was to provide an alternative financial guide to all of the "get rich quick" books. Nearly every financial book has the words "rich" or "wealth" in their titles. Americans seem to have an obsession with being rich so they keep buying all of these wonderfully entertaining books that don't seem to tell you anything practical. Oh, I know, just buy up some foreclosed rental properties and build yourself a real estate empire like Donald Trump. Real estate not your cup of tea, try your hand at day trading Internet stocks (not really a hot topic right now, but a few years ago it was all the rage in getting rich quick). It is so easy and it takes no training or special knowledge of any type!

If you have been sucked into the hype of one or more get rich quick ideas, don't feel alone. I, like most other men, have also had my share of financial misadventures that were supposed to result in nearly instant wealth with little to no work (I will elaborate on my greatest blunder shortly). I periodically run across the same infomercials you see on late night TV and I have often considered picking up the phone and ordering their package of information. They make it look so easy and they wouldn't really be lying, would they?

The media works very hard to build an addiction to their information. If there truly were a holy grail of investing (like index investing for example), the media could reasonably explain everything you need to know in one magazine. Short, to the point, and easily understandable. But what would they sell you next month? Why do you think so many magazine titles have to do with the "hottest" stock picks like "The Ten Best Stocks for 2003!" I have read many of the financial periodicals in an effort to stay on top of changes in the industry and most of the time I end up shaking my head in disappointment wondering how many readers will be hurt by the drivel that passes for media advice. You will often see articles directly contradicting each other. The classic example is an article on "buy and hold" investing in an equity index fund immediately followed by an article with the best individual stock picks for that particular month. The typical investor might get a little confused since the first article says all you need to know about investing is the 1-800 number to a no-load mutual fund company so you can buy an S&P 500 Index fund and hold it forever. Don't pick individual stocks the article goes on to say. Individual stocks are too risky and you could truly get hurt. The index is more diversified and will perform better over time. The reader might think that is great advice until she reads the next article where the magazine explains why their stock recommendations are better than the overall index and are nearly certain to outperform over at least the next six months (who knows after that). So now the reader might think buying individual stocks is the best move because index investing is too boring and the magazine virtually guarantees the reader will do great if she follows the advice of their resident stock guru.

I will certainly give the financial media credit for trying. They have made investing into America's national pastime (not everyone can play baseball, but everyone has a few bucks of "play" money they could throw in the market). Buying stocks is associated with sex, beautiful cars, mansions, even your own tropical island. You too could become an international man of mystery and intrigue, but you need to spend $3.50 on the newest financial magazine to find out how.

The media is why a good financial advisor has become a *filter* of information rather than a *source* of information. I mentioned previously you have access to nearly all the financial information I use to help make decisions for my clients. It's all there if you know where to look. The Internet is the great equalizer between the investor on Main Street and the stock broker on Wall Street. Unfortunately, very few people know how to piece all of the information together so it can benefit them. It is not because most people lack the intellect to process all of the information and use it to their benefit. Their emotions get in the way. It is human nature to be poor investors because humans in general are ruled by emotions.

YOUR EMOTIONS

I have read many articles detailing studies showing women are better long term investors than men. At the same time, men are considered more knowledgeable about investing. Shouldn't knowledge be correlated to success making men better investors than women?

The difference is emotions. For men reading this book, you are probably shaking your head right now thinking this guy is a schmuck. Not only do men know more than women, but men are less emotional so men are definitely better investors. Not so my friend. Women may be more emotional than men about many things, but investing is not one of them. Women cry at sad movies; men cry when they see sad brokerage statements.

I have mentioned several times the differences between how men and women view money and how these differences can cause friction in relationships. Since investments involve money, this is an area where disagreements often occur. In my opinion, men are much more inclined to take significant risks with their investments in order to strike it rich. Women are much more inclined to take the slow, steady approach with relatively limited risk. This can be a real problem for a lot of couples and it often creates difficulties in establishing a long term financial strategy.

Personally I have a lot of trouble working with most men in regards to their finances. Men have fantasies about wealth. They often love to talk about investments and will often brag about how they were able to turn a quick buck on a "smart" investment. They almost never talk about their losing investments because that would diminish their ego. Men are more inclined to trade often in search of a better investment that will make money faster. They often talk about investing with "play" money. When I talk about long term financial objectives, men often say things like "I want to be rich!" When I ask them what rich means, they rarely have a real answer. They might say a million dollars is rich, but if they reach a million dollars, they are more likely to think five million is rich. Men are often looking for a moving target which is ultimately unattainable because no amount of money is ever enough.

On the other hand, women think very differently than men when it comes to money and investments. They tend to associate investing with security. Women gain comfort from knowing there is a financial plan in place to meet their objectives. They generally are less willing to take risk in order to receive bigger gains. Women almost never refer to their investments as "play" money. When I talk about long-term financial objectives, women almost never say they want to be rich. It is usually easier for me to get defined objectives from women. Many of my women clients don't even bother opening the statements they receive in the mail because they know there is a plan in place and performance last quarter doesn't affect their plan. My job is much easier with most women because we can actually measure progress towards defined objectives while men consistently change the targets so often we never get a feeling of progress.

It may sound like I am bashing men, but I'm not. I am simply speaking from experience and also from my own perspectives on investing. I am a typical male investor. Risk doesn't bother me. Losing money in an investment doesn't bother me, but it would drive my wife nuts. What my wife has told me over and over is she wants to know we have a plan in place to provide for our future together. Becoming wealthy would be a pleasant surprise, but meeting our personal objectives we developed together is the ultimate reason why we invest.

I even tried my hand at day trading for awhile. I read several books about technical stock trading and how to quickly get in and out of stocks with big profits and little to no risk. The first stock I picked was an Internet search engine called Infoseek. The Internet was hot and I figured I could do no wrong. The stock more than doubled in two weeks and I sold with a tidy profit. I was a genius! I figured my days of working for a living were nearly over. If I could just double my money every two weeks, I would be rich in no time.

As the market continued to go up, I picked some winners and some losers, but overall I was doing very well until I decided to get real smart. Everyone knew Internet stocks were outrageously valued and they had to fall back to earth at some point. Since I was a genius stock picker, I figured I knew more than all of the market gurus and I was going to pick the top and bet on a decline. At this point I wasn't trading just a couple thousand per trade. My bets had increased with the size of my ego. I had a margin account with a discount broker which allowed me not only to buy stocks, but to also short stocks. Shorting a stock means you actually sell stock you do not own in anticipation of the stock price going down and then you buy the stock back resulting in a profit. It is a paper transaction because you cannot sell a stock you don't own. The downside risk on shorting a stock is unlimited because if the stock goes up in price and you have to buy it back at a much higher price, you can actually lose more than you put in (because of borrowing on margin).

Anyway, I got really brave knowing Internet stocks had to collapse at some point so I shorted a prominent Internet services company. It was an outrageously high priced stock that I figured would definitely go down in price. I invested $15,000 in this one transaction. What I did not realize was the market boom had legs and continued to rise for the next couple months before the major collapse. As the market rose, this Internet stock quickly started to go up in value which shocked the heck out of me. My losses started to mount and I got scared. Within two weeks, I had lost $10,000 and it appeared there was no end in sight so I covered my position and got out. Lucky, lucky, lucky. If I had not gotten out, I would not only have lost my original $15,000, but I would have lost at least another $15,000 on margin. The stock I picked to decline eventually quadrupled to over $200/share within a year. I was a genius all right.

Here is the truly sad part about the whole deal. I was absolutely, totally right in my reasoning. The stock was outrageously priced and it should have gone down. In fact, once the market eventually collapsed, this Internet stock went from over $200/share down to a low of about $1.30/share (a decline of over 99% of the value). The problem with short term trading is you have to be more than just right; you have to also have good timing which is the really tough part. If I had been lucky enough (and yes I mean lucky, not smart) and timed the actual peak, my $15,000 stock bet would have doubled very quickly. I was right about the stock being overvalued, but I was wrong about the market timing aspect of my investment. Fortunately, I was lucky enough to learn my lesson very early before we had truly significant money to blow on get rich quick investing.

The stock market is particularly good at playing on human emotion which is why human nature makes us all inclined to be poor investors. The stock market is a continual struggle between the two competing emotions of greed and fear. During raging bull markets, most investors swing towards greed and get suckered into buying crappy stocks at high prices. When the market collapses, fear takes over and most people sell good stocks at low prices. Investment professionals rely on the natural human tendencies of amateur investors to create the huge market swings necessary for them to collect much greater profits. Without human emotion, the stock market would slowly climb with the overall economy and there would be little to no advantage for the professionals.

The combination of media hype with human emotion can be devastating to your finances. Ultimately, the financial plan you create will be the best defense against your own natural tendencies to sabotage your finances. A coherent financial plan with well-defined objectives will allow you the luxury of focusing every financial decision you make on your own unique objectives. Without a financial plan, you are at the mercy of other people's opinions and your own fickle emotions. Your financial plan creates a system for making major financial decisions in line with objectives, allows you to measure progress, and sets a road map for making minor adjustments along the way.

Probably the greatest value a financial advisor brings to a relationship is to help clients see the big picture and step back from their emotional involvement with financial decisions. I often say my most important task when dealing with investors is to keep them somewhere in the middle between greed and fear. This is easier said than done.

◆   ◆   ◆

The next several chapters will take you through a discussion of practical investment uses to help meet your unique financial objectives. There will be some definitions, but I do not want you to get bogged down with detailed explanations for each different investment option. There are hundreds of other financial books that have already summarized comprehensive lists of investment definitions. The point of this book is to give you the practical information to apply certain investments as tools to meet the objectives you pulled together from Chapter 2.

7

Investment Vehicles

When I first became a financial advisor, a big part of my practice involved explaining a local hospital's 403b retirement program to their employees. I would sit down with people and start by defining what a 403b program was and how it worked at the hospital. After a summary description, I would ask the employee if she had any questions before we moved to a more specific discussion of her unique situation. Probably the most common question was "What kind of return can I get on a 403b account?" I immediately would know the employee did not know the difference between investments and investment vehicles. I had to explain the 403b was simply a retirement savings program provided as a benefit by the hospital. It is a division of the IRS tax code (section 403(b)) and does not have any specified return. The investment return depends on what investments are put *inside* their 403b plan.

This is a very important distinction between investment vehicles and the investments we can put inside these vehicles. For some of my more sophisticated readers, this chapter will be review material, but it is essential we all have a basic understanding of how investments can be structured to meet specific financial objectives. As an advisor, it is easy for me to assume my clients understand more than they actually know. I have found even very knowledgeable investors are often confused by the difference between investment vehicles and actual investments. Here are some examples:

Investment Vehicles	Investments
401k	Mutual Funds
IRA	Stocks
Roth IRA	Bonds
Joint Account	Real Estate
529 Plan	CDs

Note investment vehicles are types of accounts you can set up. Once the account has been established, then you put investments into the account. The investments ultimately determine the return you will receive on your money. Picking the right investment vehicle is often more important in meeting financial objectives than picking the right investments.

There are hundreds of different investment accounts that can be established. For the sake of being practical, we will focus on those types of accounts commonly used to meet your most important financial priorities established in Chapter 2. We defined three areas of your finances that directly involve investing:

- Emergency Reserves (including accumulation for certain spending priorities)

- Education

- Financial Independence (otherwise known as retirement)

We will focus on each priority separately. In some cases, the same type of account can be used to meet all three types of objectives and in other cases, there may be an account that can only be used for one objective (like an IRA being specifically used for retirement savings).

EMERGENCY RESERVE INVESTMENT ACCOUNT TYPES

Your emergency reserve is all about safety. This money needs to be there when you need it. We try to maximize returns on these accounts, but always respecting the need to have this money available to help us through the most difficult times in life. Your emergency reserve accounts are also where you will save and accumulate money for short term specific needs like saving for a house down payment, vacation money, braces for your children, etc.

There is nothing magical about the investment account types for your emergency reserve. This is the land of regular old taxable accounts at the bank and/or a mutual fund company. These accounts can be held jointly or individually and interest earned on the account is taxable in the year it is distributed to your account.

You will need three basic account types to create the structure for investing your emergency reserve.

- Checking Account

- Savings Account

- Mutual Fund Account

The checking and savings accounts will likely come from a local bank. The mutual fund account should not come from a bank, but rather should come directly from a mutual fund company of your choice.

Do not worry about the interest you make on a checking account. A checking account should be selected for convenience and look for a free account. When I say free, I mean free from all nickel and dime charges. You should be able to get free checks, free ATM privileges, free transfers, and free online banking, if possible. The fees on many checking accounts actually outweigh the interest you earn after taxes are considered and many banks require minimum balances in the account just to earn any amount of interest.

We were solicited one time from our current bank to upgrade our checking account to their "premium" account. Our current account paid no interest, but also had no minimum required balance and came with all the free perks I just mentioned. The sales rep said our average monthly balance was enough to qualify and we would get all the same benefits, but we would also start earning interest. I didn't see any harm in changing so we did. When we got our first statement after the change, I noticed the interest rate on our account was something like 0.25% annually and we had to maintain a $1,000 minimum balance. If we dropped below $1,000, even for just one day, the bank would charge us a fee of $20. This is the type of stunt banks can pull and many people fall for it (including me).

Why was this a bad deal? At least we were now earning some type of interest compared to our original account with no interest, right? Let's start with this fabulous interest. If we assume the average account balance is $3,000, we would earn a whopping $7.50 per year in interest. This is before taxes! After taxes, our actual interest would be about $5 or less. We gave up some liquidity on our account (due to the $1,000 minimum balance) and took the risk of paying a $20 fee each month in order to earn a whopping $5 per year in interest. Keep in mind this was a program being touted by the bank as a good deal for its customers! Once I realized my blunder, I called the bank and changed back to our original, no interest account. As a side note, the operator who took my cancellation call spent about fifteen minutes trying to explain to me why it was a mistake for us to switch back. The operator could not believe I would rather have an account with no interest.

Once I ran her through the above calculations, she realized it was probably a good idea.

Personally, I would consider what the bank did to be a scam. This might be strong language, but the bank was trying to get people to participate in a program with excessive fees and virtually no interest. The bank knows there are many people who don't understand how to calculate annual interest and they also know many people do a poor job of balancing their check book. In my opinion, this program was designed to generate fee business for the bank and was not in the best interest of customers.

Remember your emergency reserve objective from Chapter 2. Our emergency reserve objective was:

> Keep a minimum of one month of expenses in checking (no interest on the account)
>
> Keep a minimum of two months expenses in savings (minimal interest)
>
> Keep a minimum of nine months expenses in a joint mutual fund account

Tracy and I have a joint checking account with at least one month's worth of expenses. We also have individual checking accounts for each of us for spending money. Although both of our individual accounts have some money in them at all times, I don't count this money towards the one month's worth of expenses. Our spending accounts were specifically set aside as spending money so they cannot be considered as an emergency reserve. I repeat—none of our checking accounts earn interest, but we also do not pay any fees for our banking services including online bill pay.

That gets us to our savings account. Interest matters in a savings account, but still not as much as convenience. Your checking and savings should be linked and it should be very simple to transfer money back and forth between accounts. Rather than earn low interest from our local bank, we decided to have our savings account at a direct bank. A direct bank is essentially an online bank. There are many options to choose from, but the bank we chose pays a very competitive interest rate, is FDIC insured, and I found their system easy to coordinate with our checking account. There are no fees, no minimum balance, and I can do all of my banking online. I figure our savings account has consistently paid at least twice as much interest as the local bank and sometimes as much as four times more interest.

We tend to hold at least a couple months worth of expenses in our savings account so interest does start to add up. Earning an extra 1% per year on an average $10,000 balance will create an extra $100/year (before taxes). After taxes, we are not talking about a lot of money, but it is free money with no strings attached and no fees.

If you are starting from ground zero with no significant checking or savings account balance, proceed systematically towards your goal. Get your cash management in order first so you have positive cash flow (refer back to Chapter 4). You will slowly start to accumulate balances in your checking and savings. Do not start a mutual fund account until you consistently have at least three months' worth of expenses in some combination between checking and savings.

Checking and savings accounts are simple to understand and nearly everyone has them. Now we get to the mutual fund portion of your emergency reserve—much more confusing. Very few people ever go beyond having checking and savings accounts and most people carry almost no significant balances so they are living paycheck to paycheck. If you make it to the mutual fund point, congratulate yourself because you have accomplished a major achievement in your financial plan.

Mutual fund accounts get much more complicated, but for now, we are focusing only on the account type and not the investments inside the account (investments will be covered in the next chapter). We are looking for a regular, taxable mutual fund account with any reputable firm. If you are married, I believe the account should be held jointly and if you are single, the account will be an individual account. Often the mutual fund account can be electronically linked to checking or savings to allow electronic transfers to and from different accounts. Each mutual fund family will usually have some type of minimum balance to start an account.

How do you set up an account? Your advisor will help you select an appropriate mutual fund family, or if you do not have an advisor, you might consider researching no-load fund options (low expenses). I would love to give you some specific names to check out, but as I stated at the beginning of this book, I am not allowed to make specific fund or fund family recommendations. You may want to check out www.morningstar.com to get some ideas where to start. Morningstar provides independent research for the average investor.

How do you go about accumulating emergency reserves in a mutual fund account? There are two main ways this can be done. First, I recommend setting up some form of automatic transfer from checking into your mutual fund account. You might set up a $50 transfer each month just like paying any other bill. The amount can be increased or decreased depending on available cash flow. I like this approach because it is easy and it is systematic. The second way is to make periodic lump sum deposits in your mutual fund account. The concept is to sock away a piece of "extra" money like bonuses, tax refunds, gifts, etc. This does not work as well for most people because it is really hard to write big checks and it is more fun to spend our extra money. I believe the best approach is to set up your mutual fund account with a systematic, automatic investment plan and periodically deposit additional money when it is available. Once an account is established, you will be amazed how easy it is to find some extra money to put in the account. If an account is never established, it is much easier to spend any extra money.

We have a joint mutual fund account with over one year worth of expenses invested in a range of funds. We do not have systematic investments because my income is highly variable. We send money when there is extra available which works well for us. The account is electronically linked to our checking account for easy transfers.

I think you will find reaching your emergency reserve objective to be one of the most difficult goals to achieve. Most of my clients work towards this goal, but always seem to suffer setbacks along the way. There is always some excuse to spend money and take back what you have worked so hard to accumulate. Remember, this money is for *emergencies*. Getting the proper accounts established will be a huge step, but it will still take time to make progress. Keep in mind when you have achieved your objective, all the money you saved each month to accumulate a reserve can now be used for other important priorities.

EDUCATION INVESTMENT ACCOUNT TYPES

Saving for education has become a hot button issue the past several years with huge tuition increases at most colleges. Education costs have grown much more rapidly than overall inflation for many years and that trend is likely to continue. The government has become actively involved in encouraging parents to save for education with new incentive programs specifically designed for meeting education expenses. The emergence of new options has made education savings one of the most complicated financial decisions for many people.

I will do my best to clear up some of the confusion and explain why you might consider certain options better than others. Again, this chapter only deals with types of accounts rather than specific investment options within those accounts. The following options are most commonly used to fund education:

- Taxable accounts in the parents name only
- UGMA or UTMA accounts (taxable custodial accounts)
- 529 Plans
- Education IRAs (also known as Coverdell Education Savings Account)
- Roth IRAs

Each of these accounts varies in three important aspects: who controls the account, taxation on the account, and potential financial aid implications. Control and taxation are relatively easy to address for each option, but financial aid implications are more difficult to determine. Financial aid is an ever-changing process and varies significantly from person to person depending on your circumstances. I will give some basic direction on financial aid implications, but I recommend doing additional financial aid research before making any important education funding decisions. You will also want to contact your tax professional before implementing any of these accounts because your unique tax circumstances may result in different conclusions than those expressed in this book.

<u>Taxable accounts in the parents name only</u>:

This is essentially the exact same account you set up for emergency reserves and other short term accumulation goals. It can be some type of bank account, a mutual fund account, or some form of brokerage account. Any gains, dividends, and interest on the account are taxable to the parents when it is received. There are basically no education tax advantages. However, the parents own the account so they retain full discretion over how much is used for education and when. If your child decides not to attend college because he would rather join a band and become a rock star, you still control the money and can shift those dollars to another financial priority.

The account is an asset of the parents in financial aid calculations so it will count less in financial aid calculations than money held directly by the child. If you think your child will qualify for need-based financial aid, saving into a taxable account is not a bad way to go. However, very few of my clients end up qualifying for need based financial aid so this rarely is a huge consideration.

Saving money in a taxable account under your name is easily the most flexible way to save because you always retain complete control over all aspects of the account. Your investment options are virtually unlimited so returns on the account are also a direct result of your decisions.

<u>UGMA or UTMA Custodial Accounts</u>:

UGMA stands for Uniform Gifts to Minors Act and UTMA stands for Uniform Transfers to Minors Act. They are basically the same type of account, but have different names in different states. These are custodial accounts in the child's name, but you retain control of the account for the best interest of your child until age of majority. Once your child reaches 18, or 21 depending on your state, the account becomes his and he can use the money for whatever he likes. I often see these accounts and rarely do they have any significant advantages to anyone other than your child if he decides not to attend college.

UGMA and UTMA accounts can be some type of bank account, a mutual fund account, or some form of brokerage account and you have complete flexibility in choosing investment options. Any gains, dividends, and interest on the account are taxable, but who is responsible for the tax depends on the age of the child, and the total amount of gains, dividends, or interest in a given year. Your accountant will help you figure out the specific tax ramifications. Wealthy people will often use a custodial account to transfer income producing assets to their children as a tax reduction strategy. This is not a particularly important benefit for the rest of us who are not wealthy.

These accounts are considered assets of the child so they count more towards financial aid calculations and can directly reduce need based financial aid more than an asset of the parents.

Setting up an UGMA or UTMA account is particularly handy if your child has some type of job and wants to sock away his extra money. Otherwise, there are no significant advantages for contributing your own money to this type of account.

<u>529 Plans</u>:

A 529 plan is a state sponsored, tax advantaged way to save for college education expenses. I am not going to get into all of the specifics of these plans, but you can get a great deal of 529 information at savingforcollege.com along with many other websites dedicated to saving for college. We will touch on some of the basics.

Every state either has its own plan or is in the process of developing a plan. This makes 529 plans very confusing for most people and also for financial advisors. You do not need to select the plan in your own state! Some states offer tax advantages for their state residents, but you need to do your homework to make sure these tax advantages actually help you. Each state has some of their own rules, different investment options, different fees, etc., but all 529 plans have some common characteristics.

First off, all 529 plans have a significant tax feature. The account will grow tax deferred until withdrawn from the account. If the withdrawal is for qualified higher education expenses, all gains, dividends, and interest on the account are federally income tax free, and possibly state tax free depending on the plan and the state where you live. This is a potentially big benefit for many people particularly if they have very young children with a long time horizon until college. However, I want you to remember who normally benefits from programs with significant tax breaks—the wealthy!

Financial advisors have jumped on the 529 bandwagon the past couple years. Is it because 529 plans are the best way to save for college and they want to help their clients understand these complicated programs? We would like to think so, but it really is not true. Because 529 plans have some very attractive features for wealthy people, many advisors tout these plans as a door opener to get in front of wealthy prospects. There are definitely benefits to 529 plans, don't get me wrong. However, you need to be careful about advisors and other financial gurus touting these plans as the best thing since "sliced bread."

A 529 plan is considered an asset of the owner. Note I said owner, not necessarily a parent. Grandparents, aunts, siblings, friends of the family, etc. can all open 529 plans for a child. Maximum contributions to an account vary from state to state, but will often be $200,000 or more per account. This is another reason why 529 plans are attractive to wealthy people and why financial advisors are so high on these plans. How many people do you know can put away $200,000 for one child's education? The large contribution amount can be particularly attractive for grandparents with significant assets who want to help their grandchildren with education, but is rarely attractive for the average parent.

Since money in a 529 plan is considered an asset of the owner, financial aid calculations are difficult to determine. If your child will likely qualify for financial aid, it might make sense to have an owner other than the parent. A grandparent might be a good owner in this scenario. One thing to remember is the money becomes an asset of the child once it is gifted so gifting of a 529 may adversely affect the next year's financial aid calculation. This little catch is rarely mentioned in the mass media when discussing the tax benefits of a 529 plan. If a parent is the owner, the money counts as a parental asset that will count less in the financial aid calculation than a child's asset.

Investment options are controlled by the state sponsoring the plan. Most states offer a menu of mutual fund options varying from aggressive funds down to very conservative funds. Most people will be able to find a suitable investment option in nearly every state's plan. However, do a little research on fees. Some plans have dramatically higher investment expenses and those fees are usually hidden. I suggest you spend at least a couple hours of research before selecting a plan.

What happens if the 529 plan beneficiary decides to join a band and not attend college? You have some options. Whoever owns the plan could decide to withdraw the money, but would have to pay income tax plus a 10% penalty on any *gains* in the account. The government implements a penalty because 529 plans are meant for college, not as a tax deferred investment for the owner. I try to avoid unnecessary taxes when possible, so a better option would be to change the beneficiary on the account to another family member who will need the money for school. The plan would continue to grow tax deferred until the new beneficiary needs the money for college where the withdrawals would be federally tax free, if used for qualified higher education expenses.

A new trend in 529 plans is employer sponsored salary deferral plans. If you work for a relatively large employer, you may have the option to defer salary directly into a 529 plan. This is a great way to contribute money because it automatically comes out of your check before you see it and creates an excellent systematic investment program. Contributions are still on an after tax basis so you don't get immediate tax benefits. These programs can be a nice perk, but you still need to do your homework. There are a lot of poor 529 plans out there so you still need to determine if your employer plan is right for your circumstances.

All in all 529 plans provide a nice way to save for college, but the tax benefits for most of us are not that significant. These are truly excellent planning tools for wealthy people, which is why so many advisors are out there pushing these plans.

Education IRA (Coverdell Education Savings Account):

Education IRAs just went through a name change to the Coverdell Education Savings Account so I apologize for any confusion here, but I will refer to them as Ed IRAs in our discussion. An Ed IRA is a federally tax advantaged way to save for college. These plans are very similar to 529 plans in many regards, but are not state sponsored, so they are a little less confusing.

The primary benefit of Ed IRAs is similar to 529 plans. The account will grow tax deferred until withdrawals begin. If the withdrawal is for qualified education expenses, all gains, dividends, and interest on the account are federally income tax free. Note I said all qualified education expenses, not just higher education. This is one advantage of an Ed IRA over a 529 plan. Ed IRA money can be used prior to college for private school expenses, computers, and other expenses considered educational.

If Ed IRAs are so similar to 529 plans and actually have some additional attractive benefits, why do nearly all advisors and most media articles recommend the 529 plan? In fact, there are many times I don't even see Ed IRAs mentioned in a discussion about financing college education. The answer comes down to a single reason. Ed IRAs are not for wealthy people. They are designed for the rest of us. First off, as of 2003, you can only put up to $2,000 per year into an Ed IRA per child. There are also income limits to participate. For 2003, a single individual must have an adjusted gross income below $110,000 to make any contributions (contributions begin to get limited over $95,000) and a married couple must be under $220,000 (contributions begin to get limited over $190,000). These income restrictions are for 2003 and they may change in the future so contact your accountant if you are not sure about the current income limits. The income restrictions and the lower contribution amounts make Ed IRAs a tool for the middle class rather than the ultra wealthy. This is the primary reason most advisors favor 529 plans over Ed IRAs.

There is another disadvantage to Ed IRAs. The account is considered an asset of the child in financial aid calculations. Since children's assets count more than parent's assets in the calculation, Ed IRAs can hurt financial aid more than 529 plans. This is certainly a concern for many people who will possibly get need based financial aid.

Investment options are much more flexible in an Ed IRA. Because the plan is controlled by Federal regulations rather than State regulations, rules are consistent for all plans. You will have a wide array of investment options available to you, but mutual funds will generally be the funding mechanism of choice to keep expenses low and still provide diversification.

Comparing Ed IRAs and 529 plans is complicated enough to give most people a serious headache. If you have young children and are looking at both plans as options, you will need to make a lot of income and tax rate assumptions about the future. Whenever you make assumptions, you probably are not going to be totally accurate so the comparison may get skewed. The point here is to start a saving plan. Both options have tax benefits and provide similar mechanisms for saving and investing. Also remember you can now contribute to both an Ed IRA and a 529 plan in the same year for the same child.

Roth IRA:

Some of you might know a Roth IRA is a retirement saving vehicle and might be a little confused why I have it as a college savings option. It is early in the morning as I write this section and I am a little groggy, but no, I didn't make a mistake. The Roth IRA actually provides a very attractive college savings vehicle for the rest of us. Roth IRAs are typically a poor option for wealthy people which is why you may have never heard anyone talk about Roth IRAs to help with college funding.

I will elaborate on the retirement merits of the Roth IRA later, but for now I want to cover some of the basic characteristics of Roth IRAs. Roth IRA contributions are made on an after tax basis (no tax benefits when contributions are made). As of 2003, your contributions are limited to $3,000 per year unless you are fifty or older when you get a step up to $3,500 per year. There are income restrictions for making contributions as I previously mentioned. Roth IRA investments grow on a tax deferred basis and are tax free if withdrawn after age 59 ½. The key Roth IRA characteristic most people don't know is you can withdraw *contributions* to a Roth at any time, for any reason, without paying any taxes or penalties. Emphasis is on *contributions*, not any *growth* on your account.

Most of us do not have an unlimited source of funds to invest for all of our important financial priorities. This means we have to efficiently utilize our resources to get the most out of our money. In my opinion the Roth IRA is the most efficient investment vehicle that exists to meet various financial objectives. The tax free withdrawal of contributions allows a Roth to be considered as an emergency source of funds, a source of college money, and as a retirement savings vehicle all wrapped up in one neat little, tax efficient package.

How many people do you know that can save money to accumulate an emergency reserve while maxing out their retirement plan at work, maxing out their Roth IRAs, maxing out their Ed IRA, and still have money left over to fund a 529 plan? Ridiculous! Only very wealthy people could afford to save that amount of money and they would likely have too much income to participate in the Roth or the Ed IRA, due to the income restrictions. For the rest of us, there is never enough money to go around and that means we have to set priorities.

Here is the logic as to why Roth IRAs make great college savings vehicles. Assume a married couple maxing out Roth IRAs for each spouse, (currently $3,000 per account for a total of $6,000 per year). Roth IRAs are individual accounts so a husband and wife would need to have separate accounts. The accounts are both invested in a diversified portfolio of mutual funds. For an example, let's assume you have young kids that will start college in fifteen years. Over those fifteen years, you will have contributed $90,000 to Roth IRAs and at 8% hypothetical returns, the two accounts would each be worth about $81,500 (combined $163,000). During the accumulation period, you could have accessed the contributions for a serious emergency or for any other reason without paying taxes. If you didn't have such an emergency, you would have $90,000 available to help the children with school. There would be absolutely no taxes due, there would be no required documentation of expenses, and the money you saved would not count against financial aid calculations. That's right, because the money is in an account designated for your retirement, financial aid calculations do not count that money against you. Remember, only the contributions are available prior to age 59 ½ with no tax or penalty. Any earnings on the account should remain there until after age 59 ½.

Also, if your kids decide not to attend college, the money is in your accounts under your control at all times. You simply leave the money to accumulate and eventually withdraw it tax free when you retire after age 59 ½. It almost sounds too good to be true! If you end up withdrawing the full $90,000 available to you for education, the accounts would still have the growth money (about $73,000 between the two accounts assuming our hypothetical 8% return) that would continue to accumulate for retirement.

Many experts would argue a couple assumptions. First, they would say college will cost a heck of a lot more than $90,000 in fifteen years especially if you have more than one child. Totally true, but my contention is the rest of us will not be able to fund the entire cost of college education for more than one child without seriously impacting other financial objectives so the argument becomes somewhat irrelevant. The second argument is, if you use the money to pay for college, it isn't there for retirement. Again, absolutely true. If you plan on using Roth IRA contributions to help fund college expenses, you must account for that assumption in your overall financial plan. This means you cannot assume those contributions will also be there for retirement. We cannot count the same money for two different priorities. However, you can still assume the growth will be there for retirement. If the kids don't need the money for school (maybe they don't go to school, or they get scholarships or an inheritance), the Roth money is still in your account and you can change your financial plan to adjust your retirement assumptions.

Combining all of these benefits makes Roth IRAs a top investment vehicle for many parents no matter what their financial objectives might be.

◆   ◆   ◆

We have only talked about investment account types for education. The actual investments you put inside these accounts will determine your ultimate performance. Specific investment options and recommendations will be discussed in the next chapter. For now, let me give you some reasoning in how to select appropriate accounts for meeting education funding objectives.

The first thing you need to do is determine how much you can reasonably save for education. For most of my clients with children, they are strapped with a lot of financial challenges and can rarely put away more than a couple hundred dollars per month for education. This is also the situation for my wife and me, so trust me, I understand.

Once you know how much can be saved each month, I recommend following this strategy:

1. Save into a Roth IRA until it is being maxed out for both of you.

2. If you still have money available for education savings, start an Ed IRA.

3. If you can max out the Ed IRA and still have money available for education savings, good for you. Start a 529 plan.

Most of my clients don't make it to Step 3 in their education savings program. In fact, most of my clients don't make it past Step 1 without significantly impairing their ability to meet other financial priorities.

Let me use our situation as an example of creating an education funding strategy. My wife and I discussed our education priorities at length and came up with the following conclusions:

• We assumed two children both attending college at age eighteen with four years of college.

• We will provide a set amount of money and our kids will need to find a way to pay for any additional costs through their own means.

• We may decide to send our children to private school before college (tough to decide when your only daughter is eighteen months old!).

• After maxing out both of our Roth IRAs, we don't want to dedicate more than $2,000 per year to education accounts for each child.

- We talked to grandparents and expect they will want to contribute some money to the kids for education (probably not more than $500/year).

- We assumed our children would not qualify for need based financial aid (some merit based scholarships would be nice—a parent can always dream!)

Here is our approach. We plan to max out our Roth IRAs every year until the kids go to school, but we will assume $3,000 per year of contributions is specifically for education objectives. We anticipate using our contributions to help them with school and will only assume growth on our Roths will be available for retirement. Over the next eighteen years, our total Roth contributions will be more than $108,000. We will use one Roth for Isabella, and the other Roth for our second child (a third child will make us readjust our planning, but we are thinking two children for now and will consider a third child in the future). We will put grandparent contributions into an Ed IRA for each child and add money of our own up to the $2,000 per child limit. If we assume 8% growth on all investments in both the Roth and the Ed IRAs, we come up with the following money available for each child:

Roth IRA	$54,000 Tax Free Per Child
Ed IRA	$74,900 Tax Free Per Child
Total	$128,900 Tax Free Per Child

If this amount doesn't cut the mustard in eighteen years, the kids will each be responsible for picking up the remaining tab. We will obviously tap the Ed IRAs first and our Roth IRAs last just in case expenses are less than $128,900 per child. That way any remaining money will be left in our Roths to accumulate for our retirement objectives. We also have the flexibility to spend some or all of the Ed IRA money tax free on private school or any other educational needs prior to college. We will cross that bridge when we get to it.

Our approach is not the one and only "right" approach. It is the systematic method my wife and I agreed upon. I particularly like the flexibility of our investment options, the flexibility of withdrawals, and the potentially tax free growth on our investments (tax free has a nice ring to it). We also know exactly what our obligations are from a contribution perspective. I will describe how we invest each of these accounts in a later chapter.

RETIREMENT INVESTMENT ACCOUNT TYPES

Saving for retirement—everyone knows they need to do it, but procrastination still prevails for many people. Procrastination stems from a lack of knowledge. Action comes from getting the knowledge you need to make good decisions. Knowing your options for saving and how they work is critically important.

Retirement investments make for big business and anytime there is big money on the line, you will be bombarded with sales pitches making it difficult to keep your focus, especially over a forty year career. Not only is big business doing its best to influence your retirement savings choices, but the government is also an integral player in shaping our decisions. Ever since the Great Depression, the government has recognized the importance of people saving to secure their own retirement future. The government also took on the responsibility of creating a retirement safety net through the social security system.

Government regulation will likely be the determining factor in how you save and invest for retirement, and by government regulation, I mean taxes. There are a tremendous number of retirement saving options for the average person, but instead of giving a comprehensive review of each and every account type available, I will simplify matters based on how accounts get taxed. There are three ways to look at saving for retirement:

- Taxable Accounts—taxes are due when you receive capital gains, dividends, and interest.

- Tax Deferred Accounts—taxes are deferred until money is withdrawn from the account (examples of tax deferred accounts are IRA, 401k, 403b, 457 plans along with a variety of other company retirement plans and also annuities).

- Tax Free Accounts—only the Roth IRA fits in this category. Gains, dividends, and interest are tax free if all rules are followed.

Taxable Investment Accounts:

These are the exact same account types we reviewed for your emergency reserve investment options. There are no special tax benefits in using these accounts to save for retirement. Income taxes are due on gains, dividends, and interest in the year they are received. Accounts should be held jointly for married couples.

There are three places most people go to open some form of taxable account for retirement:

- Bank

- Mutual Fund Company

- Brokerage

The bank will offer conventional accounts like CDs and money markets, but many banks also offer mutual funds and brokerage services. You already know how I feel about banks, but let's review. I believe you should use banks for checking and savings accounts only, nothing else. That was easy! In my opinion there are a lot of reasons to avoid banks for retirement savings and only one reason to use a bank. In my opinion, the primary reason people use banks is because they know and trust their bank after years of having checking and savings accounts with them. It is a convenience issue. Most people have a general distrust for things they don't understand and most people don't have a good understanding of the mutual fund and brokerage industry. Since you are reading this book, you are not like most people, so I suggest not doing business with banks other than your checking and savings.

I said there were many reasons why you should not buy investments at a bank. It comes down to conflict of interest. In most cases, the bank rep you talk to about investments is an employee of the bank. They are paid by the bank for the things they sell. The more they sell and produce for the bank, the more they get paid. Banks tend to pay their financial advisors very low percentages so the advisor is forced to sell, sell, sell to make a decent living. I have experienced many cases where a bank advisor sold someone a totally inappropriate investment either because it paid a high commission or because the advisor didn't take the time to understand the client's situation. Many financial advisors start their careers in banks, but eventually move on after they learn the business. If you have done any long term investment business at a bank, it is likely you have had several different advisors over the years as one advisor leaves and gets replaced by a new, often less experienced, advisor. I won't even get into how banks may nickel and dime their clients to death with miscellaneous ancillary fees and expenses. In my opinion, the whole concept of banks selling investments is fundamentally flawed and should be avoided unless convenience is your primary motivation.

Mutual fund companies are another story. I recommended using mutual funds as the investment vehicle of choice for the longer term portion of your emergency reserve account. The joint mutual fund account (or individual account if you are single) you set up to accumulate emergency reserves is also where you should have your taxable retirement saving account. Mutual funds offer some very attractive features while maintaining relatively low expenses for average investors. As of this writing, the mutual fund industry is dealing with some important scandals such as market timing, late trading, excessive fees, etc., but I still believe mutual funds still offer the best investment alternative for the rest of us (even with their faults). It is important to have confidence in the fund family you choose to work with and there are still many mutual fund families available that have not been involved in any significant scandals.

If you have an account established for investing emergency reserve money, I recommend using the same fund family, and actually use the same account for your taxable retirement investments. As I mentioned before, pick one of the larger fund families that offer a comprehensive menu of fund options.

Since your taxable mutual fund account may be used to help meet several different financial objectives, I often see people setting up several different accounts each designated for a different purpose. This approach is fine, but can be cumbersome with paperwork and investment management. We deal with the same issues, but instead of setting up several accounts, we keep one joint mutual fund account and designate different mutual funds for different purposes. Most large fund families will offer a large menu of funds so you can often pick different funds within the same account to meet different objectives.

Brokerage accounts are much more difficult to analyze. Decades ago, brokerage accounts meant working with a stock or bond broker. Now the brokerage industry has changed. There are still plenty of "full service" brokers, but there is also a new wave of "discount" brokerage accounts. Brokerage accounts provide a flexible means of holding a wide array of investments in one consolidated account. You could buy nearly any type of investment through your brokerage account including money markets, CDs, mutual funds, individual stocks, bonds, and other more obscure investments.

I believe some stock brokers do a good job for high net worth individuals, but stock brokers are usually a high expense alternative for the rest of us. Stock brokers operate similar to bank representatives. Most stock brokers are employees of their firm and are trained to sell. The requirements to get started as a broker typically involve tremendous marketing and cold calling efforts in order to survive. If a young broker has to spend so much time marketing, how can they spend the time necessary to know your needs and treat you as a person rather than a potential commission? Veteran brokers are the opposite. They have built their business on the backs of regular folks as clients and now that they are successful, some of their firms teach them to slowly eliminate their smaller clients and focus on their wealthiest clients. This is why I believe high net worth clients can sometimes get nice benefits from stock brokers, but the rest of us usually cannot justify the fees.

The conflict of interest is incredible in the brokerage industry. Most firms do not promote financial planning services because it is more profitable to sell investments rather than service. The trend has been to call stock brokers "financial advisors" or "financial planners," but I do not believe they usually deserve the title.

It is my opinion most people of modest means will be better served with regular old mutual fund accounts. If you want advice, ask friends and family who they use as an advisor and try to find an independent planner rather than a stock broker or bank rep. The independent planner will generally receive a much larger piece of any fees you pay, so they have a much greater incentive to give you better service. I am a firm believer in directing as much of your expense to the person actually helping you rather than to their firm. Do you really think the VP or brokerage manager who doesn't know your name, but still receives a significant amount of your expenses, has your best interest in mind?

Discount brokers are another story. For the "do-it-yourselfers," discount brokerage accounts were a God send. These accounts do not offer advice (some say they do, but avoid discount brokers if you need help with investing or financial planning), but they are inexpensive. If you are doing all the work yourself, it definitely makes sense to keep your expenses as low as possible.

A discount brokerage account will allow you to purchase a wide variety of investment alternatives, but this is where many people make mistakes. Many people get caught up in the excitement of trading and end up buying individual stocks in their discount brokerage account. This is usually a mistake. Remember, stick to your plan. You don't need to hit home runs with stock picks; you can hit singles and doubles with much less risk and still reach your financial objectives. I recommend using your brokerage account to purchase a diversified portfolio of mutual funds. This approach may be boring, but it gets the job done while reducing your overall investment risk.

How and where do you set up a discount brokerage account? Most people opt for Charles Schwab or Fidelity, but I would tell you to investigate other options and look for a respected name with low trading expenses and no minimum required trading. I see no reason why you should pay more for the name brands of Fidelity or Charles Schwab (you are simply funding their huge marketing programs). I used to have a lesser known discount broker before I became a financial advisor and I thought the fees were reasonable and their system was relatively easy to use. They were much less expensive than Charles Schwab for similar service and options. Make sure the brokerage you use will allow you to buy the funds you want to buy (discussed in the next chapter). Some discount brokers are limited in the funds you can purchase through their system. Setting up an account is usually an easy process done over the Internet or by phone. The company you select should have a system in place to lead you through the process of establishing an account. If you find the account set up process incredibly confusing, I would recommend changing firms immediately because their other services will likely be equally disappointing.

◆   ◆   ◆

I previously mentioned my wife and I have our longer term emergency reserve account invested in mutual funds. This is the same jointly held account we also use to accumulate our taxable retirement savings.

For those readers managing investments without advice, set up a taxable account either directly with one of the major mutual fund families or with a discount broker.

Tax Deferred Accounts:

Tax deferred accounts make up the bread and butter of retirement investing. There are a variety of tax deferred accounts specifically designed for retirement savings, but most of them have the same benefit from a tax perspective. Money is normally invested in these accounts on a pre-tax basis; the investments grow on a tax deferred basis, and taxes are paid when the money is withdrawn during retirement. You receive a tax benefit from the government to encourage retirement savings. Employers have welcomed these plans with open arms and often provide some form of retirement savings plan as a benefit to their employees. Everyone with earned income has access to participate in some form of tax deferred retirement saving account. Because the government is involved in setting up the rules, and because these accounts deal with taxes, confusion is common. We want to focus on some basic rules, but more specifically, we want to discuss how these accounts fit into your financial plan for retirement.

As stated previously, you will want to consult your tax professional before implementing any investment based on tax ramifications. In order to simplify our discussion, I will break down tax deferred investment accounts into three categories:

- Individual Retirement Accounts (IRA)—personal account not offered by employers

- Employer Sponsored Plans—the most common type is a 401k plan, but also includes 403b plans, 457 plans, SEP IRAs, SIMPLE IRAs, Keogh Accounts, Profit Sharing, and some other lesser utilized plans.

- Annuities—insurance contracts specifically designed for retirement investing

Tax deferred accounts have become hugely popular over the past couple decades. These types of accounts get an enormous amount of support from the financial media and are also touted as the basis for retirement planning by most financial experts. Because of all the media hype, it is not uncommon for me to meet people who have every penny of their retirement savings in some form of tax deferred account. I am always glad to see people have saved money for retirement, but solely relying on tax deferred accounts for retirement is probably not your best move. Blasphemy, you say! How can it ever be wrong to save on taxes? I will explain why in a few moments, but first we have to see how these different accounts work.

The basic workings of an IRA and an employer sponsored plan are about the same. Money is put into the account on a pre-tax basis so you immediately save money on your taxes by making contributions (assuming you pay income taxes). The account grows (or declines) on a tax deferred basis. Any withdrawals from these accounts are income taxable in the year the withdrawal is made. Deferring taxes is nice, but the government is going to get their money eventually. Also, if you withdraw money from the account before age 59 ½, you may have to pay a 10% penalty in addition to the tax (there are some exceptions like death, disability, 72t distributions, etc. so please contact an accountant before withdrawing tax deferred money before age 59 ½).

It would truly amaze you how many people save money into their tax deferred account and then casually withdraw the money for "important" reasons before age 59 ½. It simply makes no sense and absolutely drives me nuts. These are *retirement* accounts, not "emergency reserve accounts," not "pay for wedding accounts," and definitely not "add on to your garage accounts." I had a woman call me one time who wanted to take out her 403b money to pay for an addition on their garage. She had $10,000 in her account and she thought the addition would cost about $8,000. She knew there would be taxes due, but they *really wanted* a bigger garage. I asked her some questions about their income and also found out she was 38 years old. I discovered they were in the 27% federal tax bracket and about a 7% state tax bracket. I explained to her she would only get about half of her money or about $5,000 after paying taxes and penalties on her account. I also explained it would make more sense to take a home equity line of credit or even put it on a credit card and pay it off as soon as possible. Did she listen to me? No. She raided her retirement account to pay for an addition to her garage knowing full well she would lose about half her withdrawal to the government!

The basic difference between IRAs and company sponsored retirement plans is how you contribute money. An IRA is an individual plan where you will make contributions out of your own accounts and will write off the contribution on your tax forms. Employer sponsored plans are typically funded through salary deferral. The contributions come right out of your paycheck before you ever get your hands on the money. Quick and painless, this is why most people like employer sponsored plans.

There are all kinds of rules governing both IRAs and other types of retirement plans and I definitely do not want to get you bogged down in the gory details. Remember, these are government sponsored programs so they are going to be complicated. Contribution limits are always changing so you will need to do some research on how much you can contribute to your chosen plan on a tax deferred basis. If you have a company sponsored plan, contact the person responsible for administering your plan to get specific details on how to participate. Your plan may be different from your neighbor's plan so please do not rely exclusively on third party advice. Get your information straight from the source. One of the most important details you need to know is if your employer provides some form of "match" on your retirement account. Most 401k plans provide a match (usually 50% of your contributions up to a certain limit). If your company provides some type of match, take it! This is free money. Not participating in a retirement plan with a match is like saying you would not take the time to bend over and pick up a $100 bill you found on the street!

Let me give you an example. The firm I used to work for now provides a 50% match on their 401k up to a maximum employee contribution of 4%. Let us assume you make $50,000 and contribute the 4% to get your full match from the company. You would put in $2,000 per year or about $167/month. The company would have to match half of your contribution or $1,000 per year ($83/month). Don't tell me you would pass up $1,000 just sitting there for the taking! Also, all of the money is tax deferred so you get another important benefit. If you had taken the $2,000 as income instead of saving into your retirement account, the government would have taxed you on both the state and federal level. It is likely you would pay about 1/3 of the $2,000 in taxes. This means you get to save $2,000 into an account for retirement, get an immediate 50% return on your money due to the match, and it only costs you about $1,340 from your after tax budget. Sounds like a great deal to me!

Make sure to find out if there is a vesting schedule attached to your plan for employer matching contributions. Some employers use their retirement plan as a way to retain their employees. A vesting schedule allows these employers to place a restriction on when their matching dollars become the employee's money. You will commonly see "tiered" vesting schedules. An example would be:

One Year	20% Vested
Two Years	40% Vested
Three Years	60% Vested
Four Years	80% Vested
Five Years	100% Vested

In this example, you would need to be employed for five consecutive years before you actually owned all matching contributions. If you left before five years, a portion of those matching contributions would get pulled back to the employer or to other participants according to the vesting arrangement. Make sure you fully understand any vesting restrictions on your company retirement plan before making contribution decisions.

Many financial gurus make the blanket recommendation that everyone should "max out" their tax deferred retirement plans. This is not right! How much you should contribute to your tax deferred retirement plan is entirely dependent on your unique financial situation. I would suggest nearly everyone should contribute at least what the company will match, but after that, there are a lot of other things to consider before increasing your contributions. I will elaborate further after talking about the Roth IRA, but for now, please contribute at least enough to get all of the matching money from your employer sponsored retirement plan.

If you do not have an employer sponsored plan, the government allows you to participate in an IRA. Also, if you have an employer sponsored plan, but you fall under certain income limits, you could still contribute to a personal IRA in addition to your company plan (check with your accountant for current income limitations). As of 2003, you can contribute up to $3,000 per year to a personal IRA, and $3,000 per year for a spouse's IRA even if your spouse does not have earned income. If you are over age fifty, there is a catch up provision that allows you to contribute more money. However, before you run out and start an IRA, you might want to read about Roth IRAs in the next section.

Annuities provide another form of tax deferred retirement saving account. If you are like many of my clients, you may own an annuity and not even know it. These accounts are sold by insurance people and they are incredibly confusing investment vehicles. For now I will cover some of the basics you need to understand.

An annuity is a form of life insurance contract designed for investing. Whenever you hear the words "life insurance," I want you to think expensive! Not necessarily good or bad, but expensive. The typical annuity is funded with *after tax* dollars, but grows tax deferred and only your gains are income taxable when the money is withdrawn. The reason I have to say typical is because annuities can also be used inside IRAs or other employer sponsored retirement plans in which case your contributions would be before taxes. This is just part of the reason why annuities are so confusing, not only to the general public, but also to agents who sell them.

There are hundreds, if not thousands, of different types of annuities sold by different insurance companies with all kinds of different little nuances. The basic types are fixed, variable, and equity indexed annuities. Fixed annuities work much like a CD. They pay a set amount of interest over a set period of time. All of the fees are built into the contract so you truly get whatever interest rate they say you are getting. There are also surrender charges associated with most contracts so you need to find out how long the annuity must be held before you can access the money without charges. A variable annuity has more flexible investment options. You can normally select from a menu of mutual fund subaccount options ranging from very conservative to very aggressive. The name variable means your account balance will vary with the returns you get on your investment subaccounts. The primary charge you need to be aware of with a variable annuity is something called a Mortality and Expense Risk charge, or an M&E charge. This is the life insurance component of the annuity and it directly impacts the returns you get on the contract.

Annuities are usually sold and not bought. What I mean is annuities are generally a better deal for the agent than the person buying the annuity. Of course, this is a generalization and is not always the case, but in my experience, it is most often the case. Annuities pay higher commissions than mutual funds in general so there is a financial incentive for agents to sell annuities. Also, most of the fees associated with an annuity are hidden fees so it is often easy to sell annuities without explaining overall expenses to the customer. Remember I said life insurance is expensive. How do insurance companies pay for their fancy buildings and catchy ad campaigns? Insurance companies make money, a lot of money, and they do it through charging their clients fees. In many cases these fees can be excessive and end up costing the investor a lot of money.

You may have the idea I don't like annuities. You are correct! However, there are a few circumstances where annuities have some advantages over other types of retirement investments. The first and most obvious circumstance is when you have fully funded all other retirement investment options. Since annuities have no maximum limits, you can contribute as much as you want. Unfortunately, only very high income people ever truly run into this issue. Absolutely none of my clients are in a position where they have maxed out their retirement plans at work, maxed out their Roth IRAs, accomplished their other primary financial objectives, and still have extra money lying around to put in an annuity.

The second major circumstance does actually occur for some of my clients. Because annuities are structured as life insurance contracts, they can provide some guarantees not readily available through other investments. The first guarantee is a death benefit guarantee. There are numerous types of death benefit guarantees available depending on the specific annuity, but the basic death benefit guarantees your heirs will always get back at least what you put into the contract when you die. If you are anything like me, you probably don't get real excited over this guarantee. I typically purchase investments with the hope they will increase so I would hope the contract is worth more than what I put in when I die. For this reason, I rarely consider an annuity death benefit as an attractive feature.

The next major type of guarantee is a retirement income guarantee feature. This is much more relevant for some of my clients. There are a number of retirement income guarantees available so you need to be careful to do your homework if this is something you would like. Most annuities will have some option where you will be guaranteed to get monthly income from your investment for the rest of your life no matter how long you live. This is typically called annuitization, but there are new riders available that may or may not require annuitization to get the guarantee.

Conventional annuitization allows an investor to enter an agreement with the insurance company where a certain amount of money is invested and the insurance company guarantees an income stream for the rest of your life. There are both fixed and variable annuitization options. The fixed option means you will get the same monthly payment forever. Under fixed annuitization your biggest concern should be inflation. Over time, inflation will slowly diminish the buying power of your annuity income. The variable annuitization option varies your income depending on the performance of your investments. The better your investments perform, the more income you will receive over time. However, it also works in the other direction. If your investments lose money, your income stream decreases.

Retirees often like annuitization because they are assured of income for the rest of their lives. They can never outlive their investment. However, their kids don't really care for annuitization because when the parents die, the insurance company typically keeps what is left over (if anything). Annuitization protects income for the parents, but can entirely eliminate inheritance to heirs. This is a major drawback if you die prematurely and is one reason why I typically do not recommend my clients annuitize their money. I would prefer to see my clients keep control over their money rather than passing that control to an insurance company.

There is one specific type of circumstance where I recommend annuities. During the recent bear market (from 2000–2002), many of my more skittish clients wanted completely out of stocks. Some of these clients were getting close to retirement and were scared they would lose more money and jeopardize their future retirement if they stayed in any kind of stock investment. I obviously urged them to keep some of their money in stocks or inflation would end up hurting them over the long term. What was the solution? A relatively new development in the annuity business was the development of what is called a "Retirement Income Guarantee" or a "Living Benefit Rider." This rider allows investors the ability to stay invested more aggressively than they would normally invest while maintaining some minimum guarantee on their money. Usually the guarantee is a minimum growth rate on their money like 5% or 6% annually, but the guarantee usually requires annuitization to take effect. You are probably very confused about now, but the basic premise is: You get the upside potential of your investments while maintaining downside protection. Of course this guarantee costs money and is usually a money maker for the insurance company, but it does provide a sense of security for some people. I have used this feature to help me keep skittish clients in stocks with at least some of their money. Of course it was necessary to completely disclose the increased cost associated with this rider. There is a lot more detail to these investments, but for our purposes, I simply want you to know some of these riders exist and can be attractive to certain investors.

If you are comfortably able to ride out bad investment periods without freaking out, annuities are rarely your best option for retirement savings. There are thousands of life insurance agents who would take issue with this blanket statement because their livelihood depends on investors not fully understanding the fee structure of annuities. Annuities are expensive, often pay very high commissions, and usually are in the best interest of the agent and her insurance company rather than the typical investor. Enough said.

Tax Free Accounts:

Doesn't "tax free" have a nice ring to it? Historically there have been many investments touted as effective tax shelters, particularly for wealthy people, but many of them were shams and proved to be either illegal or ineffective. However, in 1997 the government created a fully legal and fully tax free investment vehicle. It was called the Roth IRA.

I am as positive about the Roth IRA as I am negative about annuities, and I am very negative about annuities. I like to think of the Roth IRA as the all purpose investment vehicle for the rest of us. I have already described how the Roth IRA can be used as an emergency reserve fund, an education funding vehicle, and, last but not least, as a retirement savings account. In this section I will focus on the Roth IRA as a retirement account.

A Roth IRA works almost the exact opposite of your regular IRA or your company retirement plan. You fund a Roth IRA with *after tax* dollars so you do not get any immediate tax savings. The account grows tax deferred similar to a regular IRA, but the truly exciting part of a Roth IRA comes when you need the money. Qualified withdrawals are entirely *income tax free*! Yes, *tax free*.

As I previously mentioned, the contributions you make to a Roth IRA are always available to you at any time, for any reason, with no tax or penalty. However, the growth on your investments, and hopefully there is some growth, must remain in the account until after age 59 ½ to be withdrawn tax and penalty free.

A regular IRA allows you to defer taxes, but ultimately, the taxes are inevitable. You are just delaying the IRS from getting their cash. With a Roth IRA you actually get the opportunity to build wealth knowing full well that all gains will remain in your pocket rather than going to the government. This is truly a beautiful thing especially for young, low to mid income people, who have enough time for compound interest to work its magic.

Should you do tax deferred investing for retirement via an IRA or company sponsored plan or should you do tax free investing via the Roth IRA? This is a common debate and it is a much more difficult question than it seems. The common rule of thumb I hear all the time is:

- If you expect your tax bracket to be higher at retirement than it is today, use the Roth IRA.

- If you expect your tax bracket to be lower at retirement than it is today, use the IRA or company sponsored plan.

- If your tax bracket is the exact same at retirement, either plan will theoretically give you the exact same after tax outcome.

This all sounds like great advice, but rules of thumb are nearly never appropriate for everyone. I already mentioned most financial advisors have a blanket recommendation to "max out" your tax deferred plan. This advice makes a lot of sense for very high income people who might be at a lower income level during retirement and who make too much to even utilize a Roth IRA, but it does not make sense for the rest of us. Most of us are middle income people who will also be middle income people at retirement (if we do proper planning). Our tax rate will probably not change much unless the government changes the tax code, which could easily happen. No one can predict what taxes will be during retirement, but we can make some decent guesses of what you might need for money during retirement and this is the key to the decision between tax deferred accounts and the Roth IRA.

None of my clients have the exact same goals for retirement, but most of them have similar ideas on how they will spend retirement money. Everyone will need some amount of monthly income to pay recurring bills and nearly everyone will need or want some type of lump sum money to pay for non-recurring bills like buying a new car, taking a big vacation, buying a vacation place, etc. The *type* of money you will need during retirement is the key and if you take one thing away from this book, I want you to remember this:

Tax deferred accounts are very good at providing *monthly income* during retirement to help replace a paycheck. Roth IRAs are very good at providing *lump sum money* during retirement to make big purchases.

This means the two types of accounts provide a compliment to each other and the most common advice I give people in the accumulation phase is to have both types of accounts. Let me use a couple examples to illustrate why you should have both accounts:

I recently did some financial planning for a relatively wealthy retiring executive and his wife. This person had done an excellent job of saving into his company retirement plan and had accumulated about $1,000,000 in his 401k plan and ESOP (both tax deferred accounts). He was also set to receive a stock buyout big enough to pay off most of his existing debt, but would leave him with little to no money outside his tax deferred accounts. One of their primary retirement objectives was to purchase a condo in Florida as a winter home. He said it would cost about $150,000 and they really wanted to pay cash for the purchase. I explained they would need to withdraw about $250,000 from his IRA to pay cash for the condo because there would be about $100,000 withheld in taxes. A lump sum withdrawal from a tax deferred account can be devastating to your tax picture because it gets added to your current top marginal bracket and will likely boost you into higher tax brackets. Of course they were not too excited about spending 1/10 of their retirement nest egg upfront on taxes, but they didn't have a lot of choices. They had three basic options:

1. Not buy the condo (because they couldn't afford it anyway)

2. Take the lump sum withdrawal and pay the taxes (not exactly attractive)

3. Use stock money to pay off the condo instead of paying off their primary house mortgage and keep making a house payment

They really wanted the condo so I recommended Option 3. Of course they didn't listen to me and opted for Option 2 which significantly impacted their future retirement income. The basic point is tax deferred accounts and lump sum purchases do not mix well.

The second example is how Tracy and I do our retirement savings. We contribute to both tax deferred accounts and to Roth IRA accounts for both of us. The tax deferred accounts will compliment Social Security to provide us with monthly income during retirement. The Roth IRAs will be used as a tax free source of buying power to make lump sum purchases and to act as an emergency reserve during retirement. The combination of accounts is much more powerful than just picking one account because we have absolutely no clue what our tax bracket will be in thirty years and we truly don't have a great idea of what retirement might be for us.

There is another big reason to have a Roth IRA for retirement in addition to tax deferred accounts. I mentioned early in this book I may never retire which means we may never have to tap into our retirement savings. If this happens, we will be very unhappy with our tax deferred accounts and very happy with our Roths. Here's why. The government gives you a tax break on tax deferred accounts to encourage people to save for retirement, but they are only allowing you to *delay* the tax consequences. That money will eventually get taxed in one of two ways:

1. If you retire, the government forces you to take "required minimum distributions" from your tax deferred account at age 70 ½. Your accountant will tell you how much you are required to take out each year and if you don't make the required withdrawals, there is a 50% penalty imposed. Obviously, you will make the required withdrawals to avoid the penalty and pay taxes on the distributions.

2. If you are like me and might possibly never retire, you may escape the "required minimum distributions," but you will eventually die with your tax deferred accounts and your heirs will have to pay the income taxes. Unfortunately, we have no idea what tax bracket our children might be in when we die. Hopefully our kids will be very successful which means they will inherit our tax deferred money and absolutely get hammered on income taxes.

Neither option is particularly attractive to us. On the other hand, we are never forced to do anything with our Roth IRAs. We are never forced to make withdrawals and if we die with money remaining in our Roths, our children will get the money entirely income tax free. Not bad!

You might be asking "Why not just do the Roth and entirely avoid tax deferred accounts?" Good question, but again it isn't that simple. Your tax rates might go down at retirement so a regular tax deferred account turns out better than a Roth IRA or you might get matching funds to save in your company plan. As I said before, you don't want to turn down matching funds, so you should absolutely participate in your company retirement plan. Every one of you will be in different circumstances so your decision about how to save for retirement will be different from other people. One more reason you need to closely examine generic advice from media gurus who don't have a clue about your situation.

Assuming you have some cash flow available for retirement savings, here is my general advice to clients on the pecking order of retirement funding:

1. If you have a match at work, contribute enough to get the full match, but nothing more for now.

2. Fund a Roth IRA with any additional money until you can get it maxed out.

3. If you still have more money available, increase contributions to your company plan until you reach 10% withholdings. I rarely recommend people save more than 10% into their company retirement plan unless they did a poor job of saving early in their career and need to quickly catch up.

4. If you still have more money available, save into your taxable mutual fund account.

5. Almost never fund an annuity for retirement. Annuities tend to be for very high income people who cannot participate in Roth IRAs, who are looking for maximum tax deferral, and who expect their taxes to decline during retirement. Not common traits for the rest of us.

Rarely do people get past Step 2. In fact, many people don't get past Step 1. If you can get yourself to Step 3 at an early stage of your career, retirement will almost certainly not be a concern. It is nearly impossible to go straight from ground zero to Step 3 so it is incredibly important to work your way up the ladder. Baby steps work just fine, but you absolutely must make progress or you will eventually find yourself at age sixty thinking you will never be able to retire.

Most of my clients get their company contributions in the form of a pension so they do not get a match on their own retirement plan contributions. My typical approach is to determine together how much they can comfortably save for retirement and then put half in a tax deferred account and half into a Roth IRA. Once the Roth IRA is maxed out, we put the rest into their tax deferred account until they reach 10% contributions. If someone gets this far, we put remaining money into a taxable mutual fund account.

When you retire, there will be five possible sources of money:

*   Social Security—monthly income controlled by the government

*   Pension—you may or may not have one of these

*   IRA—company retirement plans should normally be rolled into a personal IRA at retirement to simplify management and to maximize personal control

*   Roth IRA—the best source of lump sum money at retirement

*   Regular taxable account—your emergency reserve account

You have no control over social security or company pension plans, but you do have control over the last three sources so make the most of them.

◆   ◆   ◆

We covered a lot of different investment vehicles in this chapter and your head may be spinning right now. It isn't as complicated as it might seem. Here is a summary of what accounts you will need to meet your previously defined objectives:

1. Emergency Reserves (including accumulation for certain spending priorities)

   • Checking account—should have at least one month worth of expenses

   • Savings account—for the remainder of your short term emergency reserve

   • Taxable mutual fund account—for longer term emergency reserves and as an accumulation vehicle for certain spending priorities

2. Education

   • Roth IRAs

   • Education IRA and/or a 529 Plan

   • Taxable mutual fund account

3. Financial Independence (otherwise known as retirement)

   • Tax deferred account—IRA or company sponsored retirement plan

   • Roth IRAs

   • Taxable mutual fund account

You probably noticed an overlap in types of accounts between your different objectives. In particular the Roth IRA and taxable mutual fund account can be used for a variety of different purposes. Flexibility is what makes these types of accounts so important to most people who are trying to perform a balancing act between different financial priorities.

The following is a summary of accounts Tracy and I have set up, where we set them up, and why they were created:

Checking Accounts (Joint, one for me, and one for Tracy)—we use a major national bank for these accounts because we particularly like their online banking feature, but normally, a bank is a bank in my opinion. Make sure your checking account is free and has the options you need. As I previously mentioned, we do not earn any interest on our checking account and it always holds at least one month worth of expenses. This account is strictly for day-to-day money management.

Savings Account—we have an online direct Money Market savings account that is electronically linked to our joint checking so money can be painlessly transferred between accounts. Our money market savings has no minimum deposit required and also no fees, but it is a bare-bones savings with no check writing privileges. This account is strictly for emergency reserves and always has at least two months worth of expenses.

Taxable Mutual Fund Account—we have this account with one of the major mutual fund families. The fund family we chose has a diverse set of investment options able to meet the needs of nearly any investment objective. This account satisfies a number of our financial needs including an emergency reserve, a slush fund for any immediate major purchases, and will likely supplement our retirement needs. We always maintain at least nine months of expenses in this account. It took us many years to slowly build up this account.

Roth IRAs (one for me and one for Tracy)—our Roth IRAs are in brokerage accounts. We probably should have these accounts in mutual funds, but we hold individual stocks and buy a new stock each year with our contributions. We "max out" our Roth contributions each year. Our Roths will also meet a number of financial objectives including education funding, retirement (specifically lump sum needs during retirement), estate planning, and, if things got real ugly, it could be used as an emergency reserve.

Tax Deferred Accounts—we have a number of these accounts due to job and career changes over the past several years—which reminds me, I need to get moving and consolidate some of these miscellaneous accounts into our IRA accounts. All of our tax deferred accounts are with mutual fund companies. Our only active tax deferred account is my SEP IRA. Our IRA accounts are with a major mutual fund family. Tracy has a SEP IRA and also a Simple IRA. When we eventually retire, all of our tax deferred accounts will be held in an IRA for me and an IRA for Tracy. Our contributions to tax deferred accounts vary depending on our financial circumstances each year. Remember, I do not get a set paycheck each month like most people so my tax deferred saving is more difficult to determine. These tax deferred accounts are strictly for retirement savings. More specifically, these accounts are for monthly income during retirement to replace work income.

Education IRA (or Coverdell Education Savings Account)—we have an Education IRA for Isabella and plan on starting one for any future children. This is yet another account we have at a major mutual fund family. We "max out" our contributions each year (current maximum is $2,000/year). This account is strictly for education funding, but not just for college. An Education IRA can also be used for valid educational expenses prior to college.

Why so many accounts? Unfortunately in our society, financial planning has become very convoluted with specific types of accounts created to meet different financial objectives. Our different accounts all offer some form of advantage in meeting our unique goals. Yes, it is a pain in the butt to keep track of them all, but it is a small price to pay for financial success. One simple way to manage your accounts is to do some research and pick one mutual fund company that offers consolidated statements. This way you can put all your various mutual fund accounts in one place and get one statement with information for the various types of accounts.

This chapter has only focused on what *types* of accounts you should realistically have in place to meet your most important financial priorities. In the next several chapters we will focus on what specific *investments* we put inside these different accounts.

8

Investment Alternatives

Now that you know what types of accounts may be appropriate for your specific financial plan, we have to discuss the specific investments to put in each account. Investment alternatives are nearly limitless which makes this aspect of planning very complicated. The best way to simplify selection of appropriate investments is to remain focused on your financial plan. Otherwise emotions will likely sabotage your investment decisions.

The most basic factor affecting what specific investment options you select is *time*. We can discuss all kinds of other investment factors like fees, tax efficiency, diversification, etc., but, ultimately, your investment decisions should be based on time. What do I mean by time? In a nutshell, time simply means how long you have before you need the money. There are short term financial objectives; there are long term financial objectives, and everything in between. Preparation of a coherent financial plan is the only way to truly define your investment time frame for each unique financial objective and defining your time frame should help focus your investment decisions.

Time is important during both the accumulation phase of investing and also during the spending phase. The accumulation phase will normally emphasize growth because we are trying to build up an asset base. The spending phase will tend to emphasize income for obvious reasons. Time defines our risk tolerance whether we are in the accumulation phase or the spending phase, and this leads us to a very important concept of investing.

RISK VERSUS VOLATILITY

"Risk" is probably the most misused investment term by both individual investors and by the media. It is important to understand the primary difference between risk, which must be accounted for in a properly constructed financial plan, and volatility, which is normal up and down noise in an investment. The basic difference is time. Risk means adding a time element to volatility. In order for risk to be properly considered, there must be a time frame involved. I don't care if the time frame is one week, one month, one year, or 100 years; there must be some element of time when considering risk. On the other hand, volatility has no element of time. It just measures the magnitude of change.

We often hear how "risky" the stock market can be. In fact, there are some people who will automatically tune me out as soon as I mention investing any portion of their money in the stock market. Nope, they say, stocks are too *risky*! Maybe, maybe not, but normally what they are referring to is *volatility* rather than *risk*. When time is considered, stocks may or may not be risky. I believe stocks are very risky as one day, one week, or one year investments, but are not very risky and, in fact, are one of the least risky investments over thirty years. This information likely contradicts what you have been taught in the past so I will illustrate with an example:

You invest $1,000 in two different alternatives that produce the following annual returns:

	Year 1	Year 2	Year 3	Year 4	Year 5
Option 1	5%	6%	7%	6%	6%
Option 2	20%	-10%	5%	18%	0%

If you were somehow "guaranteed" to get the above returns, which investment is more risky over five years? In theory, they have the same risk because the end result is the same in both options. You would end up with $1,338 in each investment. However, Option 2 is a much more volatile investment because the annual changes are much more dramatic than Option 1. Option 2 would *feel* much more risky, especially during year two when returns were negative.

The reason I am bringing up this topic is because as I write this book, we are on the back end of a major bear market in stocks and many people have seen substantial declines in the value of their investments. These declines have caused many investors to move most, or all, of their money to "safe" investments like money market funds, CDs, or bonds. The safe investments make people feel better because they no longer have to feel the uneasiness of volatility. It is a little like a roller coaster ride. There are ups and downs, twists and turns, and many people get a sick feeling when the car is racing downward, but if you stay in the car, you always return safely. Roller coasters are very volatile, but not very risky, and it is this feeling of volatility that can scare some people and excite others. These are basic human emotions, which are not a problem at a carnival, but as I previously mentioned, can be potentially devastating when investing.

The long term average annual return in the overall stock market is between ten and eleven percent, but the stock market almost never actually returns ten or eleven percent in a given year. There are ups and downs, and there always have been ups and downs, but the long term average tends to stay right around ten to eleven percent. If you have lost a lot of money in stocks the past few years, you might be getting downright irritated with me right about now, and believe me, I am not trying to downplay your losses. However, the last three horrible years were basically a return to earth after a huge bull market in the late 90's. The recent stock market declines brought us back to the long term averages.

If I generically refer to the stock market, I am normally talking about the Standard and Poor's 500 Index or S&P 500 Index. It is likely you have heard this term before because it is commonly cited as an indicator for the performance of the overall United States stock market. The S&P 500 Index is made up of 500 very large domestic publicly traded corporations. The S&P 500 Index is a very good indicator of how large company stocks are doing as a group, but is not always a good indicator for small or international stocks.

As of 6/30/03, the three year annualized return for the S&P 500 index is -11.20%. Absolutely devastating losses! One of the worst bear markets in United States history. However, over that same period, the ten year annualized return is 10.04%. The twenty year annualized return is 12.20%. The recent bear market was an offset to the huge bull market of the 80's and 90's. It was a reversion back to the normal long term return of the overall stock market. Where will the market go from here? I have absolutely no clue, but I expect, long term, the stock market will probably return about ten to eleven percent.

Most people would be thrilled to get ten to eleven percent returns over the life of their investments, but there is a problem. In our society, long term often means a year or even less. Stocks are horrible investments over one year periods because they are very volatile, but they make excellent thirty year investments where the volatility has time to work itself out of the system. The overall stock market tends to lose money about three out of every ten years or about 30% of the time. The overall stock market has never lost money over any thirty year period in United States history. It has never lost money over any twenty year period. The only time the stock market has ever lost money over a ten year period was during the Great Depression. The maximum ten year annualized loss was -0.89% from 1929–1938 (all of these statistics come from Ibbotson Associates). Are stocks risky long term investments? I don't think so.

The point of this whole discussion is volatility does not necessarily mean the same thing as risk and time is an essential element to consider when you are evaluating investments to meet your financial priorities. Keep this in mind whenever you are evaluating your investments.

The following two chapters will break down practical investment applications based on whether you are in the growth phase of investing or the spending phase. This chapter will focus on some basic investment theory to give you a general understanding of some important concepts. My focus is on simplicity. You will not see any discussion about some of the "sophisticated" investments used by wealthy people and their advisors. Options, futures, commodities, hedge funds, and limited partnerships might be appropriate for some very wealthy people, but not for the rest of us.

ASSET ALLOCATION AND DIVERSIFICATION

If you have ever talked to a financial advisor, or if you do any reading at all about investments, the terms "asset allocation" and "diversification" have probably been thrown around. Clients will often tell me "they don't want to put all their eggs in one basket" and one of the more common questions I get is "Are my investments diversified?" Everyone knows they should be diversified and they should pay attention to asset allocation, but there seems to be complete confusion in how to address these issues. Much of our investment discussion will center on creating a coherent asset allocation strategy.

Asset allocation is how you decide to distribute your money between the major asset classes of investments. Diversification comes as a natural result of proper asset allocation. For our purposes, we will stick with cash, bonds, stocks, and real estate as the major asset classes. Some gurus would argue there should be other classes in your asset allocation, but these four groups will suffice for the rest of us. Within these four groups, there are literally hundreds of subset groups which is what makes asset allocation so confusing. Asset allocation is extremely important to the ultimate success of your financial plan. In fact, asset allocation will likely be the most important financial decision you make in regard to your investments.

There was a widely referenced study done in 1991 (May/June Edition of Financial Analysts Journal) about the effects of asset allocation on the performance of an investment portfolio. The study concluded asset allocation was responsible for about 91.5% of all investment performance. Specific security selection, market timing, and expenses had little overall affect on a well diversified portfolio. This means the *types* of investments you pick over a lifetime will far outweigh the *specific* investments you pick.

You might suspect if asset allocation is so important to proper investing, there must be some expert out there who has created the one-size-fits-all asset allocation. Many "experts" have certainly tried and there is definitely an unlimited amount of asset allocation advice available to all investors. However, it just isn't that easy. Asset allocation is more of an art than a science.

There are two primary reasons why asset allocation is so misunderstood by the experts. The first reason is all analysis regarding asset allocation must be based on what has happened in the past. What if the *past* is not exactly like the *future*? Also, how far back do you look? The United States today is certainly a different place than the United States during the Great Depression. Analyzing past returns is useful, but not entirely accurate.

The second reason is asset allocation needs to account for the unique objectives and emotions of the investor. This is impossible to do on a grand scale which seems to confuse the issue with experts. If you have ever seen "asset allocation models" (very popular in 401k plans), you might know there are usually between 3–5 models available. The typical menu is: Aggressive, Moderate, and Conservative along with some variation such as Moderately Aggressive or Moderately Conservative (whatever "moderate" means). The mistake here comes from these descriptors being about human emotion rather than objectives. You might consider yourself a conservative person and select that particular model for your investments, but what if the conservative model does not meet your objectives? Maybe you are 25 years old and are using the model asset allocation to save for retirement. Clearly most financial advisors would recommend the aggressive portfolio based on your objectives, due to the long time horizon until retirement, but the descriptor "aggressive" would not match your personality and would likely make you uncomfortable. The other extreme is someone who is aggressive in nature, but is sixty years old, has a substantial nest egg, and wants to retire next year. This person might select the aggressive portfolio based on her personality, but should likely be in the conservative or moderate portfolio based on her objectives. The whole system is messed up which only leads to greater confusion and investment mistakes.

Another common way the financial services industry has addressed generic asset allocation is through rules of thumb. One common example is the old rule of thumb for determining your mix of stocks and bonds: 100 minus your age equals the allocation to stocks (under this rule a 45 year old should have 55%

stocks and 45% bonds in her portfolio). When the stock market was hot, the rule became 110 minus your age for stocks. I guess when the stock market is crappy, maybe it should be ninety minus your age. It is all arbitrary! In my opinion, model portfolios and rules of thumb are essentially worthless. Any asset allocation or diversification advice that does not specifically account for your investment objectives is likely to be flawed.

The other major problem with model portfolios is they rarely delineate between different types of investment accounts.

Let's start with short term investment alternatives. Whether you are investing for growth or investing for income, short term investments should be focused on preservation of principal rather than maximizing growth or income. The basic premise is "return of my money," not "return on my money." Nothing exciting here. In most cases, if your investment time horizon is less than one year, you should put the money in a money market account, and preferably an FDIC insured money market. You may earn relatively little short term interest, but you basically have no risk of losing money and you should have total liquidity mean-ing your money will be available when you need it.

Unfortunately we are currently in a very low interest rate environment. Our money market account pays one of the higher FDIC insured money market rates, but we are still only getting 2% right now. After taxes, our interest doesn't amount to much, but it is short term money that must be there if we need it. Because interest rates are so low, you might be tempted to take on greater risk in order to achieve higher returns. Please ask yourself why you are investing this money. It is short term money and the difference in returns over a short period of time normally does not justify any significant amount of risk. Let me give you an example:

Let us assume you have accumulated $20,000 to be used for a house down payment in about one year. Your money market account is paying 2%. You decide 2% is too low so you search for a more attractive option to grow your money. You decide on a no-load, equity income stock mutual fund paying attrac-tive dividends with excellent historical performance. The equity income fund could lose money over the next year, but, statistically speaking, it should realisti-cally outperform the money market account.

Scenario 1: The equity income fund does well and you make 10% over the twelve month period. Slap yourself on the back because it turns out you made a great investment decision. The 10% return earned you $2,000 while the 2% return would have earned only $400. However, you will have to pay taxes on your gain. Let's assume 25% total tax on your gain, so now you have $1,500 with the equity income fund and $300 with the money market fund. The difference is $1,200! You could now put down $21,500 on the house instead of $20,300. If you planned on putting 10% down on your house, you would now be able to buy a $215,000 house instead of a $203,000 house. Depending on real estate prices in your neighborhood, the difference is probably not noticeable and does not justify the added risk of the equity income fund.

Scenario 2: The stock market happens to tank over the next year and the equity income fund loses 20% over the twelve month period. Now we have a problem because your $20,000 nest egg has turned into $16,000. If you sell, there would be some tax write off for the loss, but it probably would not make you feel any better because you now might not have enough money for the down payment on your house. If you were planning on putting 10% down on the house, you went from a $203,000 house down to a $160,000 house. Depending on your neighborhood, this could make a big difference in the house you end up buying.

Basically I am trying to show you that short term investing typically does not justify the risk of losing *any* principal on your nest egg. Stick to the safe bets on your short term money and you will be happier over the long term.

As your time horizon shifts from less than one year to more of an intermediate term investment, you can begin taking some risk to help enhance investment returns. The problem here is defining what intermediate term means to you and figuring out your risk tolerance. There is no right or wrong answer and don't let any financial guru tell you different. If you are deathly afraid of losing any of your investment and the time horizon is less than five years, keep your money in money market accounts or possibly purchase a Certificate of Deposit (CD) if it pays a greater interest rate. CDs are a better option if you know exactly when the money will be needed. I do not recommend purchasing a CD with a longer term than 1–2 years. You can always buy another CD if your first one expires and you still don't need the money.

When we get beyond short term time horizons, and if you can handle some slight fluctuation of principal, we get into the real world of asset allocation. In my opinion, the only way to achieve an appropriate asset allocation is to create a financial plan outlining your specific objectives. Once the objectives are on paper, it becomes much easier to determine which investment types make sense for you. Unfortunately this process takes time which is why you have been reading for several hours and still have not reached specific investment recommendations!

Most asset allocation models include: Cash (or cash equivalents), Bonds, Stocks, and Real Assets (real estate or commodities). We have already talked extensively about cash investments and how they work. In my opinion, cash and cash equivalents do not belong in an asset allocation because they are not investments. They are safe money havens to specifically hold money that will be spent over the short term. The amount of cash you have on hand is totally dependent on your emergency reserve objectives. For this reason we will focus our asset allocation discussion on the following asset classes:

Bonds	Stocks	Real Assets
Government Bonds	Large Company Stocks	Real Estate
Corporate Bonds	Small Company Stocks	Gold
Municipal Bonds	International Stocks	Commodities
	Value Stocks	
	Growth Stocks	

Let me simplify further by eliminating the Real Asset column from most asset allocation. Real asset investments have created many very rich people. Unfortunately, real assets are very unique investments that typically involve leverage and rely heavily on factors out of our control. For most of us, we already have a significant real asset holding called our house. You might even own some type of rental real estate that also might make up a large part of your investments. Wealthy people can typically incorporate real estate and other real asset investments into their comprehensive asset allocation and still keep some balance in place. For the rest of us, real estate tends to be an "all-or-nothing" proposition. Let me explain. For people of modest means, real estate generally means buying rental properties in your local area. Rental properties take a lot of money so most people who buy real estate do not buy any other types of investments. They might own their own home and rental property meaning most or all of their asset allocation is riding on the performance of real estate in their local area. You might do very well with this strategy or you might do poorly with this strategy. If you find yourself wanting to become a real estate mogul, there are many excellent books specifically addressing how to do that, but for our purposes, real asset investing usually doesn't make much sense other than owning your home.

In a few short paragraphs our decision making process has become much clearer with only bonds and stocks remaining. Cash and real estate are separate issues from asset allocation. This doesn't mean cash and real estate are not important elements of your financial plan, but it does mean they are their own unique area of analysis and should not be confused with the stock and bond portion of your investments.

There are a few things I would like to clarify. When I talk about stocks and bonds making up your asset allocation, I mean the allocation of your investment accounts such as your 401k (or other form of company retirement plan), IRAs, Roth IRAs, variable annuities, taxable brokerage or mutual fund accounts, and education accounts like Education IRAs or 529 plans. I am not talking about checking and savings accounts or any other account at your bank. Remember banks are good for checking and savings accounts, but I do not encourage using banks for investment accounts. Checking and savings accounts make up a valuable part of a proper asset allocation, but they should be considered as a separate item as we previously discussed.

The next thing I want to clear up is the actual difference between a stock and a bond. This difference is something I believe should be taught to every person in the United States at least once per year from about sixth grade through high school graduation. The basic definition of a bond is loaning someone money (usually some government entity or a corporation) in exchange for interest payments over a set period of time. A stock represents a piece of ownership in a company. When you own a bond, you are a *creditor*. When you own a stock, you are an *owner*. Big difference!

One way to look at the difference between stocks and bonds is by comparing working for someone else to actually owning the business. If you have ever worked for someone else (we all have at some point), you performed a function to receive a set salary. You pretty much knew how much your salary would be based on the number of hours you worked. If the company did well, you may have received a bonus, but most of the time your income fluctuated very little whether the company did well or did poorly. The main risk in a job is getting laid off or fired, which is certainly a big risk, but you could always find another job somewhere else. Think about any job you have had in the past. Who was the richest person there? Was it one of the workers or was it the owner? In most cases, it is the owner. The owner directly participates in the profits of a company meaning if the company does well, so does the owner. If the company does poorly, the owner does poorly. This means owners are taking more risk than workers so the owners always take a bigger piece of the overall pie to compensate them for their risk. Bill Gates is not the wealthiest man in America because he gets a huge salary. Bill Gates is super rich because he is the largest stock holder at Microsoft and his stock has appreciated greatly as Microsoft grew from a small start up company into a huge corporation. Granted, there are many Microsoft employees who also became wealthy along the way, but only those employees who owned stock really made huge amounts of money.

The beautiful thing about the American way of life is we can all choose to own a piece of Microsoft if we want. You could literally go out and buy one share of Microsoft stock (selling for $27.52 per share on the date of this writing—you can look it up in a financial newspaper like The Wall Street Journal or Investors Business Daily or on the Internet at Yahoo!Finance under the Nasdaq stock symbol MSFT). Your one share of stock would allow you to make a profit whenever Bill Gates makes a profit on his stock. Sure, your piddly one share of stock pales in comparison to the millions of shares owned by Bill Gates, but you are still sharing in the wealth of his company. Next week you could probably buy another share of stock, maybe in Microsoft or maybe in another entirely different company. It doesn't take much money and you begin to become an owner rather than a worker. Yes, you take more risk as an owner, but risk is the only way to reap greater rewards over long periods of time.

I am not one of those people that think we should all start our own business and get fabulously wealthy. Jobs are great. They provide a set salary, usually provide decent benefits, and jobs provide security for millions of families. However, I believe everyone in this country should own some shares of stock so they can become *owners* rather than *workers* in our society. There is this mystique out there that only the rich can own stock. Hogwash! Anyone can and should own stock at some point in their lives. Stock ownership is one of the best ways to understand the American business culture of free markets and entrepreneurial spirit.

The truth is most American workers have been getting the shaft for a long time. The United States economy has grown by about 5% annually over the past thirty years while the stock market has gained about 11% per year over that span. At the same time, real wages have actually *declined* over the same period. Real wages account for inflation. This means the fat cats of corporate America are keeping a bigger and bigger piece of the overall economic pie. This is why you often hear about the unequal distribution of wealth getting larger in the United States (rich getting richer and poor getting poorer). The most obvious solution to this problem is starting your own business, but that is easier said than done and is fraught with all sorts of risk. In my opinion, the next best option to get out of the worker doldrums is to become an owner through the purchase of stock. I don't care whether you buy individual stocks or mutual funds that own stocks. You can do this in your 401k, in an IRA, or in a taxable brokerage or mutual fund account. Either way, you are becoming one of the owners in our society and ownership will allow you to reap rewards over time.

All of this discussion leads to the basic premise:

Stocks are better for growing money while bonds are better for preserving money.

Always keep this in mind as you create and periodically modify your investment asset allocation.

The next step is to understand some of the investment options available when we talk about stocks and bonds. I will do my best to stay with simple definitions and provide only the necessary information you will need to understand how to construct an investment portfolio.

BOND INVESTMENT OPTIONS

Option 1: Short term bond mutual funds—these funds generally invest in short term government or corporate bonds. They will generally have higher yields than money markets or CDs, but your principal is not guaranteed. If interest rates decline, the fund will get an enhanced return and you will be happy. If interest rates rise, the fund could lose money. Normally your losses would be very small because any loss of principal would be offset by the interest you are earning. We are currently in a very low interest rate environment which should mean the chance of rising rates is relatively high. I would avoid short term bond funds until interest rates rise substantially from their current low levels.

Option 2: Floating rate funds or loan participation mutual funds—these funds go by many names so they might get confusing. They generally invest in very short term corporate loans (short normally being less than one year and often ninety days or less). These investments are designed to "float" with interest rates so they should perform better during a rising interest rate environment. Some of these funds have limited liquidity where money can only be withdrawn once per quarter or some other form of restriction. In the past I have owned one of these funds and have been satisfied. Our fund currently yields 2.6% and it has daily liquidity. Floating rate funds with more limited liquidity will likely pay you a higher yield. There is some risk with these investments, but I believe the risk is pretty minimal. I like this option for investment time frames between six months and two years.

Option 3: Intermediate to long term bonds—intermediate to long term bonds will come in a wide variety of flavors. The first decision is whether you want to purchase individual bonds directly or purchase a bond mutual fund. This can become a complicated debate, but I believe it does not have to be complicated. I have personally never recommended a client purchase individual bonds. Buying individual bonds is a difficult endeavor where you better have a firm grasp on what you are doing or you will likely end up disappointed with your results. Do you have a solid understanding of bond prices, competitive yields, credit risk, duration, inflation risk, maturities, etc.? I would say 100% of my clients do not fully understand these issues and that includes me! I am not a full time bond trader and I would not consider myself knowledgeable enough about individual bonds to properly construct a competitive bond portfolio for a client. This means I always use bond mutual funds for the intermediate to long term bond portion of asset allocation.

A bond mutual fund is a professionally managed pool of money invested for the benefit of the individual shareholders. The main attraction to bond funds is convenience. The professional money manager and his staff are paid to create a properly constructed portfolio of bonds to meet the investment objective of the particular fund. You do not need to become an expert to invest in bond funds. However, convenience always comes at a price and there are two primary draw-backs to bond mutual funds.

1. Bond mutual funds can lose money. Most people purchase bonds to cre-ate income in their investment portfolio or to offset the risk of other investments like stocks. If you buy individual bonds and hold them to maturity, you get the interest payment over the life of the bond and, if everything works as planned, you also get back your original investment when the bond is sold. Unfortunately this is not how bond funds work. Bond funds are constantly buying and selling bonds to reposition their overall portfolio. When a fund sells a bond, there can be profit or loss on the sale depending how attractive the bond is on the open market. The profit or loss means you may or may not get back all of your original investment. The attractiveness of a bond on the open market is prima-rily determined by interest rate fluctuations. The general rule you need to understand is the inverse relationship of bond prices to bond interest rates. *If interest rates rise, bond prices will fall. If interest rates fall, bond prices will rise. If interest rates do nothing, bond prices will remain flat.* If

you expect interest rates to rise, be prepared to have periodic losses in your bond mutual fund.

In the late 70's and early 80's, interest rates were very high with government bonds paying double digit interest. I have heard many clients talk about their first mortgage at 14% or more. Over the past twenty years or so, interest rates have steadily declined to the current very low levels. As I write this, thirty year mortgages are about 6% or so and ten year government bonds are yielding about 4.25%. The steady decline in interest rates over such a long period of time created a tremendous bull market for bonds and was a huge incentive to purchase bond funds. As the rates declined, bond prices went up which gave you both a high yield and also capital appreciation on the bonds. Nice combination. As an example, one diversified bond mutual fund I have used with clients had an average annual return of 11.71% over the past twenty years (measured through 6/30/03). Of course there were a couple years when this fund actually lost money for investors, but I think most investors would be thrilled with double digit gains on what is considered the conservative portion of their overall asset allocation.

Unfortunately, I believe the long term bull market for bonds has likely come to an end. In the current low interest rate environment, we are at the opposite end of the spectrum. Most prudent investors expect interest rates will likely rise over the next couple decades (or at least remain flat). This interest rate environment is horrible for the overall bond market because not only are you getting very low interest yields on your investment, but you can also lose money on your bond holdings if interest rates do rise. In my mind, intermediate to long term bonds are relatively dangerous holdings over the long term which means you will need to be very careful in how you fill this portion of your asset allocation.

2. Bond mutual funds are often more expensive than purchasing individual bonds. Professional money management and the conveniences of bond mutual funds do not come without a price. The fund company gets paid not only for management, but also for all of the administrative chores like sending out statements, reinvesting dividends, trading the bonds, and keeping track of the fund portfolio. The "expense" ratio of the mutual fund will eat into the overall returns of your investment.

Remember there are fees associated with all investments and they must be considered in your overall plan.

Another expense of bond mutual funds is the commission if you are using a financial advisor or broker. There are also commissions if you buy individual bonds through a broker. Make sure you understand how your advisor is being paid for the purchase of any investment they recommend.

None of my clients aspire to become experts in bond trading so I always recommend bond mutual funds. However, there are a couple of scenarios where buying individual bonds may be attractive for you. If you are looking for bonds with essentially no credit risk such as United States Treasury Bonds, United States Agency Bonds, or insured bonds, you might consider buying individual bonds. One of the attractive features of bond mutual funds is diversification away from credit risk. Since U.S. government bonds are backed by the U.S. government, they have little to no credit risk (credit risk is the chance of default on the bonds). If these bonds are held to maturity, you will get interest payments along with the return of principal when the bond matures. Bond mutual funds have a difficult time adding value to bonds with no credit risk, especially in low interest rate environments when fund expenses eat away at your returns. Individuals can purchase U.S. Treasury Bonds directly from the government without a broker via Treasury Direct.

If you go with individual bonds, I do recommend laddering your holdings which is simply a strategy for buying bonds with different maturities. A typical laddered portfolio might have equal investments in five or more different maturities. An example using a $50,000 investment:

$10,000 invested in bonds maturing in two years
$10,000 maturing in four years
$10,000 maturing in six years
$10,000 maturing in eight years
$10,000 maturing in ten years

When the two year bonds mature, they are reinvested in ten year bonds and the ladder stays intact. This allows you to spread your interest rate risk. If rates rise, the newly purchased ten year bonds will take advantage of higher interest payments. If interest rates fall, some of your older bonds will remain paying higher yields. There are investment books written specifically to address concepts like bond laddering so I won't go into more detail. I think you get the general idea.

For our purposes, you will likely want to stick with bond mutual funds for the intermediate to long term bond portion of your investments.

STOCK INVESTMENT OPTIONS

I personally do not believe most people are well suited to buy individual stocks so I normally recommend purchasing stock mutual funds for my clients. If you want to become a stock picker, go ahead and try your luck, but I would strongly recommend buying larger, well established companies rather than trying to pick the next high flier. Mutual funds are well suited for the rest of us because they provide an inexpensive way to get professional money management, diversification, liquidity, and ease of administration in one neat little package.

Now is a good time to define a mutual fund because I think most people have heard the term, but do not have a firm grasp on how a mutual fund actually works. For some strange reason, many people seem to have the idea a mutual fund is a specific stock or a specific bond. This is not the case. When you buy shares in a mutual fund, you are pooling your money along with other investors in a professionally managed investment. The pooled money is used to purchase whatever asset the fund focuses on such as stocks, bonds, real estate, etc. The typical stock mutual fund will hold a large number of stocks and will periodically buy and sell different stocks for the fund as the money manager deems appropriate for the shareholders. Mutual funds were created to allow smaller investors to combine their assets in one fund and become larger investors for the purposes of reducing investment expenses, creating greater diversification potential, and for convenience.

Let me use a personal example so you get a better understanding of how a mutual fund works. One of the stock funds I own is considered a large company growth fund. Growth investing has been horrible the past three years so the fund has poor short term performance, but still has an excellent long term track record. As of June 30, 2003, the fund's top ten holdings were:

Stock Holding	Industry	% of Fund
Pfizer	Pharmaceutical	5.23%
Microsoft	Software	4.47%

Merck	Pharmaceutical	3.26%
Johnson and Johnson	Health/Consumer Goods	3.14%
WalMart	Retail	2.81%
Intel	Semiconductor	2.31%
Dell	Computer	1.96%
AIG	Insurance	1.95%
Wyeth	Pharmaceutical/Health	1.77%
General Electric	Diversified	1.69%

In light of the recent mutual fund scandals, I often get the question, "Can I lose all of my money in a mutual fund?" I suppose you could if every single stock in the fund were to go bankrupt at the same time. Possible, but not likely. In fact, if every one of the above companies went bankrupt, I would contend you have a lot worse things to worry about than your investment losses. Our country would literally fall apart at the seams. Have you been in an *empty* WalMart lately? Do you think computers might still be used next year or maybe the year after? Are people going to need medications for the next couple years? I don't think any of the ten holdings mentioned above are going bankrupt anytime soon. However, you are probably thinking, "What about Enron, or Kmart, or MCI? They were all large companies that went kaput!" Enron is the exact reason why mutual funds make good sense compared to buying individual stocks. If one of the top ten holdings comes out with an accounting irregularity and goes bankrupt tomorrow, my growth fund would lose only a small percentage (assuming all other holdings stayed flat). Granted I would not be happy, but at least I didn't lose a majority of my investment. *If all ten top holdings went bankrupt, I would lose only 29% of my investment!* The point is the combination of professional money management, low expenses, and diversification makes mutual funds an excellent investment option for the rest of us.

There are a wide number of opinions on how to construct a stock mutual fund portfolio and I certainly do not claim to have a magical asset allocation answer. However, there is some agreement from the experts that most people should try to diversify their stock holdings which means accumulating a wide variety of stocks fitting in different categories. I use the following categories to explain diversification with stocks:

Size	Valuation	Location
Large Companies	Growth	Domestic (U.S.)
Mid Size Companies	Blend	Global (both U.S. and foreign)
Small Companies	Value	International (only foreign)

Let me explain some of the differences so you get a better understanding how these categories fit together like pieces in a puzzle.

Category 1: Size matters—large company stocks as a group are less risky than mid or small size stocks. The Microsoft's of the world hold dominant positions in their market and are well established. Small and mid size companies are fighting for their piece of the pie and have a greater likelihood of failure. The greater risk involved with small and mid sized stocks means they tend to have greater long term returns. Small company stocks have averaged about 12% since 1926 while large company stocks returned about 10 ½%. Your stock asset allocation should have a core holding of solid large company stocks complemented by lesser holdings in small and mid size stocks.

Category 2: Valuation is critical—this is a tougher area to address because there is no black and white definition of growth versus value. I tend to think of value companies as mature companies that usually distribute profits to shareholders in the form of dividends. Value companies are usually slow, but consistent, growers. I think of growth as companies that have not matured yet. These companies typically pay little or no dividend because most of their cash gets reinvested back into the business to help maintain their rapid growth. Growth and value compliment each other very well with value companies usually doing better when times are tough (like 2000–2002) and growth companies doing better when the economy is doing well (like 1995–1999). Many stock mutual funds are considered blend funds because their managers will "cherry pick" their favorite stocks from both the growth and value categories so they have exposure to both groups.

Category 3: Location, location, location—the final piece of the diversification puzzle with stocks is U.S. companies versus international companies. Location has become difficult to determine with today's global economy. Coca Cola is technically headquartered in Atlanta which makes it a domestic company, but Coke products are sold throughout the world. Would Coca Cola be considered a domestic or global business? In general, international companies will tend to be more volatile than American businesses due in part to the size and stability of the

U.S. economy. However, there are many times when international will help stabilize a stock portfolio when the United States is suffering and may enhance returns when the world economy is strong. I believe U.S. stocks should be the cornerstone of all portfolios, but I also believe all stock investors should have some exposure to international companies. I don't like when experts make predictions, so I normally do not pull out my crystal ball, but my guess is that international stocks will outperform U.S. stocks over the next decade. There are a number of reasons for this prediction, and I could certainly be wrong. Either way, exposure to international stocks will likely enhance your portfolio over the long term.

Here are some guidelines I commonly use when constructing the *stock* portion of client portfolios (remember stocks might only make up a piece of your overall portfolio). These are my beliefs in my practice and are guidelines only that may be modified based on the unique needs of each client:

1. Focus your core holdings on larger companies—a typical split might be 60%–70% large and 30%–40% small and mid size companies. Small size companies have historically outperformed large companies, but with substantially greater volatility.

2. Try to balance growth versus value (50/50 split) across all of your stock holdings (large, small, mid, domestic, and foreign stocks)

3. Focus more on U.S. stocks, but always have some exposure to international stocks—a typical split might be 70%–85% domestic and 15%–30% foreign

4. The more conservative you are, the more you should shift towards large, value stocks—stay towards the low end of the recommended range in small-mid size and international stocks

5. The more aggressive you are, the more you can shift towards more volatile stocks—stay towards the high end of the range in small-mid size and international stocks

No matter what you do, pick an allocation you feel comfortable with and stick to it through both good and bad times. This means you periodically need to tweak your investments, but do not make wholesale changes due to emotions. There is rarely a reason to modify more than 10%–20% of a well diversified portfolio in any given year.

REBALANCING

Another major mistake made by most individual investors is not periodically rebalancing their portfolio. You may have never heard this term before because very few people actually do periodic rebalancing with their investments. Rebalancing is the process of tweaking your investments back to your original allocation when things get out of whack. A simple example would be someone who has decided they should own 50% stocks and 50% bonds in her $100,000 IRA account. For illustrative purposes we assume the stock portion was made up of the S&P 500 Index and the bond portion was an actively managed, diversified bond mutual fund.

1998—the S&P 500 rose 28.6% and the bond fund rose 3.65%. At the end of the year, our hero looks at her portfolio and sees her stocks have grown faster than the bonds. There is $64,300 in stocks and $51,825 in bonds or about 55.4% stocks and 44.6% bonds. The portfolio is out of whack. Our hero sells $6,238 of stock and uses the proceeds to buy bonds. Now the portfolio is back to 50% stocks and 50% bonds.

2002—the S&P 500 Index declined 22.1% and the bond fund rose 8.4%. At the end of the year, the portfolio is way out of whack with stocks at about 41.8% and bonds at about 58.2%. Our hero sells bonds and buys stocks to get back to the original 50/50 split.

One thing you might notice from the rebalancing examples is our hero was probably tweaking her portfolio in the opposite direction you were moving your portfolio in 1998 and in 2002. *Most* people have a tendency to move money towards their *best* performing investment and away from their worst performing investment. Rebalancing does the exact opposite which means with rebalancing you are *selling high and buying low*. Human nature is to buy high and sell low which is counter to productive investing, but it is one of the primary reasons why most investors experience poor overall investment performance.

In fact, rebalancing is the only "buy low and sell high" strategy that works on a consistent basis. There are many experts (and many amateurs) that believe they can time the markets to get in near the low point and get out at the high point. Some of them are even right sometimes, but the problem is no one has been right all the time and when they are wrong, they tend to get burned in a big way. The beauty of rebalancing is it takes most of the emotion out of investing so you can maintain investment discipline. This is extremely difficult to do without first creating a coherent plan.

Last, but not least, rebalancing provides an automatic element of risk control. If someone had actually done rebalancing in the late 90's, he would have been slowly moving his profits out of growth stocks and into bonds and value stocks. When the crash hit, his overall losses would likely have been significantly reduced. Rebalancing is a systematic approach to lessening the highs and lows of a portfolio which also helps create more disciplined investing. Our greed factor gets stronger with higher highs, and our fear factor gets worse with lower lows. Smoothing out the peaks and valleys helps us control these natural human emotions.

To summarize, rebalancing is a systematic method for selling your winners to buy your losers in order to get back to your original investment allocation. Rebalancing provides the following benefits over the long term:

- Automated buy low, sell high strategy
- Helps maintain investment discipline
- Element of risk control

If you only take away a couple ideas from reading this book, rebalancing should be one of them. This very basic investment theory will definitely serve you well in achieving your investment objectives. The concept is a simple one and most people understand why it works when it is properly explained, but there is always the same question, "How often should I rebalance?" This is another one of those impossible questions with no right answer. In a perfect world you should rebalance whenever your account gets even slightly out of whack, but that is not realistic. I recommend reviewing your accounts at least once per year and I don't care which time of year. If any of your holdings are more than 5% off the original allocation, rebalance. If the account is still about where you started, put your statements away and wait until another day to review. Notice, I did not say you needed to review your accounts every day, every week, or every month. Once you have a plan and have implemented your investments to meet your objectives, things are nearly on auto-pilot. Only infrequent, tiny modifications are necessary to keep you on course.

I also need to mention that rebalancing works best in some form of tax deferred account like your 401k, IRAs, Roth IRAs, or variable annuities. When you rebalance in a taxable account, you will often incur a taxable event because you may be selling an appreciated investment. The tax ramifications will tend to negate some of the rebalancing benefits. You never have to worry about tax ramifications when rebalancing in a tax deferred account.

◆   ◆   ◆

You now have a basic understanding of the investment pieces that will be used to complete your financial puzzle. The next two chapters will get into specific investment recommendations based on whether you are in the accumulation phase of your plan or in the spending phase. This chapter covers a handful of basic beliefs I think will help you understand more specific recommendations still to come:

1. In my opinion, the premise of basic investing is: **Stocks are better for growing money while bonds are better for preserving money.**

2. Understand the difference between risk and volatility. Risk adds a time element to volatility. Many investments (stocks in particular) are volatile investments that contain significant risk over short periods of time, but become less risky over a longer time horizon.

3. Mutual funds are commonly a better option than individual security selection for the rest of us. The most important benefit of mutual funds is diversification, but you also get professional money management, reduced expenses, and simplicity.

4. When deciding on an appropriate asset allocation, your short term money should be separated from long term money. Emergency reserves and short term savings should be invested for preservation of principal rather than growth. Longer term money will need to follow an asset allocation strategy.

5. Your stock allocation should be broadly diversified by size (large, mid, and small), valuation (growth versus value), and location (domestic versus international). Diversification across these three areas will help reduce overall volatility and may enhance long term investment returns.

6. Rebalance, rebalance, rebalance. Almost no one does it, but rebalancing can provide a systematic approach to "buy low and sell high", helps maintain investment discipline, and provides an element of risk control. Rebalancing works best in tax deferred accounts like 401k plans, IRAs, Roth IRAs, and variable annuities.

I will also summarize a couple basic investment predictions that may impact your long term investment decisions. These predictions are simply my opinion and do not constitute specific investment recommendations. My crystal ball can be just as cloudy as the "experts."

- Interest rates are at extreme lows and will likely rise slowly over the next couple decades. A rise in interest rates hurts long term government bonds because bond prices move opposite interest rates. Although bonds are considered "safe" investments, long term government bond funds will likely be a poor investment over the next ten to twenty years (at least until rates rise significantly from current levels).

- International stocks will likely outperform U.S. stocks over the next decade. Stocks tend to move in long cycles and the U.S. has significantly outperformed international stocks over the past fifteen years. I see this trend changing over the next ten to twenty years.

- As the economy improves, small and mid size stocks should outperform large company stocks. When the economy is back on track, large stocks will likely catch up.

- *None of these trends will happen in a nice, neat, straight line which is why diversification works.*

9

The Accumulation Phase "Investing for Long Term Growth"

You have probably heard some variation of the saying "make your money work as hard for you as you work for your money." Sounds great, but what the heck does it mean? I am not absolutely sure, but the one thing I know is you have to save money first before you can grow money. Simple concept, but not easy to do for the rest of us.

In Chapter 7 we talked about the three primary reasons for investing:

- Emergency Reserves
- Education
- Retirement

Emergency reserves are split into short term money that should be held in your checking account, money market savings account, or possibly in CDs. Long-term money should be held in a mutual fund account. We will touch on the mutual fund portion of your emergency reserves in this chapter, but it truly is not a big "accumulation" vehicle. You still want this money to be reasonably safe because it is considered emergency reserves and could theoretically be needed at any time, but on the other hand, it will probably end up being a long term investment. It will be important to seek decent long term returns in the mutual fund portion of your emergency reserves while still respecting the need for safety.

Education and retirement objectives both require an accumulation phase and a spending phase of investing so these are the two areas we will focus on in this chapter and the next chapter. There are some other investment objectives that could be considered long term, like saving for a house, saving to buy a vacation

home, or saving for your child's wedding. Our focus will be on specific investment recommendations to meet education and retirement goals, but some of
these recommendations could certainly be adapted for other long term investment objectives.

I recently was fortunate to attend an excellent seminar on the philosophy of
financial planning. A big part of the discussion was focused on William James'
idea of "Precursive Faith." Mr. James apparently did a lengthy study of why some
athletes become champions while others with equal ability never attain greatness.
He interviewed a number of great champions from a wide range of athletic activities and found most, if not all, great champions expressed some form of precursive faith. Precursive faith is having belief before success. Great champions were
able to visualize their future success before ever realizing success. Apparently,
visualizing yourself with success is a strong move towards achieving those dreams.

This simple concept really hit home with me because I realized most people
struggle to have precursive faith in their financial planning, and particularly in
their investing. Tracy and I have always talked about being financially successful
together. We have a plan and just assume we will eventually reach our most
important objectives. I can't say how we know, but we basically have faith that
good things will happen over our lifetimes. Most of our investments so far have
done poorly due to the prolonged bear market and yet we still have not wavered
in our faith of the future. We continue to invest knowing times will eventually
improve (don't know when) and our hard work will be rewarded. This is precursive faith in the future. Unfortunately, most people have a difficult time being
positive about their financial futures after suffering through a long, dismal bear
market with overwhelming investment losses. We maintain a different perspective. While our losses were also substantial, we viewed the bear market as a huge
buying opportunity for *long term* investments.

We as a society seem to have difficulty with long term objectives. Most people,
including me, tend to do best at tasks with known deadlines and specific objectives. When these deadlines are short term, we can see the finish line ahead and
gain immediate gratification by accomplishing our task. Saving for long term
financial objectives like retirement is difficult because we do not get immediate
gratification and retirement objectives are usually difficult to define. How does a
25 year old know what she wants in retirement when she just started her career?

Many people do not buy into the concept of saving today for a payoff in the
distant future. Saving for pleasure tomorrow means pain today especially when
the saving part must be done when cash is at a premium. We start out our adult
life at our lowest earning potential and yet our cash needs are at their greatest

level for raising a family, buying a home, and saving for the future. This combination severely handicaps our ability to have precursive faith in our financial futures. This is yet another reason why financial planning becomes so critical for our eventual success, especially when it comes to investing.

How depressing is it when you hear from an investment guru that you will need $1,000,000 or more to comfortably retire and your bank account has $100? Many planners are now telling their twenty something clients that $3,000,000 will be needed for a comfortable retirement at age 65. How overwhelming is that? My question is, "How do the experts know how much you will need unless they know your financial objectives?" (other than Suze Orman who has the uncanny ability to make specific investment recommendations after hearing thirty seconds worth of information about a person—yes, I am being sarcastic!). Most of these projections are so reliant on a wide array of arbitrary assumptions that they become almost meaningless. As a planner we have to "guess" at your assumed rate of growth, inflation rates for the next 35 years, social security, and your life expectancy. After making all of these assumptions, we tell you down to the dollar, how much you will need to have a comfortable retirement. Do you really think all of those assumptions will play out *exactly* as planned? I don't think so!

After reading this far, you should know enough to take the generic advice of financial experts and financial media with a "grain of salt." Hopefully you are in the process of creating your own unique financial plan which will allow you to pick out pieces of advice relevant to your plan and discard the useless advice that does not make sense for your circumstances, but might make sense for someone else. You now have specific long term financial priorities in place. While these priorities might not be set in stone (retirement objectives tend to change as we get older), we at least have a consistent target to move towards.

One important piece of advice that might help before we get into the specifics of investing for the long term is to approach your investments from a "divide and conquer" perspective. It is very difficult to visualize accumulating $1,000,000 when you may have nothing right now. However, it probably isn't too daunting to save $100. Once you get to $100, then shoot for $1,000. You will achieve these small goals quickly and your success will encourage you to bigger goals like $10,000 which will almost magically turn into $100,000 over time. I think you get the idea. One million dollars is seemingly unattainable, but $1,000 is achievable. Small steps will eventually get you to your goal.

WHAT IS LONG TERM?

I have read and heard a lot of different ideas about how long "long term" really is. I do my financial planning process a little different than most advisors because I base my asset allocation recommendations on *accumulation versus spending phases* rather than just based on *time*. What I mean is nearly everyone is considered a long term investor, but some are in the accumulation phase while others are in the spending phase. If you base investments strictly on time, I believe you will make some important mistakes. Let me use an example to help clarify this point.

Let's assume we have two women who are both concerned about their retirement objectives. One is forty and hopes to retire by age 62. The other woman is sixty and hopes to retire by 62. Most advisors would say the forty year old can be quite aggressive because she has 22 years before needing the money. Those same advisors would say the sixty year old is a short term investor because she needs the money in two years. I would say they are *both* long term investors, but one is in the accumulation phase and the other is very close to the spending phase. The sixty year old has an estimated life expectancy to age 83 and could easily live longer. I would probably base her planning on living to at least age ninety. This means she still has the potential for thirty or more years of investing ahead of her. Thirty years makes her a long term investor, but she will need to adjust her investments based on her spending habits during retirement.

Most people I meet think investing ends on the day you retire. In our previous example, the sixty year old would likely tell me she has two years to invest so we better make the most of it. My recommended investments change dramatically for a two year time horizon compared to a thirty year time horizon. If she truly had only two years for investing, I would probably put nearly all of her money in principal preservation investments like money markets, CDs, or fixed annuities. She would find her money would be very "safe," but she could be devastated by inflation as she got older and could ultimately learn that safe investing can really hurt long term investors.

On the other hand, we can use the example of two people saving for an education funding objective. Assume one family has a two year old and another family has a sixteen year old and both families want to have money set aside to pay ½ of their child's college education. Now we truly have a difference based on time because the first family is obviously in long term accumulation mode. They will not need the money for at least sixteen years. The family with the sixteen year old would be considered short term investors because not only will they enter the spending phase in two years, but the whole college process should be done in another four or five years (we hope). Their entire college savings plan will probably be spent by the time their child is 22 or 23, or about six to seven years. They are truly short-term investors.

My point is you need to define, in realistic terms, what your time horizon is for your long term financial objectives. Then you need to decide when the accumulation phase needs to begin transitioning into the spending phase. This is relatively easy to do with college expense planning, but can be very difficult with retirement planning. Notice I said "transitioning" from accumulation into spending. The change from accumulation mode into spending mode should be a gradual shift and there is no black and white answer to how this shift should be made. I have seen a lot of people who were invested 100% in stocks for accumulation right up to the day they retired and then put 100% of their money in bonds or CDs for income production during retirement. There is huge potential for a devastating mistake by taking this "all-or-nothing," black and white approach. In the next chapter I will show you a technique for making the transition from accumulation to spending that will help reduce the risk of making a major mistake with your investments.

Let's get back to the original question of "What is long term?" I typically use a guideline of ten years as a separator between the accumulation phase and the spending phase. Remember, the accumulation phase requires more aggressive investments with greater risk because you are trying to get the biggest bang for your buck. The spending phase requires much more conservative investments to help protect your nest egg and to provide income needed for spending money. In my opinion you are solidly in the accumulation phase until you get to ten years from when the actual spending phase will begin. The forty year old who wanted to retire at age 62 will be in pure accumulation mode for the next twelve years until she is 52. Then the transition from accumulation to spending mode (becoming more conservative with her investments) will last until retirement at age 62 when she is fully in the spending phase of retirement. The growth phase is easy and the spending phase is relatively easy, but the transition phase will be difficult to explain.

I have to admit, ten years is a totally arbitrary number. There is no scientific reason for selecting ten years as a reasonable time frame to define long term investing. You are welcome to use five years if you are more aggressive and fifteen years if you are more conservative. I have found the ten year time frame provides a reasonable balance between risk and return for most portfolios. You will see why in a moment.

EMERGENCY RESERVE MUTUAL FUND ACCOUNT

Before we get into investing for growth in your education and retirement accounts, we have to address the mutual fund portion of your emergency reserve account. There is no special guideline here because there is no defined time when you will need the money. We obviously have no way of knowing when a serious emergency might occur like a major health issue or getting laid off from work, but we do know these events are infrequent. With a little luck, we hope to never actually need the mutual fund portion of our emergency reserve, unless the money is specifically being set aside to help with education or retirement objectives. This creates a long term investment that could be needed at any given time. We have created an investment paradox, which makes this a difficult account to invest.

I think the best way to start is by explaining how Tracy and I have invested our taxable mutual fund account. I remind you again that what we do is neither right nor wrong, but I believe people learn best through specific examples. Our joint mutual fund account has the following holdings:

Type of Fund	Percentage of Account
Large Cap Growth	22.6%
Large Cap Blend	25.7%
Mid-Large Cap Blend	20.4%
Small-Mid Cap Blend	20.3%
Sector Fund—Technology	11.0%

All of these funds are stock mutual funds and most of them are geared more towards growth than towards value. This is very aggressive compared to what I would normally recommend for clients. The reason we can be more aggressive with this account is because we hold so much of our emergency reserve in a guaranteed money market account. The absolute safety and liquidity of the money market account gives us greater freedom to take risks with the longer term portion of our emergency reserve.

We have the Technology Fund as a relatively small fund that should take full advantage of the crash in technology stocks and provide solid growth from current relatively low prices. I do not recommend sector funds for most people, but if you decide you want to live a little on the wild side, I would stick with health care, technology, and financial sector funds. These three areas consistently provide an excellent opportunity for growth over the long term. I believe health care funds are particularly attractive over the next twenty years as the baby boomers age and start running into more serious health care issues. I beg you not to put more than a small percentage of your nest egg into sector funds. Sector funds by their very nature are not diversified and suffer from more extreme volatility than the overall stock market.

As I said, our emergency reserve mutual fund account is much more aggressive than I would recommend for clients. I think there are two very good investment ideas for most people's taxable mutual fund account: equity income stock mutual funds and balanced mutual funds. Equity income funds come in a variety of flavors, but most of them will focus their holdings on very large, dividend paying companies. Some of these funds will also buy some bonds which makes them more of a balanced fund. Equity income funds are the least risky form of stock fund so they generally do not have huge fluctuations up or down. This is a good trait to have in an emergency reserve fund where you may need the money with relatively short notice. Most major fund families will offer some form of equity income fund. Some equity income funds are more aggressive than others so you need to do some checking before you invest. For example, some funds will nearly always be fully invested in stocks while others will hold some balance of stocks and bonds.

Balanced mutual funds also have the trait of low volatility which makes them an excellent option for a basic taxable mutual fund emergency reserve account. These funds are very similar to equity income funds and, actually, I would classify many equity income funds as balanced funds. Most balanced funds will shoot for a mix of diversified stocks and bonds with the professional money manager making selections on the shareholder's behalf. Both equity income and balanced funds provide a simple way to get solid long term growth with relatively low risk.

If you want some additional safety and decide to go with a bond fund for a portion of your emergency reserve, I recommend using one of the relatively new inflation protected government bond funds. One of the dangers inherent with bond funds is the risk of rising inflation taking a bite out of your returns. The inflation protected bonds, otherwise known as TIPs for Treasury Inflation Protected, provide a built in hedge against rising inflation. These are low risk investments that provide a nice compliment to higher volatility stock funds.

You could always design your own personal balanced or equity income fund by selecting from a mix of large cap value funds and a diversified group of bond funds. I don't see why you need to reinvent the wheel when most reputable mutual fund companies have already done the work for you. Just make sure you are keeping the emergency reserve money liquid and respect the need for safety while still trying to achieve some growth.

ACCUMULATION RECOMMENDATIONS

The two primary accumulation objectives are education and retirement. Retirement is actually much easier to plan for because, for most of us, it is further out in the future than education goals. This means you should have more time to put away money resulting in smaller required contributions to meet your objective and more time to ride out poor market conditions. The second reason is retirement is for you and your spouse, not someone else (namely your children). It is much easier for most people to focus and avoid procrastination when they will be the direct benefactor of their planning efforts.

Most retirement plans will look at about a forty year career starting somewhere between 22–25 years old and ending around 62–65. The pure accumulation phase of investing will last about thirty years before slowly transitioning from accumulation to the spending phase. Remember from Chapter 7 that I recommend the following *types* of accounts to save for retirement:

- Tax deferred account—IRA or company sponsored retirement plan
- Roth IRAs
- Taxable mutual fund account

Accumulating money for education is much different. For most parents, there is a relatively short accumulation phase for education savings. There are only about eight to ten years where the sole investment focus should be on growth and then we get into the transition phase between accumulation and spending. For this reason it is absolutely critical for parents to start saving early when their baby is born.

Remember from Chapter 7 that I recommend the following *types* of accounts to save for education:

- Roth IRAs
- Education IRA and/or a 529 Plan
- Taxable mutual fund account

We have already gone through appropriate investments for the taxable mutual fund account so our focus in this section will be on tax deferred accounts for retirement, Education IRAs and/or 529 Plans for education, and Roth IRAs for both objectives. I stress these recommendations must be for *long term* investments only and should be confined to only the account types listed above.

ASSET ALLOCATION

We need to revisit the basic investment premise:

Stocks are better for growing money while bonds are better for preserving money.

An accumulation portfolio should be 100% stocks. No if's, and's, or but's. After experiencing one of the longest and harshest bear markets in history, you might think I am nuts. In the previous chapter we looked at risk versus volatility and I touched on why stocks can be poor short term investments because they are very volatile. However, when you look at long periods of time (ten years or greater), stocks are not particularly risky and have consistently provided the best source of growth for long term investors trying to accumulate money. If you don't believe me, please take the time to read "Stocks for the Long Run" by Jeremy Siegel. I normally check out financial books at the local library, but this was one book I decided to buy for myself because the information was excellent. Mr. Siegel does get a bit too analytical and some of his material is difficult to understand, but the basic concepts are worth noting. Stocks provide the best long term investment for accumulating wealth when all factors are considered.

It is absolutely necessary to look back at history to get an idea why stocks are such a good long term growth strategy compared to "safer" investments. History does not tell us what stocks or bonds will return in the future because our country, and the world in general, is constantly changing. History does give us an idea of relative performance meaning how well stocks might do in comparison to other asset classes. The following tables are taken directly from Ibbotson and Associates 2000 Yearbook which contains market results from 1926–1999.

Asset Class	Geometric Annual Mean (Annual Average Return)	Standard Deviation (Measure of Volatility)
Large Company Stocks	11.3%	20.1%
Small Company Stocks	12.6%	33.6%
Long Term Corporate Bonds	5.6%	8.7%
Long Term Government Bonds	5.1%	9.3%
Intermediate Government Bonds	5.2%	5.8%
U.S. Treasury Bills (1 Year)	3.8%	3.2%
Inflation	3.1%	4.5%

It is important to note that long term stock returns (both large and small stocks) are more than twice as great as bonds of all types. However, it is also important to note that volatility of stocks is more than twice as great as bonds. Most experts equate standard deviation to "risk," but it really measures volatility because there is no time component. A time component would be necessary to quantify true risk. Basically it is necessary for stocks to produce greater returns than bonds because they are more volatile. If stocks did not provide greater returns than bonds over long periods of time, no one would buy them. This idea is called the equity risk premium. If stocks are perceived as having greater risk than bonds, they must have a greater return. Equity risk premium is inherent in a free market society because no one is ever forced to buy a certain investment. There must be an additional incentive for people to take on greater risk.

Compound Annual Rates of Return for Various Asset Classes by Decade (%)

Asset Class	1930's	1940's	1950's	1960's	1970's	1980's	1990's
Large Company Stocks	-0.1	9.2	19.4	7.8	5.9	17.5	18.2
Small Company Stocks	1.4	20.7	16.9	15.5	11.5	15.8	15.1
Long Term Corporate Bonds	6.9	2.7	1.0	1.7	6.2	13.0	8.4
Long Term Government Bonds	4.9	3.2	-0.1	1.4	5.5	12.6	8.8

Intermediate Government Bonds	4.6	1.8	1.3	3.5	7.0	11.9	7.2
U.S. Treasury Bills (1 Year)	0.6	0.4	1.9	3.9	6.3	8.9	4.9
Inflation	-2.0	5.4	2.2	2.5	7.4	5.1	2.9

A mix of large and small company stocks would have outperformed all other bond classes in every decade except the 1930's during the Great Depression. It is also very important to note how a mix of large and small stocks would have out-paced inflation in every decade including the 1930's when inflation was negative (deflation). There are several decades when bonds would have actually lost ground to inflation. The relative performance compared to inflation is called the "real" rate of investment return because it is an indicator of true buying power. The ability for stocks to consistently outperform other asset classes on a "real" return basis is the primary reason for the long term attractiveness of stocks during the accumulation phase of investing.

Our final table shows what $1 invested at the end of 1925 would have grown to by the end of 1999 on both an absolute (nominal return not adjusted for inflation) and on a relative basis (real return after adjusting for inflation).

Asset Class	Nominal Total Return (1926–1999)	Real Total Return (1926–1999)
Large Company Stocks	$2,845.63	$303.09
Small Company Stocks	$6,640.79	$707.33
Long Term Corporate Bonds	$56.77	$6.05
Long Term Government Bonds	$40.22	$4.28
Intermediate Government Bonds	$43.15	$4.60
U.S. Treasury Bills (1 Year)	$15.64	$1.67

If this table doesn't make a compelling case for investing in stocks for long term growth, I don't know what else to say. Yes, bonds are less volatile, but this is ridiculous. A combination of large and small company stocks would have produced nearly 100 times more wealth than government bonds from 1926–1999.

Another interesting point is how U.S. Treasury Bills did on a real return basis. They just barely eked out a positive return when inflation was considered. U.S. Treasury Bills are comparable to one year CDs at the bank and return slightly better over time than a money market savings account. These safe money investments are excellent for preservation of principal over short periods of time, but they will devastate your portfolio over long periods of time when inflation is considered. The reason I point this out is because an incredible number of people have moved their retirement accounts into these safe money investments due to fear of the stock market. This could be a potentially huge mistake!

I previously mentioned an explanation why I use ten years as my arbitrary transition period between accumulation and spending. Ibbotson provides an interesting analysis of stock market returns over "rolling" periods of time. Since the end of 1925, large company stocks have had positive one year returns 54 out of 77 years, or about 70% of the time. If we look at rolling five year periods, large company stocks had positive returns 65 out of 73 periods, or about 89% of the time. When we get to ten year rolling periods, large company stocks had positive returns 66 out of 68 times, or about 97% of the time. The only two times we have experienced ten year periods of time when large company stocks lost money were during the Great Depression. From 1929–1938 large stocks lost 0.89% average annually and from 1930–1939, they lost 0.05% average annually. Amazingly, on a real return basis (accounting for inflation), large stocks would have still provided positive returns in these two periods of time because inflation was more negative than the stock market. This means your buying power would have still improved as you were losing principal! Ten year periods have historically provided enough recovery time to ride out even the worst stock market crashes and still achieve a positive result.

The tables and analytical stuff can get boring, but I needed to back up my point. Now we can get back to the present. I want to start with the reader who is just beginning her financial plan and is basically starting her investments from ground zero. Your portfolio should be 100% in stocks because you literally will benefit whether the market goes up or down over the short term. You might be a little confused by the last statement. It makes sense that you would benefit when the stock market goes up because your investments would rise in value, but how can you benefit when the market declines? This is important so pay close attention.

Let us assume you are just getting started so you have no invested money and you have concluded from your financial planning that you are able to contribute $100/month to your 401k plan at work. The company will match 50% of your contribution so your actual contributions are $150/month. You decide to invest 100% in stock funds knowing they are volatile investments. If the stock market goes down the first month, you will have lost some amount of your first $150 contribution, but *your next $150 contribution will purchase less expensive shares of stock. You get more shares for the same amount of money!* When you are first getting started, you should be *hoping* the market will *decline* because you have virtually nothing to lose right away (your account balance is minimal) and you get to buy stock at lower prices. Wouldn't you rather buy on sale?

Stocks are one of the few things we like to buy when it is expensive rather than inexpensive. If we are shopping for groceries, and hamburger is normally $2.00/lb., but our local grocer is running a 50% off sale for $1.00/lb., we rush out and stock our freezer with hamburger (vegetarian readers can think of soy patties or brussel sprouts; the concept is the same). It's the same hamburger; it just makes sense to buy when it is cheap. With stocks it is the exact opposite. When Cisco Systems was selling for around $80/share back in 2000, everyone wanted to buy. During the recent stock market crash, Cisco sold for less than $10/share in October of 2002. It's the same company making the same products in the same marketplace! I would rather buy at $10 than at $80! Cisco is now selling for around $24/share (as of 12/31/03) for a 140% gain over the past fourteen months or so. *The best time to buy stocks is when no one else wants to buy stocks!*

Now you might be asking how a *rising* stock market would benefit you because now you have to buy each month at *higher* prices and you would prefer to buy at lower prices. Good question. While you really don't want stocks to rise early in the investment process, a rising stock market will make you *feel* better about your financial plan. Emphasis on "feel" better because your account is rising and it appears you are making progress, but there will eventually be a stock market decline where you will "feel" bad, but get to buy more shares at lower prices. A rising market makes us feel good, but a declining market provides us with the opportunity to buy at a better price. Both rising and falling markets have benefits for the beginning investor.

The process of consistently making contributions whether the stock market is rising or falling is called "dollar cost averaging" in the investment industry. Your same contribution buys fewer shares when the market is up and more shares when the market is down. You have probably heard about dollar cost averaging, because most experts over-hype the concept. As a beginning investor, don't worry about stock prices. Your job is to create a coherent financial plan, establish defined objectives, implement your plan, and consistently invest towards your goals. The stock market will take care of itself over time.

On the other hand, there are readers who have done their work and have accumulated a sizable nest egg. These investors actually have something to lose if the stock market goes down. Major market declines don't feel like buying opportunities anymore because the losses are substantial enough to make us sick. The reason for the ten year transition period is to allow investors enough time to recover from major market declines before entering the spending phase. However, the bigger your nest egg balance is compared to your consistent investments, you want to move more and more towards less volatile investments. This might be another confusing statement. You might be asking "I thought you said to invest 100% in stocks during the accumulation phase. How do I reduce volatility as my nest egg grows?" Another good question. An important concept for the rest of us to understand is:

Not all stocks are created equal!

I have already commented on small and international stocks being more volatile than large company, U.S. stocks. As your nest egg gets larger, your stock holdings should be moving more towards *larger company value stocks* rather than small or international growth stocks. This means you are still 100% invested in stocks, but the gradual move to less volatile stocks will help reduce short term volatility while still retaining the potential for long term growth.

During the huge bull market of the late 1990's, everyone seemed to forget that not all stocks are created equal. Growth stocks, and particularly technology stocks, were the place to invest no matter what the cost. Value stocks were ignored for the most part. Risk was not even a consideration because everyone was making money in growth stocks. Market gurus told people we had entered a new investment paradigm where the good times would never end and you should buy even more on any dips in the market. When the first major stock market decline occurred in March of 2000, most people thought it was just another good buying opportunity. Unfortunately the gurus did not tell investors the stock market doesn't work that way, and the basic workings of the stock market had not changed. It was like leading lambs to the slaughter as average, everyday investors put their life savings into pure growth. Asset allocation and diversification were non-existent. The losses mounted and some people were hurt irreparably. Greed and misinformation were the primary drivers.

It seems now after three years of market declines, we are on the other side of the fence with people telling me they want out of stocks, all stocks, not just growth stocks. I have to continually remind people that value stocks, and particularly small cap value stocks, actually held up pretty well during the decline and the real problem was not that they held stocks, but they only held *growth* stocks. They had abandoned the basic investment concept of diversification and it reared up and bit them in the butt! Hard!

It is interesting to note, after such a devastating market decline the past three years, the S&P 500 Index has *averaged positive 10.04% annually over the past ten years* (through 6/30/03). When put in this perspective, most people might admit stocks are not so bad after all.

Enough commentary. Back to our story. It is possible to be 100% invested in stocks and still retain the concept of asset allocation and diversification. You simply are not using *bonds* as the diversification element. You are using *size, valuation and location* as the diversifiers per our discussion in the last chapter. The best way I know to illustrate this concept is by using a Morningstar box. I use this illustration with every client I talk to about stock market investing.

Stocks by Style

Large Cap Value	Large Cap Blend	Large Cap Growth
Mid Cap Value	Mid Cap Blend	Mid Cap Growth
Small Cap Value	Small Cap Blend	Small Cap Growth

The nine different boxes represent the different kinds of either domestic or international stocks. I use this illustration only for the domestic stock portion of an allocation because I normally stick to one, or maybe two, broadly diversified international funds to cover that element of the stock portfolio. Some stock mutual funds will fit nicely into a single style box while others might cover three or more boxes. By having some funds from each category, you will generally have a much more versatile asset allocation with lower overall volatility than selecting one or more funds from the same style box.

Your goal should be to have some exposure to all nine style boxes. Add in a broadly diversified international stock fund and you should be adequately diversified to reduce overall volatility while still getting the enhanced return of stocks. You do not need to buy a mutual fund representing each style box. Most mutual funds will have holdings from several boxes so you could literally accomplish your diversification goal with three mutual funds: a large cap blend fund, a small-mid cap blend fund, and a diversified international fund.

As you accumulate a larger nest egg, I would normally recommend a transition from blend funds to more focused mutual funds. I like to use a "T" approach with many clients. Envision a capital "T" on the style box table and you will get the idea. We want to focus our holdings on the large company stocks across the top so we do equal amounts in a large cap value fund, a large cap blend fund, and a large cap growth fund. This is the top of the "T." We make the stem of the "T" with either a single small-mid cap blend fund or you could use two funds including a true mid cap blend fund and a small cap blend fund. Finish out the portfolio with a diversified international fund and you have an excellent long term stock asset allocation. The typical five fund approach would look like this:

20% Large Cap Value Fund
20% Large Cap Blend Fund
20% Large Cap Growth Fund
20% Small-Mid Cap Blend Fund
20% Diversified International Fund

Your advisor should be able to easily help you compile a set of funds meeting the above criteria with any major mutual fund family. If you are a do-it-yourselfer, you should be using no-load funds. You can always do the research to pick your own funds (the Internet has more mutual fund research tools than you can imagine). Call one of the major no-load fund families and ask them for a list of funds that fit the categories you want.

Most financial media experts will push heavily on the no-load side because they typically have lower expenses than load funds used by advisors. Let me give the do-it-yourselfers out there another idea. If your biggest concern is total investment expenses (personally I believe your biggest concern should be net investment returns, but that's just me), consider a portfolio of exchange traded funds (otherwise referred to as ETFs). ETFs are a relatively new creation designed to compete for index fund investors seeking low overall expenses. I won't get into the specifics of ETFs, but they might be worth investigating if low fees are your primary objective.

Remember, most of your performance will come simply from the asset allocation you pick and not the specific funds or fund family you pick. Fees do play a role in total net returns, but you have to be careful when evaluating investments strictly from a total fee perspective because you might end up with a cheap portfolio of poor funds. Sometimes fees are legitimately used to provide portfolio enhancing services that make sense. Other times fees are purely to put profit in the pocket of the fund families or advisors. Use fees as a secondary analysis tool for picking your investments.

For some strange reason, it is apparently human nature to "collect" mutual funds. Collecting funds means buying a different fund or funds each time you evaluate investments and eventually you have fifteen different mutual funds in your portfolio. I see this all the time! People end up with a huge mess of funds scattered across several different accounts. Eventually your total number of holdings gets too big to conveniently administer. How the heck do you rebalance holdings across fifteen different funds held with different fund families in different accounts?

There is absolutely no reason to ever own more than ten mutual funds in any one account at any given time!

I normally recommend between three and eight mutual funds for the accumulation phase with the average around five. You will need more funds during the transition and spending phase of investing because you will be adding a bond component to the portfolio. Keep your funds consolidated with *one* fund family so your portfolio can be easily administered.

Obviously you will have more than one account so there may be different funds in different accounts. Invest each account as its own portfolio. If you follow my recommendations, it is likely you will have four different retirement accounts at any given time during the accumulation phase: an IRA, a company sponsored retirement plan like a 401k or 403b, a Roth IRA, and a taxable mutual fund account. The Roth and the taxable mutual fund account might have other uses than retirement so the asset allocation in these accounts might be different than the IRA and the company sponsored plan.

Allocate each of your long term accounts separately based on the ultimate financial objective designated for that particular account.

Your IRA and your 401k should nearly always have the same general asset allocation because they are normally designated to meet the same retirement objectives. The reason I say "nearly always" instead of "always" is because there is one instance where the allocation should be different in these two accounts. You normally cannot control which funds are allowed as investment options in your company retirement plan. Many employers do a less than adequate job of selecting and periodically reviewing their plan investment options so it is likely you have some major deficiencies in your company sponsored plan. A deficiency means there might not be a decent international fund or maybe the only small cap fund is really poor. If this is the case with your company retirement plan, you will need to do some extra work. The proper way to handle this situation is to first let your benefits people know their plan needs to be improved. Since that plea may fall on deaf ears, you will need to take matters into your own hands.

Sit down with your IRA and your 401k plan and figure out where the holes are in your 401k. Add the two accounts together as if it were one account and figure out how much money should go into each style of fund. Use the IRA money to fill the deficiencies of your 401k. You always have control over your IRA investment options so there should always be a decent investment option available in every style of fund. Let me give you an example how this might work:

You are forty years old. You have $15,000 in an IRA rolled over from a previous job. You also have $25,000 in your current 401k plan at work. Your 401k plan is not good, but it offers an S&P 500 Index fund which could serve as a large cap blend fund. All of the other funds are high expense, poor performing funds (very common in 401k plans especially with small employers). The first thing you do is add the two accounts together:

IRA	$15,000
401k	$25,000
Total	$40,000

Let us assume you want the following allocation:

Large Cap Stocks	60%	$24,000 (0.6 x $40,000)
Small-Mid Cap Stocks	20%	$ 8,000 (0.2 x $40,000)
International Stocks	20%	$ 8,000 (0.2 x $40,000)

Your 401k has an S&P 500 Index fund so you can at least cover the large cap portion of your allocation using the index fund. My recommendation is to put the full $25,000 of the 401k into the S&P 500 Index fund and put half of the IRA in a small-mid cap blend fund and the other half into a diversified international fund. Granted your allocation will not exactly match your intended mix, but this is not rocket science so there is no magical right answer.

There would be two variations on this example. The first variation is all of your money is in a 401k so there is no IRA for you to mix and match. Sadly this is often the case where you are stuck in a poor plan and have no control over your investment options. There is nothing you can do in this case other than complain to your company about improving the plan. Make the most of a bad situation and try to create an asset allocation that fits your needs. If the plan offers an index fund and the other options are poor, do not hesitate to put all your money in the index fund. The S&P 500 Index will hold 500 stocks so you will still have broad diversification and most index funds offer relatively low expenses. This is not the optimum solution, but all you can do is play with the cards you have been dealt.

The other variation is where your IRA is much larger than the 401k. This is a much easier scenario to work with and obtain a desirable result. In the previous example, let us assume the IRA is $30,000 and the 401k is $10,000. You could put the 401k entirely in the S&P 500 index fund which fills some of your large cap allocation. I would invest in the following funds in your IRA to complete the portfolio:

$7,000 in a large cap value fund
$7,000 in a large cap growth fund
$8,000 in a small-mid cap blend fund
$8,000 in a diversified international fund

The composite portfolio should do an excellent job for you over the long term.

The next issue is rebalancing. In this particular example, the 401k plan would be getting contributions each pay period and the IRA would not be getting any contributions. Obviously the 401k plan will eventually become a much larger piece of the puzzle over time. Simply rebalance the two accounts periodically to stay as close as possible to your original asset allocation objective. You may have your own definition of periodically, but it should be reviewed at least one time per year. *Nobody ever rebalances retirement accounts!* Take a half hour one time per year and rebalance your accounts. You will probably never be able to quantify how rebalancing actually reduced your volatility without hurting returns, but you will need to trust me on this very important piece of advice.

Using your IRA to fill in the holes of your company sponsored retirement plan leads most people into a common mistake. You must evaluate the performance of your *entire* portfolio rather than each individual piece. If you are properly diversified, it is a given that some of your funds will do better than others every year. That is the whole point of diversifying in the first place. One year large cap growth might be your best performer (like in the late 90's) while international or small cap might do poorly. The next year might be the exact opposite with small cap leading the way while large cap growth suffers. Human nature will drive you to focus on the best performing fund. You will almost surely want to sell the poor performing fund and buy more of the best performing fund. This is one of the worst things you can do when investing. It is generally called "chasing performance." You are always buying high and selling low which basically means you are always late for the show. If I have not been clear, one of the most important aspects of creating a financial plan is to provide a guideline for investment discipline. Focus on your objectives and overall asset allocation designed to meet those objectives and stick with your plan through thick and thin. Investments tend to move in cycles so just when you thought your international fund was never going to do well, it might surprise you. Whatever allocation you pick, stay consistent, and focus on rebalancing rather than chasing the next "hot" investment.

The worst culprit for "chasing performance" is the financial media. They must write or tell you about something new all the time or you would quit buying their product. Obviously they are going to follow the hottest investments or trends to satisfy their customers. When stocks were doing well, they told you about the hottest growth funds to have in your portfolio (usually focusing on technology). When stocks do poorly, they tell you about the best bond funds for your portfolio. The media is never accountable to anybody for anything they do. If you follow their advice, you would always be one step behind and your portfolio would change faster than dirty diapers (a little new parent lingo). Please ignore the end of year magazine issues that have the "Best Stocks to Own for 200_!" or "Best Mutual Funds to Own for 200_!" Having a written plan should give you the confidence to stick to your guns and become a really successful long term investor rather than a short term speculator.

Some readers might find 100% stock investing does not fit their conservative personality. This is our natural human emotions getting in the way of financial planning. If it is difficult for you to emotionally handle the bad times with stock investing, there are a couple options. The first option might sound stupid, but I think it actually works for some people. *Set your initial diversified asset allocation; rebalance your account one time per year, and ignore investment performance.* Some of the best investors rarely review their accounts. You should still review all statements to be sure that there are no unauthorized trades, deposits or withdrawals and, more likely, posting mistakes. However, some people will see a particularly bad quarterly statement and will make emotional decisions that end up adversely affecting their long term financial health. You absolutely must stay consistent with your investment strategy.

When I get investment statements I look at them for about thirty seconds and throw them away (obviously you should not throw away important documents for tax or record keeping purposes!). I do keep the annual statements for record keeping purposes, but I have no idea why I even bother opening quarterly statements because they mean almost nothing to me. I guess curiosity gets the best of me. Daily, monthly, and quarterly fluctuations do not mean anything in the grand scheme of things so I ignore them.

The other option is to give in to your emotions and not follow my advice. There are many people who will not be able to ignore the fluctuations and will accept lower returns from a less volatile portfolio. There is nothing wrong with this approach as long as you can accept the lower returns without getting sucked in when times are good. Consistency is the key. Once you pick an allocation that fits your unique style, stick with it when times get tough with only minor modifications. If I am describing you, my recommendation is to pick a balanced fund. This might be the same balanced fund I previously recommended for your taxable mutual fund account.

As I mentioned before, balanced funds provide a well diversified portfolio of stocks and bonds wrapped up in one nice, neat package. They are generally much less volatile than 100% stock portfolios, but still offer competitive returns over the long term. You will likely have some losing years, but they will be rare. For example, one prominent balanced fund I have used with clients has made money 25 out of the last 27 years or about 92% of the time. The worst one year period in this fund was March 2002–March 2003 where you would have lost 11.61%. However, the worst three year period returned positive 8.56%. Not too bad. This particular fund has averaged 11.44% after all fees and expenses over the past twenty years! I don't think anyone would criticize you for picking this fund (or a comparable fund) as your accumulation vehicle of choice.

◆   ◆   ◆

I hope this chapter answered your nagging questions about what investments to pick in your IRA or your company sponsored retirement plan. Accumulation is all about achieving the greatest possible long term returns with an acceptable level of risk which generally means investing in stocks.

I would like to list the mutual funds in all of our various retirement plans, but we have a number of different accounts and I think it would be more confusing than useful (also, I would likely get in trouble from a compliance standpoint). Our retirement accounts are invested 100% in stocks and will remain 100% in stocks until we are at least fifty years old. I don't expect to make many changes other than annual rebalancing for at least another ten years (I will be 42). I anticipate slowly moving some of our more aggressive growth stock holdings towards more conservative value stocks as we get closer to age fifty. This will help reduce volatility in our portfolio as our nest egg grows.

Our primary retirement investment is with a major fund family that offers some excellent value funds with long histories of excellent performance. The value funds help to balance our more aggressive growth funds in some of the other accounts.

We are also in the accumulation phase of investing for Isabella's college funding. We put $2,000 per year into the account (maximum allowable annual contribution as of 2003) and I chose the following types of mutual funds:

Large Cap Stock Blend	40%
Small-Mid Cap Stock Blend	30%
Diversified International Stock	30%

Her account is small right now because she is only eighteen months old and we have only contributed $4,000 so far. I don't anticipate making any changes to her account other than annual rebalancing as needed until she is at least ten years old. Hopefully her account is worth at least $30,000 by age ten (assumed hypothetical 8% growth rate). At age ten, we plan on entering the transition phase where we will slowly move her stock money into safer investments to help protect what has been accumulated.

I already told you how we invest our taxable mutual fund account. This money is invested 100% in diversified stock mutual funds. I have not rebalanced these funds so far because rebalancing would result in a taxable event. I don't want to deal with tax ramifications so I am letting our funds ride for now. There will not be many changes to this account over the next twenty years.

Unfortunately we do not follow my own advice about consolidating accounts with one mutual fund family. We probably should, but there is a method to our madness. I use many of the same funds that I use for my clients. I practice what I preach so our accounts are spread among various fund families. Periodically reviewing the performance of our various accounts gives me some added perspective on how my clients are doing. Our accounts would be consolidated with one fund family if there was no business advantage for me to keep them separated.

Let me summarize some of the more important points made about investing during the accumulation phase.

- Accumulation requires "precursive faith" which means visualizing your future investment success before it occurs. Be optimistic. Your commitment to investing will pay off over the long haul.

- Divide and conquer—it is easier to achieve big accumulation objectives by breaking them down into smaller, more achievable objectives. Once you accumulate $100, you can set your sights on $1,000, and so on until your ultimate goal is reached.

- Set your own definition of "long term"—I use ten years as a general guideline for long term investments.

- Create an accumulation asset allocation plan and stick with it through thick and thin—consistency will pay off over long periods of time and will keep you from chasing the next "hot" investment.

- Accumulation is best done with stock mutual funds—the greater long term return of stocks does not come without greater volatility.

- Equity income and balanced mutual funds are excellent options for your taxable mutual fund account.

- The best time to buy stocks is when no one else wants them—it is almost always better to buy when stocks are cheap.

- Not all stocks are created equal—large company stocks and value stocks tend to be less volatile than smaller stocks, international stocks, or growth stocks. As your nest egg grows and you get closer to the transition phase, move assets gradually towards larger company stocks and value stocks.

- Use size, valuation, and location to diversify your stock holdings—try to get exposure to all of the Morningstar style boxes. This will help reduce overall volatility without sacrificing long term returns.

- You do not need more than one fund family and you will rarely need more than five mutual funds in any given account during the accumulation phase.

- Allocate each of your accounts separately based on the unique objective designated for that particular account.

- Be sure to periodically rebalance your tax deferred accounts like IRAs, company retirement plans, Roth IRAs, Education IRAs, and 529 plans. Rebalancing does not necessarily enhance returns, but it does help reduce volatility. It is the only buy low, sell high strategy I know of that actually works consistently. Rebalancing also helps maintain investment discipline so you don't end up making big mistakes by chasing performance.

Once you have done the hard job of accumulating assets, we get to the fun part of spending the money. The next chapter will discuss how to plan for the spending phase of investing and will describe how to make the all important transition from accumulation to spending.

10

The Spending Phase "Investing for Long Term Income"

I expect most readers are still actively in the accumulation phase and may not enter the transition or spending phase of investing for many years. Everyone out there will ultimately find themselves in the transition and spending phase, but for now, there are two reasons for reading and understanding this information.

The first reason is you probably have parents, other relatives, or friends who are already done with accumulating assets for their goals. It has been my experience many of these people are not maximizing their financial resources. It is very important you let these people know this information is available to help them. Talking about personal finances has always been a taboo subject, but financial decisions have become increasingly complex and people need someone they trust to help them through the process. Unfortunately, some financial advisors are not trustworthy enough to effectively meet this challenge without some supervision. I strongly encourage all families to openly discuss personal finance with each other. It may be uncomfortable at first, but having these discussions can help build a stronger bond between family members. It is also likely you may someday end up having to help manage assets for an ailing parent. I have had many clients who ended up with this overwhelming responsibility. Many people feel they are in over their heads when dealing with money issues, but they will not ask for help. Knowing they have someone they trust to confide in can really make a difference in their lives and in yours. It is my hope this book can help instigate discussions among family members and serve as a framework for establishing a plan together.

You will also need this information for your own transition/spending plan in the future. Understanding how your portfolio will change over time is important as you accumulate assets. It gives you a better understanding of the timeline involved in the evolution of your investments. You may not understand all the information right now, but it will make more sense in the future as you implement various strategies and get firsthand experience. I suspect this is one chapter that will need to be revisited many times in the future until the concepts become totally ingrained in your financial plan.

You may not believe me, but the accumulation part of investing should be the easy part. The transition and spending phases are much more difficult to explain and also to implement. The reason? The transition and spending phases normally involve much larger sums of money and shorter time horizons. This combination will lead most investors to be overly conservative in an attempt to achieve a "guaranteed" stream of income.

When I meet with a 25 year old and we get started on an accumulation investment program, it is relatively easy to explain how stocks are excellent long term growth investments. I rarely get disagreement when I recommend a 100% stock portfolio because the 25 year old is not concerned about losing money (they have little or nothing to lose), and they know retirement is a long way off in the distant future. However, it is a different story when I meet with a fifty year old who has $100,000 in his retirement plan and he wants to retire by age 62. His perception is skewed because he looks at periodic short term investment losses, any losses, as directly impacting his retirement. Every dollar lost is not a buying opportunity, but a direct loss of income during retirement. Many retirees seem to believe their investment lives end when they quit work, so they perceive their time horizon as being much shorter than it actually is.

I have talked extensively about human nature and emotions when dealing with money. It is my experience these emotions get magnified as we get older and as the sums of money become larger. Investing is controlled by the two extreme human emotions of fear and greed. Normally I see greed controlling the accumulation phase, while fear is more dominant during the spending phase. Many people have fear of losing money, fear of spending too much, fear of living too long, and fear of taking any action where a mistake could be made. Since it is doubtful you will see a therapist to help overcome your fears, we must deal with it ourselves. It won't be easy, but I think there are a couple things we can do together to help.

The premise of this book is proper financial planning can change your life for the better. I believe this is particularly true when dealing with the transition and spending phase of investing. Having an action plan in place will give you the confidence to overcome normal anxiety associated with difficult investment decisions. A coherent plan will help strike a balance in your life and discourages extreme decisions that ultimately sabotage the spending phase of investing.

I offer volunteer financial advice sessions the last Friday of each month at a local community senior center. The seniors who take advantage of this program generally do not have a lot of money so they usually do not have any sort of financial advisor. Many of their questions concern Social Security, estate planning, and long term care. They almost never ask questions about investing which surprises me. I figured these people were solidly in the spending phase of retirement which is a complicated endeavor, so I just assumed they would be looking for advice on investing. I have done this volunteer session for several years and have come to realize why these seniors never ask about investing—they don't have any actual investments! Nearly all of them have every last penny at the bank in their checking, savings, and in CDs. They might have some fixed annuities (basically just longer term CDs, but with some tax deferral and with an insurance component) and some savings bonds, but they almost never own mutual funds and the only stock they own was inherited and they never got around to selling it.

As interest rates have gone down, down, down over the past several years, I figured there would be more investing questions because money market accounts, CDs, and fixed annuities were paying lower interest to these seniors. In fact, interest rates have become ridiculously low with one year CDs paying about 0.65% at the time of this writing and that is *before taxes!* While I write this, a five year CD is paying about 2.25%. Better, but still does not provide a heck of a lot of income. I thought these people would be looking for alternatives to keep their income at or near levels they had when interest rates were higher. Nope! Still no investing questions.

It finally dawned on me why there were no questions. *The seniors seeking my advice were not spending any money!* They had money to spend, but they just don't spend it. Remember, these are not wealthy people. Their fear of running out of money is so strong; they cannot bring themselves to spend even the minimal interest they accumulate. Most of them are living on their social security and a small pension and many of the people coming to see me would be right at, or slightly above, the poverty line. They are not concerned about the interest they earn because they don't use it anyway. In the rare occasion where they spend some or all of their interest, they cut back when interest rates fall and maybe kick spending up a notch when interest rates are higher. Their fear often controls their decisions about spending and some of them live a "poor" lifestyle where they struggle to pay for medications, skimp on any entertainment, and generally don't feel they can spend money on themselves.

My father-in-law gave me the perfect example to illustrate what I am trying to explain. As you already know, he is also a financial planner. His practice is more mature than mine so he works with a large percentage of retired people in the spending phase of their lives. The other day he was visiting with a prospective client and the gentleman said he wanted to kill Alan Greenspan for driving down interest rates. Ken (my father-in-law) learned this guy had $100,000 sitting at the local bank earning less than 1% annual interest. This person was an older senior so Ken knew any advice should not involve any risk of losing money. He recommended moving the money to a FDIC insured direct money market account paying 2% interest. Ken was basically showing the guy how to more than double his current income without any fees or minimum balances, with total liquidity, and in something FDIC insured similar to his current bank account. The gentleman thought it sounded good and told Ken to call him the next day to set an appointment. When Ken called the next day, this person told him he had thought about it and didn't want to make a change. Ken was flabbergasted why this person would not want to double his income without taking any risk! The reason the man gave was he wanted to keep his options open for when the interest rate environment improved. Ken explained the money market account would increase its interest rates if short term rates went up and also told him again about having complete liquidity at any time to do anything he wanted with the money. The guy was adamant about not wanting to change anything. He would keep his money at the bank earning almost nothing, but still keep complaining about the low rates he was getting. Strange!

I don't know if there is a moral to this story, but it gives you an idea how scary the spending phase of investing can be for most people. This person was tremendously upset by the low interest he was getting paid at the bank, but when offered a better option without any additional risk, he opted to stay at the bank out of fear—fear of making a mistake. He also didn't spend any of his current interest so he really did not care if his money earned 1% or 2%. It just sits in the account anyway! In fact, I have actually had seniors tell me they didn't want to earn *more* interest because they would have to pay more taxes! Can you believe that statement? Why would someone say something so incredibly silly, but yet still complain about the poor interest they are earning at the bank? I have found Alan Greenspan to be almost universally despised by the senior community because in their minds he destroyed their retirement income. Of course, he didn't actually do anything to hurt them, but that is not their perception. They never created a plan for retirement and now they are hurting because of it and are looking for someone to blame. I don't want you or your parents to end up in this situation.

I have found it almost impossible to discuss investments with anyone over the age of 70. They tell me things like:

"I want to earn a high interest rate with no risk and I want guarantees so the rate can never fall."—if that investment option existed, wouldn't everyone be in it already? Guaranteed high returns with no risk? Where do I sign up? If I talk about any investment without a guarantee, they will never actually follow my advice. They absolutely must have a guarantee no matter how expensive or how poor the investment!

"I don't need the money and I want to protect it from long term care expenses." I might recommend gifting some money to kids or grandkids. No, they say. We might need the money. I thought you said you don't need the money. We don't, but we might. This is where I start rubbing my forehead and reach for the aspirin bottle.

I eventually learned these ambiguous investment objectives result from never creating a plan in the first place. This is also part of the reason many seniors fall victim to scams. When you have no plan, you have no reason to be disciplined. When you have no investment discipline, you will make mistakes like falling for the fast talk of a scam artist.

In this chapter I will show you a systematic approach for taking your hard earned nest egg and positioning the money to provide income during the transition and spending phase of your life. Because it is systematic, it will give you the confidence to remain disciplined. *This approach will absolutely not work unless you take the time and effort to examine your own situation and establish defined, realistic spending objectives.* Establishing defined, realistic spending objectives is one of the most important services performed by financial advisors and, unfortunately, many advisors will not actually take the time and effort to help their clients with this critical aspect of their lives. Your financial advisor should be willing to help guide you through this process. If your advisor only sells you investments and does not discuss your spending objectives, fire him, because he is not doing the most important part of his job. If an advisor does not meet with you for more than an hour at a time, fire him, because this process will take some time.

If you do not have an advisor, I will do my best to explain the process, but it will be different for every one of you. There is no rule of thumb to guide you. There is no "canned" plan that will give you success. Also remember as you go through this process, I am talking specifically about the rest of us. Wealthy people would certainly benefit from the following plan, but they are wealthy, which means they are still going to do well even if they make mistakes. The rest of us cannot afford to make mistakes. Mistakes during the spending phase directly affect our quality of life.

The spending phase occurs in both our education planning and our retirement planning. While the accumulation phase was similar for both of these important financial objectives, the spending phase is very different. With education you have a defined spending period (or you should) of four or five years. With retirement, we can make lifespan estimates, but unless you know exactly when you will die, they are just estimates. I have not had a client commit to a date of death in their financial plan! Anytime you have a defined objective it is easier to create a plan, so our education spending plan will be relatively simple. Creating a retirement income plan has a lot more variables which makes mistakes more common. We will focus most of our attention on retirement planning, but I want to start with education.

CREATE A SPENDING PLAN FOR EDUCATION

In the last chapter we set the investment time period of pure accumulation through age ten for education savings. Age ten is an arbitrary age and is certainly open to debate. I selected ten based on someone who started saving when their child is a baby. If you start saving when your children are older, I recommend using a rule of thumb to delineate between the spending and transition phase. Subtract their current age from eighteen (the assumed age when they will start college) and divide by two. This will give you the length of years for accumulation and the length of years for the transition phase. Here is an example:

> You start saving when your daughter is eight years old. Take: 18-8 = 10 years
> Divide 10 years by 2 = 5 years
> The accumulation period is five years and the transition period should be five years
> Follow the advice in the accumulation chapter for the first five years of investing and then use this chapter for the transition and spending phase

In this chapter we need to cover the transition period from the end of accumulation through the beginning of freshman year and also the spending period from freshman year until your child graduates (or until you cut them off, whichever comes first).

Hopefully you have created a coherent financial plan for helping your children get through college. Obviously if you don't have any financial desire to help the kids, you can skip this section. If education is one of your primary objectives, you should have a defined, written spending goal in mind (refer back to Chapter 2).

Most of my clients want to provide some fraction of the typical *public* college education cost like 1/3, 1/2, or 2/3. Use your goal to estimate specific dollar amounts you will need. Our goal was to provide the full cost of four years at an in-state public school for all of our children (Isabella and we assumed at least one other child). We used the University of Minnesota as our guideline and assumed 6% annual inflation. This calculation resulted in the following specific dollar amounts needed for Isabella:

Year 1 = $29,620
Year 2 = $31,400
Year 3 = $33,280
Year 4 = $35,300
Year 5 and beyond = Her problem!

If you remember from Chapter 7, our plan was to fund an Education IRA with $2,000/year and also to use the contributions to our Roth IRAs to help fund education, if needed. Our taxable mutual fund emergency reserve account could theoretically be used to pick up any additional need, but probably will not be needed.

We have Isabella's Education IRA invested in 100% diversified stock mutual funds. We will maintain this strategy until she is ten and then we will get into the transition phase. The Roth IRAs are invested 100% in stocks and because of the unique ability for Roths to meet both education and retirement objectives, we will keep this account in stocks until Isabella reaches college. Our spending plan assumes the Education IRA will be spent first with our Roths picking up the difference.

In our strategy, the transition and spending plans will only be important for the Education IRA account as you will see. This may not be the case in your scenario, but it should help give you an idea of how the system works.

Transition Phase

If things have gone well, we hopefully will get an average 10% return in stocks over the next ten years. We don't know if this will happen, but that is the low end of long term stock market returns. At $2,000 per year and 10% annual returns, Isabella's balance would be about $37,000 by her age ten. Maybe her balance will be higher; maybe her balance will be lower. Her balance will not change our planning and we will remain consistently invested 100% in stock mutual funds through thick and thin during the accumulation phase.

At age ten we reach the transition phase. We start at 100% stocks, but where do we end? My recommendation is to have no more than 20% in stocks when you begin the spending phase at your child's age eighteen (or whenever withdrawals will begin). This means we have to transition gradually down from 100% stocks to 20% stocks over the eight year period.

There is no right or wrong way to make the transition and nothing is set in stone, but here is *our* plan:

Age 10–12   80% diversified stock funds/20% diversified bond funds

Age 13–15   60% diversified stock funds/40% diversified bond funds

Age 15–18   40% diversified stock funds/60% diversified bond funds

Age 18+   20% equity income stock funds/80% short term bond funds and money market

Critics will say this approach could result in losses because both the bond fund allocation and the stock fund allocation could theoretically lose money in any given year. If a significant loss occurs at age eighteen, our education savings plan could be hurt. You know what, they are right! There is always a chance your plans will not work out the way you would have liked. My approach will result in some excellent years where you are extremely happy and will result in poor years when you will question the approach. Consistency will be the key to success. The gradual transition reduces volatility over time as your nest egg grows and still gives you the opportunity to earn a competitive return over the entire eight year transition period. The ages for each transition are somewhat arbitrary, so don't feel tied to these specific recommendations. There is room for flexibility in designing your own plan.

Spending Phase

We figure Isabella's Education IRA will have about $74,900 by her age eighteen. If we get 10% annual returns during the accumulation phase, we would need to get about 5.23% during the eight years of the transition phase to reach our objective. We consider these assumptions to be reasonable. If her Education IRA has $74,900, it will get us through about 2 ½ years of anticipated college expenses. We will maintain the allocation listed above for age 18+ during the entire spending phase.

Spending will come out of the short term bond fund and/or money market account. I suggest rebalancing Education IRAs, 529 plans, or Roth IRAs at the end of each year maintaining the 20% equity income fund and 80% short term bond fund and/or money market account. These accounts allow rebalancing with no tax ramifications. If your education savings is in a taxable account, you might not rebalance each year because of tax ramifications. Be sure to consult your tax professional if you have concerns about rebalancing in a taxable account.

After 2 ½ years, her Education IRA will be completely gone and we will start dipping into Tracy's Roth IRA (or my Roth IRA—it really doesn't matter). This is where things might get a little tricky. Remember, our Roth IRAs will still be 100% in stocks because they will still be considered long term accounts based on our retirement objectives. We plan on selling stocks to create cash *three separate times* to finish off paying for Isabella's education. The first sale will happen in the fall of her Junior year to pay for the spring semester of her Junior year, after her Education IRA runs out of money. The second sale would occur the summer before her Senior year and would pay for the fall semester. The third sale would occur late fall of her Senior year to finish off her final semester. Obviously we hope these sales occur when the stock market is high so we are getting a premium on our investments, but we also understand we may end up selling low. The reason I am not worried is because each sale will only constitute a fraction of our Roth IRA balance. Also, we may sell earlier than needed if the stock market goes on a huge run like it did in the late 1990's. I know this may sound like market timing, but why get greedy. If we know the money will be needed to help Isabella, I will lock in some of our gains and make sure it will be there to help her.

We will establish Education IRAs for any future children. If we decide to have more than two kids, we will need to re-evaluate our plan about using the Roth IRA accounts. It works great with two kids because one parent's Roth is for one child and the other parent's Roth is for the second child. If we had three children, we would make some modifications to our spending plan so each one gets a fair amount. None of the recommendations would change, but we would have to pay close attention to total distributions so everything was equal for each child.

There are two main reasons for recommending mutual funds compared to other investment vehicles: simplicity and diversification. You can use zero coupon bonds for the fixed income allocation; you could buy ETFs for the stock portion, or you could buy individual bonds and individual stocks as you see fit. All of these options require brokerage accounts rather than mutual fund accounts. You will have some trading fees and usually some account maintenance fees. Maybe these options would be better for your situation, but for most people, the simplicity of mutual funds is the most attractive feature.

The main reason why education planning is relatively simple lies with most people's objectives. Most parents want the *ability* to help their children, but if they can't do as much as they planned, the kids will just have to make do for the rest. If the parents make a mistake and don't reach their goal, it is too bad for their *children*, not the parents. The parents might feel bad, but it is likely *their* parents never helped them and they turned out fine. Kids can work; they can take loans, or they can get financial aid to help pay their own way. Most parents do not pay for the entire cost of college anyway. We may ultimately decide not to pay the full amount for Isabella's education, but we want the *ability* to pay it all if we decide to go that route. Hopefully she will work hard and get scholarships so our portion will not be so great. If that happens, we will have more in our Roth IRAs for retirement. If it doesn't happen, we won't be caught by surprise which is one of the best rewards for creating and implementing a plan.

Create a Spending Plan for Retirement

Retirement spending is much more complicated than education spending because mistakes directly affect our *own* quality of life. If you are one of those people who got greedy in the late 1990's and had all your retirement money in tech stocks, it is very likely your retirement plans have been seriously impacted. While I can sympathize with your situation, I know there was something that could have been done to avoid the situation in the first place. I am tired of hearing on TV about some couple who retired in 2000 with a large retirement nest egg only to lose most of their money by investing in tech stocks. Now they are on the news because of their tragic story. One or both of them is working at Wal-Mart as a greeter just to supplement their retirement income. They don't know what they are going to do. Someone else is always responsible for destroying their retirement. They blame their company (Enron, MCI, etc.), Alan Greenspan, President Bush, terrorists, and the list goes on and on, but *they almost never blame themselves.*

Maybe I am a little cold, but they only have themselves to blame. They got greedy! Plain and simple truth. They did not have the discipline to create a financial plan and approach their investments in a systematic manner geared to meet their objectives. Many of them wanted to get rich quick which almost never works and almost always ends with bad results. This type of thing happens every so often and it is the same story every time. People get enticed into the "hot" investment du jour and end up getting destroyed financially while other investors don't buy the hype, stick to their tried and true investment plan, and ultimately reach their goals. Are we really supposed to feel sorry for the people who did not take the time or effort to do a little homework and create a plan?

It is likely the most important reason you purchased this book was for retirement planning. Obviously you have learned much more, but if all you get from your hours of reading is how to create an accumulation, transition, and spending plan for retirement, it was worth your time and money. Just simply creating a written plan for these important financial objectives will put you well ahead of the average investor.

<u>Transition Phase</u>

We assume you have done a good job of accumulating money for retirement and now you have a sizable nest egg with about ten years left until your planned retirement date. You have been primarily invested in 100% diversified stock mutual funds; you periodically rebalanced your holdings, and now we need to begin protecting some of the assets before the spending phase begins.

As you might expect, the first step is to sit down and take a good hard look at what you will want from retirement. You will need to create a tentative budget estimate for the type of retirement lifestyle you desire. There will be assumptions to make, and you certainly won't know the details of retirement when you are still ten years away, but be conservative in your estimates. I find the easiest way to create an estimate is to imagine yourself retired today. Work in today's dollars and don't worry about inflation right now. How much would you realistically need on a monthly basis to live a comfortable retirement *today*? If there are bills you know will either go away, or possibly go up at retirement, subtract or add them into today's estimate. For example, if you know the mortgage will be paid off sometime in the next ten years, but there are still payments being made today, subtract the principal and interest payments from your estimate (make sure to keep taxes and insurance in your estimate because those payments won't go away). On the other hand, if you plan on retiring before age 65, you will need to account for health insurance as an expense that will likely be greater ten years from now than it is today.

It is probably easy for you to pull together typical monthly bills, but it is much more difficult to estimate what you will realistically need for spending money. The one thing I remind you—*during retirement there will be seven days per week to spend money.* This is important! Today you are working and most people don't spend much money while at work. When you are retired, almost everything you do will cost money and, if you are an active retiree, you will do a lot of things to fill the time. I have gone through this exercise many times with clients and it is common for people to double their spending money allowance to account for greater entertainment expenses during retirement. I don't care how much you use for the estimate, but make sure you account for this issue in your planning process.

Also, you will need to make some allowance for taxes. It is likely your income will decline during retirement so you might drop into a lower tax bracket. If you have done an excellent job during the accumulation phase, it is likely you will remain in the same tax bracket. Either way, make sure your monthly retirement budget estimate has an allowance for taxes.

At this point there should be a tentative budget number written down. We don't know if this number will be accurate ten years from now, but it is a great place to start. *As an example, let us assume you came up with an estimated need of $5,000/month.*

Now we need to figure out what amount of your budget will need to come from your retirement investments. To do this we need to know what you will get from Social Security along with any other retirement income you plan to receive. For most people I am talking about a pension or possibly part time work, but everyone is different. Maybe you have parents who are well off that gift you a certain amount of money every year. As long as it is consistent money you can count on, write it down as income. If it is a one time gift or inheritance, don't include it in your planning.

Social Security sends out periodic statements detailing your estimated retirement benefits. If you have a current statement on hand, great! You can use the number they give you as an estimate of retirement benefits. If you are like most people and throw away your statements, you can always call the local Social Security office and they will be more than happy to explain your options and how much you can expect to receive at retirement. Their whole job is explaining Social Security benefits to regular folks so please utilize them for information. There is a lot of misinformation surrounding the Social Security program so it is always a good idea to confirm your assumptions with the local Social Security office.

Make sure you are using the number for the year you will be retiring. For example, full retirement age is now different for many people. For my parents, full retirement age is 66. For Tracy and me, full retirement age is 67. However, you might be retiring at age 62. Make sure the estimate you use is for the age when you plan to retire. The earliest you can receive Social Security benefits is age 62 so if you plan on retiring earlier than 62, you will need to pull more from investments until Social Security begins.

There are two questions I consistently get about Social Security: When should I take benefits and will Social Security be there for me when I retire? The first question is easier to answer than the second question. My advice for most people is to take Social Security benefits as soon as possible once you have completely stopped earning income. If you are still working full or part time and are *under full retirement age*, I normally recommend not taking benefits unless you absolutely need them. If you reach *full* retirement age, start taking benefits immediately even if you are still working. If you are no longer earning income (or maybe earning only a very small income—less than $1,000/month or so), than take Social Security as early as possible. When you start Social Security benefits early, the total payment gets reduced, but you get those reduced payments for a longer period of time. Waiting until full retirement age before collecting payments will give you a bigger check each month, but you will have to wait longer for those larger payments. In many cases taking the smaller payment early will result in more income over the remainder of your life expectancy and will allow many people to retire sooner. Just remember, age 62 is the earliest you can collect reduced Social Security benefits.

The second question is tougher to answer because no one can know for sure what will happen to Social Security in the future. If I had to guess, I expect Social Security will be around for all current generations. If you are a twenty year old, I expect Social Security will be there for you in some form or another. However, I would say the program will likely change dramatically between now and your retirement age. There may be reduced benefits; there may be greater taxes to support the system; people who have done a good job of saving for themselves may get penalized, and part of the program may ultimately get privatized. There is no way to know what will happen. If you are fifty years old, I think you can safely expect to get Social Security in its current form throughout your retirement. If you are under age fifty, I believe you should use more conservative estimates for the benefits you plan to receive. I *do not* think Social Security will go broke. In my opinion most of the debate surrounding Social Security and running out of money is just political rhetoric designed to scare people into voting one way or another. Social Security will not go broke because it is a government funded program. Unless you think taxes are going to end at some point, Social Security will always have a source of funding. Benefits may have to be reduced or changed in some other way, but the Social Security system will likely be around for many decades to come.

Once you have a solid estimate for Social Security benefits, write that number down as an income source. Some of you may also have a pension plan through your employer. If you do, please contact your benefits department to get an estimate of what you will receive based on your planned retirement age. This process will probably feel like pulling teeth because most benefits people are not as helpful as the local Social Security office. You will probably have to follow up a couple times to get the information you need. The benefits people will talk about several different ways you can get the pension money. Some typical options would be lump sum or monthly payment options. Lump sum is simple enough. You will get a one time check and will need to invest that money yourself to provide income during retirement. The monthly payment options are a little more complicated because you will need to pick from several different options that affect how much you will get each month. If you are single, it is easy. Pick the single life only option which gives you the largest monthly payment, but when you die, the payments end. If you are married, you have a more difficult decision.

Married people with pension plans normally have to pick from three or more payment plans. The most common options include: your life only, joint with a 50% survivor benefit, and joint with a 100% survivor benefit. Your plan might have other options, but these are the most common. The vast majority of married people select the joint with 100% survivor benefits to protect their spouse. This option gives a smaller monthly benefit, but guarantees those same payments will last for as long as you or your spouse are living. This might sound like "life insurance" to you. A pension is a form of life insurance and it is actually an undesirable form of life insurance that can be very expensive, but is sometimes very necessary which makes the decision making process extremely difficult. Selecting the option on your life only will give you the biggest monthly check because you basically are not buying life insurance for your spouse, but the payments end when you die leaving your spouse with nothing. Choosing your pension option is normally a one time decision, meaning you only get one chance to pick what is right for you and your family. Once you decide, there is generally no going back. I strongly recommend consulting a competent financial advisor to help guide you through the pension decision making process.

Hopefully you now have come up with an estimate for Social Security and any pension or work income you might receive at retirement. Subtract these benefits from the total estimated need.

We assumed total need was:	$5000/month
Assumed example: husband's Social Security	-$1,500/month
Assumed example: spouse's Social Security	-$1,250/month
Assumed example: spouse's pension plan through work	-$800/month
Income needed from retirement investments	$1,450/month

This is how much you would theoretically need to withdraw from investments in the first year of retirement. The reason I say "first year" is because inflation will likely force you to increase withdrawals after year one to maintain the same lifestyle. It is also important to note that pensions often provide fixed payments without any cost of living adjustments. Social Security does have some cost of living adjustment built into the program.

We allocate your retirement investments based on the income you need, but first we have to decide whether your goals are realistic. I believe people can realistically withdraw up to 7% of their investment account per year, but I normally recommend 6% so there is a built in safety factor. I have seen recommended withdrawal rates as low as 4% (usually in the media). Personally I think a 4% withdrawal rate is unnecessarily conservative and will result in too little income for many seniors. In my opinion, a 6% or 7% withdrawal rate is more realistic while still being conservative. In our example, you would likely need *at least* $250,000 specifically set aside for retirement to meet the income objective.

$1,450/month x 12 months divided by 0.07 = $248,571

If we assume the more conservative 6% withdrawal factor, you would need about $290,000 in retirement savings. The objective is to meet your desired monthly income level without digging into principal over time.

In our example, if you have less than $250,000 in your retirement accounts, you need to realistically adjust your spending habits to fit within available retirement resources. For example, if you had $150,000 of savings, realistic monthly income would be $875/month at a 7% withdrawal rate or about $750/month at a 6% withdrawal rate. You must spend within your means or risk running out of money during retirement. Running out of money would not be good!

For illustrative purposes, let us assume you have $290,000 or more in your retirement savings accounts and you want to do a 6% withdrawal rate. The million dollar question is how do we allocate your investments to meet this long term income goal? How do you balance income and safety needs with some long term growth necessary to counter inflation? I use an approach designed to calculate the amount you should have in fixed income assets (primarily bonds and money market accounts) and the rest should be in a diversified portfolio of stock mutual funds.

It works like this. In the accumulation chapter we talked about stock investments being appropriate for investors with ten years or longer time horizon. Obviously if you are in the transition phase, you have less than ten years until income will be required so you should not be 100% in stocks. However, not all of your money will be spent within ten years so there should definitely be some allocation to stocks. *If you put enough money in fixed income to cover anticipated expenditures for ten years, the rest can be put in stocks.* By doing this you are essentially protecting any money needed within a ten year period and using the rest for growth. This gives you the time needed to ride out particularly bad stock market periods.

The tough part is running the calculation to figure out what you need in the fixed income part of your allocation because we theoretically need to account for an assumed interest rate, an assumed inflation rate, and an assumed income need (along with your personal risk tolerance). Accounting for all these assumptions makes for a difficult calculation. You don't need to be exact in this calculation because none of the assumptions are going to be precise anyway, so I recommend a simple guideline approach. We need to calculate the *present value* of the income you need over a ten year period. The present value is calculated with an assumed interest rate, a future value of zero, the monthly payments you need, and a ten year time period. If you are knowledgeable about financial calculators or if you use a financial advisor, this step is simple. If not, it actually gets quite complicated, but there are a lot of calculator tools on the Internet available to help you. Find a loan amortization calculator and input your data as if it were a mortgage to solve for the initial loan amount. You are basically being your own bank in this calculation and loaning yourself money for retirement spending. The loan amount is what you would need to put in the fixed income portion of your allocation. Our example is based on the following:

$1,450/month gets input as the loan *payment*
6% gets input for the *interest rate* (or whatever you choose as a withdrawal rate)
120 months or ten years gets input for the *length of loan*

Once you input the assumptions, press calculate, and it should give you a balance of $130,606. I used a loan amortization calculator at www.dinkytown.net

(click on "amortizing loan calculator" under the heading of loan calculators), but there are numerous Internet sites with loan calculators. I also confirmed the calculation with my financial calculator.

If you used 7%, the balance is $124,883. If you used 5%, the balance is $136,708. The more conservative you are, the lower the rate you should use so you get a larger portion of the allocation in fixed income. As you can see, there is no right or wrong answer here. For this particular example, your calculation would result in a retirement spending allocation of 55% stocks and 45% bonds:

($130,606/$290,000) x 100 = <u>45% in fixed income</u> (100% - 45% = <u>55% in stocks</u>)

This allocation is for the spending phase and not the transition phase, so how do you go from 100% stocks during accumulation to only 55% stocks needed for spending? We make gradual changes to the portfolio over the course of the ten year transition period. The transition should look something like this:

Transition Year	% in Stock Funds	% in Fixed Income
1	85	15
2	85	15
3	75	25
4	75	25
5	75	25
6	65	35
7	65	35
8	60	40
9	60	40
10	55	45

At the end of the transition period, you should have reached your anticipated spending asset allocation. This is simply a guideline approach because there is no scientific method for making the change from an accumulation portfolio to a spending portfolio. The basic idea is to make a gradual change every couple years towards fixed income until you reach the target asset allocation.

If you are more aggressive, I don't recommend using less than a ten year period for this calculation. However, since there is no right or wrong answer to this problem, you could just skew the stock numbers a little higher. Say, for example, you end up with 65% in stocks after ten years. It won't dramatically change your portfolio, but it would increase volatility which is dangerous during the spending phase. The more money you have in stocks, the more damage could be caused by severe stock market fluctuations. We are looking for a balanced approach that minimizes risk of loss while maximizing the potential for growth.

On the other hand, there are many readers who might want to be more conservative. Conservative investors get really messed up when the stock market declines because they tend to want *all* of their money in safe investments like CDs or money market accounts. My approach will be particularly helpful to you over the long term because sticking to a systematic method for choosing your asset allocation will help overcome investment emotions. I must repeat, helpful over the *long term*! There are times your portfolio will lose money over short periods like one or two years and you will begin to question your investment decisions. You need to stick with a consistent approach or volatility could hurt your overall returns.

There is a better way to do the above calculations for more conservative investors. *Pick a longer fixed income period.* I would never use more than twenty years for the fixed income calculation so consider this your worst case, conservative scenario. Inputting 240 months or twenty years into our loan calculator gives us a greater percentage allocated to fixed income which naturally results in a lower volatility portfolio more suitable for conservative investors. For illustrative purposes, I will also reduce the interest rate to 5% instead of 6%:

> $1,450/month gets input as the loan *payment*
> 5% gets input for the *interest rate* (or whatever you choose as a withdrawal rate)
> 240 months or twenty years gets input for the *length of loan*

The result is $219,712. If you went this route you would end up with a 76% fixed income allocation and a 24% stock allocation.

($219,712/$290,000) x 100 = <u>76% in fixed income</u> (100% - 76% = <u>24% in stocks</u>)

Modify the numbers to meet your personal views on investing, but do not fall too far out of the window created between the ten year and the twenty year time periods. If you put it all together, I believe all investors should have an allocation somewhere in the following guidelines:

	More Conservative Investor	More Aggressive Investor
Stocks	25–40%	40–60%
Fixed Income	60–75%	40–60%

We are still in the transition period right now so you set the asset allocation for your projected spending phase and work down gradually from your 100% stock *accumulation* portfolio towards the desired *spending* allocation. Nothing exciting here, but everything you do needs to be systematic so emotions don't take over during bad times or during good times (fear and greed).

Spending Phase

If your planning has gone well, the spending phase is a natural result of the transition period. At this point, your investment allocations should be right where you wanted them to begin the distributions necessary to spend during retirement. There are two things we really need to remember as we begin the spending phase:

Review
Rebalance

With relatively conservative planning, you should have more than enough money to meet your retirement spending objectives, but what if things have not gone well. It is essential to go through another comprehensive spending review before beginning distributions. We need to go through our *budgeting* calculations again and compare them to our *income* calculations to determine how much is needed from investment income. Run through the calculations listed above for the transition period and come up with a revised fixed income percentage for your allocation. By the way, this might sound like a lot of work, but it really isn't. You should be able to pull all of this information together and run the calculations within an hour or two. If it takes more than two hours, you need to simplify your retirement investments. If numbers aren't your thing, I strongly recommend consulting a competent financial advisor to help you with this process.

If the new calculation matches your previous plan, no significant changes are necessary, but it is likely your investment allocation will be slightly different from the new calculation. If it is, just tweak the portfolio to the revised allocation. Now you are ready to begin taking distributions during retirement.

Mutual funds are great investments for accumulating money, but they might actually be better for distributions than for accumulation. Most major mutual fund companies make it very easy and inexpensive to get your money out. I suggest setting up a monthly systematic transfer (or quarterly, semi-annually, or annually) directly from your mutual fund accounts to your checking account (just like direct deposit for your paycheck). There should be no cost for this service and it should only require filling out one or two forms. Have the distributions automatically come out of the *fixed income* portion of your funds rather than the stock portion.

Obviously, taking distributions from the fixed income portion of your mutual fund account(s) will eventually take its toll and distort your allocation. There will be a natural tendency for the stock portion to become larger which means we need to periodically rebalance. I have already talked about rebalancing under the chapter on accumulation, but I believe it is actually more beneficial to rebalance during the spending phase than during the accumulation phase. There are many benefits to rebalancing, but the most important reason is to maintain investment discipline while you take income.

For example, let us assume you started out with 50% fixed income and 50% stocks when you began retirement distributions. Now you have been taking money for six months and the stock market just happened to go up during that period. You might have 45% fixed income and 55% stocks (just for arguments sake). Rebalance back to your original 50/50 allocation by selling 5% from the stocks and buying fixed income.

What if the stock market declined during the past six months? If the market declined enough, your allocation will likely still be very close to the 50/50 starting point. You lost money in stocks and spent money from fixed income. Your overall portfolio is down, but the original asset allocation will probably be close to where you started. Hang in there as the stock market recovers! Only rebalance if the allocations are +/- 5% from your original allocation. *The only time I would change this recommendation is if your retirement objectives change!* There is no other reason for fiddling with the portfolio asset allocation.

I recommend reviewing your investments more often during the spending phase, partly because you probably have more time to look at statements, and partly because rebalancing is more important during the spending phase. I recommend a portfolio review quarterly, but if you really don't like to do this kind of thing, it is still fine to do annual reviews. Please do *at least annual reviews* or things can really get out of whack. If you have an advisor, he or she should be helping to decide when rebalancing is necessary and a review might be a simple ten minute phone call or might require a sit down meeting.

I believe this approach will give you a relatively simple, yet systematic, method for figuring out an appropriate asset allocation during retirement. The topic of retirement investing can be incredibly confusing which is why so many people make mistakes. It is also fraught with ranges of emotion that can really mess up your situation. Find an allocation within your comfort level and stick with it no matter what you read in the media or what you hear from your neighbor. Your plan is your plan. What might be appropriate for meeting your objectives might not be appropriate for other people and vice versa.

IMPLEMENTATION OF A SPENDING PHASE PORTFOLIO

This whole chapter has talked about generic stock mutual funds and fixed income mutual funds. If I don't elaborate further, some people will end up with a really dreadful implementation of the spending concept. During the spending phase we always want to error on the conservative side when picking investments so when I talk about stocks, I am talking about more *conservative* stocks. When I talk about fixed income, I am talking about a diversified mix of fixed income (bonds).

Let's go back to our original example with $290,000 and with a 55% stock allocation and 45% fixed income allocation. We are setting up two separate portfolios within the same mutual fund account: a stock portfolio and a fixed income portfolio. Consider them two separate "accounts" used to accomplish two separate objectives. Fixed income is specifically for kicking off the income you need during retirement. Stocks are for growing money over the long term to help counteract inflation. Do not evaluate the two accounts against each other except for rebalancing purposes! You cannot compare stocks to fixed income because it is an apples to oranges comparison with totally different time horizons and objectives. Evaluate the effectiveness of each type of holding separately.

So how do you implement a spending approach? We can start with the stock portion. We need to get 55% of the allocation into stocks, or about $159,500 of our $290,000. Build the stock allocation around large cap value or blend funds. These tend to be the most conservative stock funds which will help keep volatility down in the account. Supplement with smaller portions in large cap growth, mid cap, small cap, and international to provide essential diversification (in an effort to reduce overall volatility). A typical recommendation might look like this:

Mutual Fund Style	% of Stocks	% of Overall Portfolio	$ Amount
Large Cap Value	25%	13.8%	$39,875
Large Cap Blend	25%	13.8%	$39,875
Large Cap Growth	15%	8.2%	$23,925
Mid Cap Blend	10%	5.5%	$15,950
Small Cap Blend	10%	5.5%	$15,950
International	15%	8.2%	$23,925
Totals	100%	55%	$159,500

I really don't care which fund family you use to accomplish this allocation. Your advisor should definitely be able to guide you in the right direction, but if you do not have an advisor, call your mutual fund company and tell them the type of allocation you desire. They should be able to list their more popular funds in each specific allocation style.

I find most people understand the reasons for picking different types of stock funds and they understand how each different style is invested, but most people (including many advisors) have no clue when it comes to fixed income. During retirement you don't want to get crazy with fixed income. The hottest thing going the past few years has been emerging market income funds with huge annual returns. *Don't get enamored with the latest and greatest investment idea.* Your fixed income investments should focus mostly on what is called investment grade bonds. Investment grade bonds typically include government and government agency bonds and high quality corporate bonds. Non-investment grade bonds are usually termed "junk" bonds because of their lower quality. Lower quality means there is a greater chance for these corporate bonds to default. If a bond defaults, you lose some, or all, of the principal originally invested in that particular bond. Mutual funds create a diversified portfolio of bonds for you so risk may be reduced over purchasing individual bonds on your own.

With mutual funds, I normally recommend only a couple types of bond funds to make up the fixed income allocation during retirement. The focus is always on diversified high quality bonds specifically to reduce volatility. There is a lot of flexibility in how you create a fixed income portfolio, but a typical recommendation might look something like this:

Mutual Fund Style	% of Fixed Income	% of Overall Portfolio	$ Amount
Short Fixed Income	25%	11.25%	$32,625
Intermediate Investment Grade	25%	11.25%	$32,625
Strategic Income	25%	11.25%	$32,625
TIPS Fund	25%	11.25%	$32,625
Totals	100%	45%	$130,500

The best way to take distributions is equally from each fixed income fund. These four basic fixed income holdings will give a broad range of diversification across both government and corporate holdings along with a broad range of maturities from very short term to longer term.

Short Fixed Income Funds—the objective of these funds is primarily preservation of principal with a focus on short duration, high quality bonds (average maturity will normally be 1–3 years). This is the safest bond fund mentioned due to short duration and generally high quality bond holdings. Another good option for this type of fund is a floating rate high income fund. Floating rate funds are short term bond funds that invest in corporate paper rather than government paper so they tend to pay a slightly higher interest rate without significant added risk.

Intermediate Investment Grade Bond Funds—the objective of these funds is to generate a higher yield with longer maturity, high quality bonds. You might see the average maturity of this type of fund between five and ten years. Intermediate term funds are more susceptible to interest rate fluctuations than short term funds and will occasionally lose money when rates rise quickly. If interest rates decline, this type of fund will usually generate both income and capital gains for investors.

Strategic Income Funds—the objective of these funds is to generate high income and possibly capital appreciation. Strategic income funds tend to be broadly diversified across both maturities and quality. If you picked only one bond fund for your portfolio, I would generally recommend a strategic income fund due to the broad range of bond holdings. This is the riskiest type of bond fund mentioned because strategic income funds will commonly put some allocation towards high yield bonds (lower quality), foreign securities, and emerging market bonds. Due to the greater potential risk, it is very important to select a strategic income fund with a long track record of consistent performance without any significant one year losses.

Treasury Inflation Protected (TIPs) Bond Funds—the objective of these funds is to generate high quality income that fluctuates with inflation. The higher inflation goes, the higher your income. When inflation is low, yields will be low. These are relatively low risk funds because they focus on government bonds and have less risk during a rising interest rate environment generally associated with inflation. Since these funds are relatively new, you won't be able to look at long term track records as comparison criteria. Many fund families have not rolled out a TIPs fund yet, but all the major fund families should have one.

There are a number of other fixed income bond fund types available that I did not mention. Most of them are of a riskier nature like high yield funds, emerging market funds, etc. Because they are riskier, these funds tend to generate higher income which attracts many retired investors. Putting a small percentage of your fixed income allocation into these riskier funds is fine, but focus the bulk of your bond holdings on higher quality bond funds with less fluctuation of principal. Remember, your *stock* holdings are for *growth*, while your *bond* holdings are mainly for *income and protection of principal.*

Critics will argue my recommendation to use bond funds is inappropriate because they would say *all* investors should use a laddered portfolio of individual bonds rather than bond funds. I mentioned this concept earlier and I absolutely agree it is a better income producing approach for people who totally understand how individual bonds work. Since I am not a bond expert and most of my clients would have no idea how to structure an individual bond portfolio, I focus on bond funds. They are simple to understand, can fit in the same mutual fund account as your stock holdings, have professional management, and are more diversified. The main drawback is fluctuating principal when interest rates change and also potentially higher cost.

You may also hear about immediate annuities for producing a guaranteed income stream during retirement. An immediate annuity works much like a personal pension plan where you give a chunk of money to an insurance company in exchange for income over the remainder of your life or for some defined period of time. Once you send the money to the annuity company, your principal is essentially gone. You don't get it back and neither do your heirs. It is meant strictly for production of guaranteed income. I have never sold one of these products because most of my retired clients already have a pension plan through work. It is not a bad concept, but please don't get talked into putting more than half of your retirement money into this type of approach. The guaranteed income with immediate annuities is usually lower than you can generate with your own broadly diversified investment portfolio when you consider your money is *entirely gone* when you eventually die or the contract period ends. You take more risk when you control the money, rather than transferring that risk to an insurance company. However, insurance companies generally don't do anything for free, so if they provide a guarantee, you are paying for it.

◆   ◆   ◆

You may need to read this chapter a couple times to fully understand how the concept works in real life. Spending money is all about balance. Creating a systematic approach with consistent results will help you maintain the discipline necessary to remain balanced. Spending on a defined goal like education is relatively easy. Creating a spending plan for retirement is much more complicated because there are so many variables that could screw up our assumptions. The fear of making a mistake causes many people to hoard their retirement money and not spend anything. I hope implementation of the spending strategies in this chapter give you and your loved ones the confidence to use the money you worked so hard to accumulate. *Creating and implementing a spending plan is one of the best ways I know to directly impact your quality of life.*

Since my family is firmly entrenched in accumulation mode, I cannot share our personal retirement spending strategies with you. Creating a coherent spending plan really isn't as hard as it might sound, but it does take some work upfront. Once the strategies are in place, all you need is a periodic review and rebalance to keep things working smoothly.

Remember from Chapter 1, implementation of a plan is more important than the plan itself. In general, doing something is better than doing nothing. A poor plan in action can be changed, but a good plan with no action is worthless.

11

Conclusion

"Be quick, but don't hurry." John Wooden, Legendary UCLA Basketball Coach

Financial planning is truly a life long journey. It never ends until we meet our maker. The financial decisions you make will directly impact the quality of life for you and your family. While everyone would agree making wise financial decisions is important, there is rarely talk about doing the planning necessary to make these decisions. We are not taught about these issues in school. Parents rarely talk about these issues with their children (kudos to those of you who do). The media only provides generic information that tends to be geared towards wealthy people rather than the rest of us.

You now have the tools necessary to create and implement a coherent financial strategy. There should be carefully considered life objectives *written down* to help guide your decisions. You should have a checklist of implementation items to accomplish as you work towards your financial priorities. It is one thing to create a plan, but remember, a good plan without action is worse than a bad plan with action. You can always review and revise a bad plan, but without action, even a good plan can never succeed.

I particularly like the quote from Mr. Wooden, "Be quick, but don't hurry" as it relates to our finances. I believe prompt action is necessary so it is critical to be quick and decisive with your finances. "Hurrying" implies being out of control where mistakes are more likely to occur. In my mind, some examples of "hurrying" are get rich quick schemes like day trading, commodities trading, Internet stocks, etc. "Quick" implies getting things done in a consistent, systematic manner where mistakes are less likely. It is easy to procrastinate about money. It is human nature to procrastinate about things we don't fully understand, but having a systematic approach will help you defeat procrastination about your finances.

I have tried to make this book about real world solutions to real world financial problems common to the rest of us. I have read many financial books that provide plenty of theory and their concepts are sound, but they still leave people wondering how to implement those concepts. I believe people learn best by *seeing* specific examples of a concept and then *doing* those activities for themselves. The appendix contains a summary case study example using our unique financial plan with objectives and implementation items. Take the various examples in this book and apply them to your own situation with modifications for your unique circumstances. Eventually financial plan reviews will be a consistent habit like spring cleaning or servicing your car.

I want to leave you with one final thought. It is easy to become great in our society, but unfortunately, our definition of greatness has been distorted beyond belief. Most people believe greatness is defined by the toys you own, the money you make, how far you can drive a golf ball, and the size of your house. I believe greatness should be measured in much less dramatic terms. Living your life in a personally responsible manner, making a difference in the lives of your children, and caring for less fortunate people make you great in my book.

One of the first steps toward greatness is being financially successful for you and your family. Financial success does not mean becoming "rich," but it does mean providing food, shelter, and clothing for your family. Success means setting financial priorities like educating your children, protecting your family in case of misfortune, and setting the foundation for taking care of your own needs when you are no longer able to work so you do not become a burden to others. These basic elements of life may sound simple, but are surprisingly difficult to achieve.

You have taken the first steps toward financial freedom by creating a plan for your future. Consistent focus and persistent effort will allow you to achieve your objectives. This may not make you great in the eyes of a society focused on material wealth, high fashion, sports stars, and sex symbols, but it makes you great in my eyes, and more importantly, will ultimately make you great in the eyes of your family.

Best wishes on your journey!

APPENDIX

Case Study Example

The following case study is a summary of our family's unique financial plan. Keep in mind this is a summary only and does not encompass all aspects of financial planning, but has been included as a basic guideline of how and why you should create a comprehensive plan. The implementation aspect of this case study does not represent specific recommendations to readers as it is unique to our situation.

Case Study—Our Family Plan

Dan—Age 32
Tracy—Age 30
Isabella—Age 2
Anticipate one or two future children

Objectives:

1. Periodically review our cash flow and establish the following emergency reserve accounts:

    Accumulate and maintain a minimum of one month of expenses in checking

    Accumulate and maintain a minimum of two months expenses in savings

    Accumulate a minimum of nine months expenses in a joint mutual fund account

2. Have the ability to fund 100% of the cost for four years of college at the University of Minnesota ($11,000/year in today's dollars). We assume a 6% inflation rate and two kids.

3. Review our risk management plan

    A. Maintain health insurance coverage for our family

    B. Consider purchasing a disability insurance policy on me. We determined $2,000 of coverage with benefits payable until age 65 would be adequate.

    C. Determine the appropriate amount of life insurance

        If I die first:

        Tracy would like to be able to stay home with our kids until at least school age, but we want enough insurance to give her the option to not work full time until the kids go to college. We also have to make sure Tracy will have enough for retirement since she may not be working much during her primary earning years.

        If Tracy dies first:

        I want to continue my profession, but I want all debts paid off and money set aside for the children's education.

4. Our retirement objective, although I may never formally retire, would be $4,600/month of expenses or about $6,150/month of gross income ($73,800/year) in today's dollars. We assume a retirement age of 62 for me and sixty for Tracy. We also assume a 4% inflation rate up to retirement and 3% inflation after retirement. Our inflation assumption means we would need about $240,000/year thirty years from now.

5. Estate Planning—our objective is to create wills, health care directives, health care power of attorney and durable power of attorney for both of us. We want to make sure these documents address our desire to take care of our children in case something happens to Tracy and me.

Assumed *net* income is $6,000/month.

Anticipated Monthly Expenses

House	$2,400
Vehicles	$ 600
Spending Money	$1,000
Food	$ 300
Miscellaneous	$ 300
	$4,600

Free cash flow is approximately $1,400/month.

Implementation Items:

1. Our emergency reserve has been established so there is no need for additional monthly savings toward this goal. Our various checking accounts typically have a minimum balance of $5,000. Our money market savings account has a typical minimum balance of $10,000. The remainder of our emergency reserve is invested in a joint mutual fund account with a 100% stock asset allocation. We currently have about twelve months of expenses in our joint mutual fund account. We own the following types of diversified stock mutual funds in our joint emergency reserve account:

Type of Fund	Percentage of Account
Large Cap Growth	22.6%
Large Cap Blend	25.7%
Mid-Large Cap Blend	20.4%
Small-Mid Cap Blend	20.3%
Sector Fund—Technology	11.0%

2. We established Roth IRAs for both Tracy and me and make maximum allowable contributions each year. The Roth IRA accounts will be used to help meet both our education and retirement objectives. We assume the *contribution* portion of these accounts will be used to help meet education objectives while the *growth* component will be used to help meet retirement

objectives. These accounts were established as brokerage accounts and are invested 100% in various individual stocks (no mutual funds).

3. We established an Education IRA (Coverdell ESA) for Isabella and fund this account with $2,000 per year. We anticipate doing the same thing for any future children. This account is solely for meeting education funding objectives. Isabella's Education IRA is invested 100% in diversified stock mutual funds.

4. We maintain health insurance coverage. Our monthly premiums are $305 and we have a $5,000 maximum annual family out of pocket expense.

5. We purchased a long term disability insurance policy on me. This policy provides a $2,000/month benefit after a 180 day wait. Benefits are payable to age 65 and are paid if I cannot perform my own occupation. This policy does not have a built in inflation rider to increase benefits over time, but I do have the option to periodically purchase additional coverage as needed. The annual premium for my disability insurance policy is $470.

6. We determined $800,000 of life insurance was necessary on my life to meet Tracy's survivor objectives. We determined $250,000 of life insurance was necessary on Tracy's life to meet my survivor objectives. We structured our personal life insurance portfolio with the following policies:

My Policies	Amount	Expiration Date	Annual Premium
Thirty Year Level Term	$150,000	2029	$145.50
Twenty Year Level Term	$500,000	2021	$305.00
Equity Indexed Universal	$150,000	Permanent	$960.00
	$800,000		$1,410.50

Tracy's Policies	Amount	Expiration Date	Annual Premium
Thirty Year Level Term	$100,000	2029	$114.00
Twenty Year Level Term	$150,000	2021	$126.00
	$250,000		$240.00

7. Tracy and I each have several tax deferred retirement saving accounts. Our retirement accounts are invested 100% in diversified stock mutual funds and

will remain 100% in stocks until we are at least fifty years old. Our various tax deferred retirement accounts have a combined balance of approximately $46,500 and we make contributions of at least $3,000/year (usually more) depending on our cash flow situation.

8. We consulted an attorney to implement our estate planning documents including wills, health care directives, health care power of attorney for both of us and durable power of attorney for both of us. The implementation of this step cost us $1,000. We expect little to no revisions to our estate plan until our children have grown up.

Critics might argue that our current plan for retirement will not be adequate to meet our objectives. Again, the critics are absolutely right. However, retirement funding is not our most immediate or most important financial objective at this time. It is very likely I will not quit working by age 62 which allows us more time to save and accumulate for retirement. Also, there will come a time when our education objectives have been met and we can focus nearly all of our remaining financial resources on our retirement goals. This is a classic trade-off that must be made when creating a comprehensive financial plan. It is one thing to create your objectives, but it is another thing to prioritize those objectives. One of the most difficult aspects of financial planning is directing your financial resources to various objectives according to their relative priority.

Bibliography

Clements, Jonathan. *When Variable Annuities Make Sense.* Wall Street Journal. Reprinted by Minneapolis Star Tribune: January 13, 2001.

Cooley, Phillip L., Hubbard, Carl M. and Walz, Daniel T. *Retirement Savings: Choosing a Withdrawal Rate That Is Sustainable.* AAII Journal: February, 1998.

Edwards, Carolina and Martin, Ray. *The Rookies Guide to Money Management.* The Princeton Review: 1997.

Farrell, Paul B. *When Annuities Make Sense: Pros and Cons of Buying Funds, Insurance as a Package.* CBS Marketwatch: May 23, 2001.

Gibbs, Lisa. *Miller: He Did It Again.* CNN Money: January 11, 2004.

Greer, Carolyn. *The Great Annuity Rip-off.* Forbes Magazine: February 9, 1998.

Jaffe, Chuck. *Fund Managers' Most Common Mistakes.* CBS Marketwatch: July 13, 2003.

Loeb, Marshall. *Are Annuities Too Good to be True.* CBS Marketwatch: March 20, 2000.

Loeb, Marshall. *Ten Investment Axioms to Live By.* CBS Marketwatch: April 6, 2001.

Molinski, Michael. *The Real Reason to Buy Mutual Funds.* CBS Marketwatch: November 2, 2000.

Siegel, Jeremy J. *Stocks for the Long Run.* McGraw-Hill: New York, 1998.

Stocks, Bonds, Bills, and Inflation 2000 Yearbook. Ibbotson Associates: Chicago, 2000.

White, Rich. *Scratching Beneath the Surface of Mutual Fund Costs.* Prospecting
    and Sales Insight: Volume I, Issue #9: May, 2003.

Websites commonly reviewed or used by the author for financial information:

www.americasaves.org
www.cbsmarketwatch.com
www.efmoody.com
http://finance.yahoo.com
http://money.cnn.com
www.savingforcollege.com

Author Biography

Daniel Dorval is an independent Certified Financial Planner professional who has spent his career helping his clients create and implement unique financial plans. His clients consist of middle income, mainstream American families primarily in the nursing and engineering professions. Before being reincarnated as a financial advisor, Mr. Dorval was a professional Civil Engineer who holds a B.S. degree in Civil Engineering and an M.S. degree in Environmental Engineering. Much of his professional attention is focused on changing the tone of the American financial discussion from one of purchasing random financial products over a lifetime to one of creating and implementing a personal plan for achieving financial success. Mr. Dorval lives in Otsego, Minnesota, with his wife Tracy and their beautiful daughter Isabella. Their family is one example of the group referred to throughout this book as "the rest of us."

0-595-31307-8

Printed in the United States
25573LVS00004B/234